French Women Authors

French Women Authors

The Significance of the Spiritual (1400–2000)

Edited by Kelsey L. Haskett and
Holly Faith Nelson

UNIVERSITY OF DELAWARE PRESS
Newark

Published by University of Delaware Press
Co-published with The Rowman & Littlefield Publishing Group, Inc.
4501 Forbes Boulevard, Suite 200, Lanham, Maryland 20706
www.rowman.com

10 Thornbury Road, Plymouth PL6 7PP, United Kingdom

Copyright © 2013 by The Rowman & Littlefield Publishing Group, Inc.

All rights reserved. No part of this book may be reproduced in any form or by any electronic or mechanical means, including information storage and retrieval systems, without written permission from the publisher, except by a reviewer who may quote passages in a review.

British Library Cataloguing in Publication Information Available

Library of Congress Cataloging-in-Publication Data

French women authors : the significance of the spiritual (1400–2000) / edited by Kelsey L. Haskett and Holly Faith Nelson.
p. cm.
Includes bibliographical references and index.
ISBN 978-1-61149-428-0 (cloth : alk. paper)—ISBN 978-1-61149-429-7 (electronic)
1. French literature—Women authors—History and criticism. 2. Spiritual life in literature. I. Haskett, Kelsey L. (Kelsey Lee) II. Nelson, Holly Faith, 1966–
PQ149.F726 2013
840.9'9287--dc23
2012034161

♾️ The paper used in this publication meets the minimum requirements of American National Standard for Information Sciences Permanence of Paper for Printed Library Materials, ANSI/NISO Z39.48-1992.

Printed in the United States of America

To Frances Shirley Haskett,
whose life was a great spiritual inspiration to many,
and to Caleb and Faith Nelson,
constant sources of spiritual illumination and delight.

Contents

Acknowledgments — ix

List of Figures — xi

Note on Translation — xiii

The Spiritual Quest of French Women Authors: An Introduction — 1
Kelsey L. Haskett and Holly Faith Nelson

1. "Spiritum nolite extinguere": Reading Religion in the Works of Christine de Pizan — 15
   Holly Faith Nelson and Katharine Bubel

2. Rhetorical and Editorial Strategies of Spreading l'*Évangile* in Marguerite de Navarre's *Le Miroir* — 33
   Sinda Vanderpool

3. Stars, Stones, Ships, and Suckling Children: Guyon's Metaphorical Journeys toward Union with God — 49
   Deborah Sullivan-Trainor

4. Neither Prude nor Coquette: The Heroine's Spiritual Journey in Lafayette's *La Princesse de Clèves* — 63
   Hadley Wood

5. Tempered Witness to the Power of the Soul in Enlightenment France: Four Novels by Charrière, Cottin, and Guérin de Tencin — 89
   Joanne M. McKeown

6. Spirituality and Social Justice in the Novels of George Sand — 105
   Kelsey L. Haskett

7	Simone Weil: Ambivalence in Search of God *Anne M. François*	131
8	Duras and the Desire for Spiritual Transformation *Kelsey L. Haskett*	149
9	Spiritual Desire and Domestic Life in Malika Mokeddem's *La Nuit de la lézarde* *Susan Udry*	171

Bibliography	191
Index	199
About the Contributors	207

Acknowledgments

We would like to thank the North American Christian Foreign Language Association (NACFLA), as it was at their meetings that the earliest material for this volume began to take shape. We are most grateful to our exceptional research assistants on this project: Juliet Henderson-Rahbar and Chance Pahl. Their invaluable assistance ensured that the production of the book moved forward at a steady pace. Our thanks are also due to the skilled and supportive librarians and library staff at the Norma Marion Alloway Library at Trinity Western University, above all to Sharon Vose and Ken Pearson, experts at securing much-needed resources through the interlibrary loans process. We also appreciate the permission granted to us (a) by the Bibliothèque nationale de France to reproduce images from *Le Miroir de lame pecheresse* (Alençon: Simon Du Bois, 1531) and MS Lat. 8775, f. 1v; (b) by the *Journal of Christianity and Foreign Languages* 8 (Spring 2007): 47–60, to reproduce and adapt portions of Kelsey L. Haskett's "Spirituality and Feminism in George Sand's *Indiana*"; (c) by Éditions Gallimard for permission to cite and translate passages from Marguerite Duras's *La Vie tranquille*, © Éditions Gallimard, Paris, 1944; and (d) by Éditions Grasset & Fasquelle to cite and translate passages from Malika Mokeddem's *La nuit de la lézarde*, © Editions Grasset & Fasquelle, 1998. As ever, Holly Faith Nelson is grateful for the steadfast encouragement and support of Russell Nelson. Our greatest debt is to the contributors to this collection, whose expertise on French women writers and patience with the editing process made the volume a pleasure to assemble.

List of Figures

Fig. 2.1	Title Page. *Le Miroir de lame pecheresse.* Alençon: Simon Du Bois, 1531.	36
Fig. 2.2	*Le Miroir de lame pecheresse.* Alençon: Simon Du Bois, 1531.	38
Fig. 2.3	MS Lat. 8775, f. 1v.	42

Note on Translation

When a passage from a French edition of a primary source is reproduced, an English translation enclosed in square brackets immediately follows. Unless otherwise noted, this translation has been produced by the author of the chapter in which it appears. When a passage from an English edition of a primary source is reproduced, the original French is only provided in square brackets where it is of critical importance to the argument of the chapter in which it is cited. When a passage from a French secondary source is cited, only the English translation appears, not the original French. Unless otherwise noted, this translation has been produced by the author of the chapter in which it appears.

The Spiritual Quest of French Women Authors

An Introduction

Kelsey L. Haskett and Holly Faith Nelson

The title chosen for this volume, *French Women Authors: The Significance of the Spiritual* (*1400–2000*), suggests two possible avenues of exploration: what role, if any, has spirituality played in forming and informing the works of French women authors, and what role have these female writers assumed in producing works that have modified or influenced in some way spiritual perceptions in literature and society? Just how significant is the spiritual dimension of life to women authors of French expression? Has their approach to spirituality affected their own culture and do their spiritual reflections or interrogations have anything to say to us today? To begin to answer these questions, the chapters that follow examine the lives and works of a number of prominent women authors in France, spanning the centuries from the Middle Ages up to the present. Each of these authors has invested her work with some form of spiritual meaning, be it in an overt manner or in a less conspicuous way. Each one calls us to consider the role of the spiritual, whether in regard to moral and ethical issues, the search for absolutes, the quest for transcendence or inner transformation, or other facets of spiritual inquiry. The importance of inner as opposed to outer life is a constant with all the authors included in this study, while the necessity of changing society through the integration of restorative, spiritual values such as peace and justice is also a reoccurring theme. The worth attributed to the individual by these authors, especially to women and their spiritual and emotional fulfillment, is often denied by the social and religious context in which they or their characters are situated, thus blatantly or tacitly pointing to reforms that will bring about more freedom and equality in society. Not only is the longing for the divine present in many of these women's writings, but the societal implications of spiritual well-being also infuse their works.

From a historical perspective, the ideological terrain in which each of these authors is grounded reveals a steady distancing from a world that embraces the spiritual, providing a rocky road for some and determining for all the manner in which the topic of spirituality is broached or incorporated into their works. Our first author, Christine de Pizan, belongs to a time in which Christianity, and in particular Catholicism, penetrated every aspect of life in one way or another. The dominant, unifying force in French society was the Church, around which all cultural, social, political, and economic activities were centered. As a result, the entire fabric of Christine de Pizan's works is interwoven with the threads of faith, making modern-day distinctions such as secular and spiritual virtually meaningless in relation to her writings. For her, prayer, politics, and every other activity in life are viewed as a spiritual exercise. This overwhelming consensus regarding the role of Christianity in society is gradually broken down, however, with the rise of humanism, rationalism, and other forces which start to transform society, leaving a much weaker form of religion and a growing secularism that eventually characterizes French society. The demise of European Christianity over the centuries, as evidenced in the various time periods of the authors studied in this book, does not erase, however, the aspiration for the spiritual that permeates their works. Often counter-culturally, these women strive to expose the very core of existence as they perceive it, seeking deeper meaning and a truer form of spirituality than that which surrounds them or provides, in many cases, the backdrop for their fictional characters. Their insights and desire for an eternal perspective are either expressed in direct discourse or poetic language, or portrayed through prose fictional narratives, surfacing even in the works of those, like Marguerite Duras, who no longer believe in spiritual reality or relate to any form of recognized religion. Notably, by the time Christianity appears to be all but buried by the secularist forces of twentieth-century Europe, a new religious force has begun to emerge, commanding the same kind of total devotion from its faithful as did medieval Christianity, and rendering the division between the spiritual and non-spiritual once again insignificant. As a key representative of this new religious culture in France, Malika Mokeddem, an Islamic Francophone and our final author, has, nevertheless, much in common with other women writers in this study who seek to transcend the parameters of prescribed religion with its evident failings, and to discover that which can genuinely meet the individual's innermost needs, while at the same time addressing society's needs for the spiritually rooted values of truth, peace, justice, and compassion.

Beginning our study in the late Middle Ages, at a time when France was ravaged by civil wars, epidemics, famines, and the Hundred Years War, we encounter an extraordinary woman whose writings exemplify the highest ideals in relation to both women's condition and the integration of Christian values into society. Christine de Pizan has the distinction of being the first woman in French history to live by her pen, and that at a time when women rarely supported themselves by any means, due to deeply embedded socioeconomic structures. Although the spiritual side of her work has not always been recognized by critics, recent trends in literary theory have created renewed interest in her spiritual thought, which Holly Faith Nelson and Katharine Bubel, in the first chapter in this book, aptly bring out as they explore "the complex ways in which the spiritual and the worldly intersect" in her writings. Living in a society in which the "language of religion," emanating from the teachings of the Catholic Church, constituted an immutable authority for thinkers in every sphere of life, Christine de Pizan cannot help but express herself in and through this language, whether her subject matter be viewed as spiritual or not. Even her writings on courtly love, Nelson and Bubel maintain, are informed by her spiritual perspective, for they include injunctions to prayer and virtuous conduct, and challenge the frequent degradation of women by male poets. Nelson and Bubel remind us that the secular, which in her day implied life "in the world," as opposed to the spiritual, which referred to a life of ecclesiastical service, are both approved of by Christine, who believed that the contemplative life and the active life are simply two ways of serving God.

Nelson and Bubel demonstrate that ethics are the central concern in the major part of Christine's works. Her thought, they observe, focuses mainly on "moral wisdom," with which she seeks to "instruct the public." For Christine, they contend, "ethical behavior built on scriptural principles was essential for her own and the nation's salvation." Addressing princes and subjects of all levels of society, she seeks to become a "moral spokesperson" for France in some of its darkest hours. Although she participates fully in the philosophical debates of her time, which often concern theological matters, she remains focused on the practical application of spiritual truths, using, as Nelson and Bubel explain, "the interpretive resources of wisdom, narrative, and prophecy (derived from biblical interpretation) to imagine and articulate her aspirations for inclusion, dignity, and hope," particularly for women. For Christine de Pizan, as for later writers in this study (such as George Sand), Christianity is viewed as a vehicle by which to surmount oppressive institutions and forces, and her writing becomes a means of influencing every sector of society, in her own day and for many years to come.

The three writers who follow, Marguerite de Navarre of the sixteenth century, and Madame Guyon and Madame de Lafayette of the seventeenth century, illustrate women's involvement in the two dimensions of life described by Christine de Pizan—the contemplative life and life in the world, with all its conflicts and moral dilemmas. First, Marguerite de Navarre was certainly well placed to understand life in the "world," as the sister of Francis I, the influential monarch of the French Renaissance. In fact, when the king was out of the country on military campaigns, Marguerite was the strongest leader in the nation. Although a well-educated, powerful woman, an author and patron of the arts, she chose nevertheless to cultivate the inner life, as Sinda Vanderpool indicates in the second chapter of this volume, thereby having a major impact on the reform movement in France. Commissioned by the Bishop of Meaux to act as the "public figurehead" of France's spiritual reformation, she wrote with the intention of providing "spiritual leadership" for her people, censuring the Church's corruption but trying to reform it from within.

In "The Mirror of the Sinful Soul," the first poem distributed in print form under her name, Marguerite de Navarre employs the "personal voice" in an "inward examination" of her soul, with the goal of moving the reader to do the same, as Vanderpool explains. By revealing the "transformative process of her own soul," reflects Vanderpool, "Marguerite desired to stir other hearts to deeper devotion to God." Like Christine de Pizan, Marguerite stresses that she is a member of the audience to whom she writes, unveiling her inner self in order to connect with her readers and convince them that they, too, can experience the soul's transformation from sinfulness to perfection through grace. Vanderpool examines the way that Marguerite "personalizes the speculum tradition" by creating a relationship with her readers, just as she seeks to help them develop a relationship with God. In the process, Vanderpool notes the major role played by Scripture in Marguerite's life and art, considering the French scriptural references in the margins of certain editions of her poems and revealing that the 1531 edition of *The Mirror* highlights the notion of mirroring by placing Scriptures that inspire her thinking on the right hand side of the page, where they "occupy nearly one-third of the space." This was definitely a perilous practice, because translating the Bible into the French vernacular was highly contentious at this historical moment. Jacques Lefèvre d'Étaples issued his 1523 New Testament in French under the protection of Marguerite, eliciting condemnation from the Sorbonne and persecution that caused a number of French authors and printers to flee the country. *The Mirror* did not manage to escape the scrutiny of the Sorbonne, despite its royal author, and some of those connected to its publication were executed or exiled. Despite her privileged status, Vanderpool reminds us, Marguerite could no longer outwardly support Lefèvre and other reformers hoping to renew the Church from within, although this courageous woman continued to write and teach and to reinforce her words with personal example.

The following century was also a dangerous one for anyone who did not follow the exact path of prescribed religion. In an era when temporal and ecclesiastical power were concentrated in the hands of an absolute monarch, Louis XIV, the idea that one could pray one's own personal, inner prayers and achieve union with God without the aid of the Church, its ministers, and its formulaic prayers was considered heresy. Yet Madame Guyon dared to write a handbook on prayer, *A Short and Easy Method of Prayer*, in which she advocates a simple method of prayer based more on inner stillness before God in an attitude of love and worship, than on actively seeking him with petitions. For this seemingly harmless book on prayer she suffered much persecution, as did her followers, who were many. Deborah Sullivan-Trainor explains in the third chapter in this book that Madame Guyon, as a leading advocate of *quietism* in France, insisted on the personal relationship that all believers can have with God through passively quieting themselves before Him and letting Him act upon their souls. By her inclusiveness, Guyon follows in the steps of Marguerite de Navarre, making reference, as well, to her own experiences as she seeks to enter into a relationship with her readers. "Prayer for Guyon is a relational experience," Sullivan-Trainor notes, "first with God in prayer, and then with other believers through her text." Like her predecessor, Guyon relied heavily on Scripture, and developed a distinct tropology, according to Sullivan-Trainor, to communicate her thoughts about union with God through a love relationship. She also believed her teachings were consistent with the doctrines of the Catholic Church, and did not want to leave the Church but to teach those within it to have more fulfilling spiritual lives. Among those she influenced were Madame de Maintenon, Louis XIV's second wife; the young women of the Saint Cyr school, which Madame de Maintenon had established; and François de Salignac de la Mothe-Fénelon, whom she mentored. Fenelon also defended her when she was attacked, particularly by Jacques-Bénigne Bossuet, who denounced the kind of interior prayer she promoted. Suffering both imprisonment and long-term confinement for her faith, she nevertheless became a significant influence on ordinary Christians and spiritual leaders in many countries, with her works being sold and read right up to the present day.

Turning to a renowned woman novelist of the same century, we discover that the pursuit of virtue is not limited to the seemingly religious sphere. However, the complementarity of religious and secular thought and practice that was taken for granted by Christine de Pizan in medieval France becomes a source of tension for Madame de Lafayette in the seventeenth century, when living a virtuous life becomes antithetical to living in the world, represented by the all-powerful court. While Madame Guyon seeks to renew inner spirituality through personal prayer and piety, but experiences great opposition, particularly from the Church, Madame de Lafayette's fictional Princesse de Clèves struggles to maintain purity of thought and action, in the midst of a world that would pull her in to its duplicity. It would not be difficult to conclude that these conflicts have come about because of the diminishing role of the spiritual in everyday life, although the role of the Church in society still stands unquestioned. Official religion, however, seems more preoccupied with outer form than with personal spirituality. This dichotomy is portrayed again in the nineteenth century by George Sand, in *Indiana*, where the female character condemns the religious institutions of her day, created by men, and embraces true religion of the heart and a relationship with God, rather than outward adherence to a social structure meant largely to reinforce patriarchal power.

In the fourth chapter in this volume, the challenge to the heroine in Madame de Lafayette's *La Princesse de Clèves* does not come from the Church, but from a society and environment purporting to be Christian but at the same time indulging in every whim of passion, to the detriment of marital fidelity, which the heroine courageously struggles to uphold in her own life. Having been introduced to court life when she is quite suitably married to the Prince de Clèves, whom she respects, the Princess encounters conflict when she meets the dashing and seductive Duc de Nemours, who falls wildly in love with her and pursues her with persistence and passion. The tension of the novel results, as Hadley Wood points out, "from the dissonance between the Princess's moral stance and the values of the court, values which Nemours exemplifies to perfection." As the Princess passes through various phases of self-analysis in her attempts to resist the Duke, the inner conflicts and soul-searching she experiences give rise to what has become known as the first psychological novel in France, written by a woman for whom the reality and integrity of inner life once again take precedence over outer life, with its frequent false appearances. The lengths to which the Princess goes to avoid succumbing inwardly and outwardly to the Duke and his almost irresistible charm have caused skepticism on the part of critics, mainly modern, who question her real motives, but Wood's reading of the novel reveals a young woman driven by a genuine spiritual imperative that goes beyond the simple classical formula that places virtue above pleasure, duty above desire. The Princess's realization that the passions of the court are destructive to her inner peace and personal integrity increasingly directs her mind and her will, and sets her apart from her male counterpart and most of the court. The theme of the necessity of virtue which ran through Christine de Pizan's works comes to the fore again in this work, as an antidote to the inescapable forces of power and love that dominated aristocratic life in Madame de Lafayette's day. That the Princess should choose to renounce the world and marriage to Nemours after her husband's death, although possibly a shock and disappointment to the contemporary reader, is nevertheless the logical outcome of the author's reasoning about the superficiality and inconsistency of passionate love, as illustrated throughout the novel. A life totally cut off from the world and devoted to religious service is the means, Wood claims, that the author chooses for her heroine to come to peace with herself and God and to avoid certain, future heartbreak.

The idea of entering a convent to elude both worldly struggles and emotional pain becomes a persistent theme in women's novels as we move into the eighteenth century, although the impulse to flee to the convent usually stems from less rigorous moral interrogations than those portrayed in Madame de Lafayette's classic novel. During the Enlightenment, when the *philosophes* put all forms of authority to the test and found them wanting, including that of the Church, the female writers dealt with in the fifth chapter in this book by Joanne M. McKeown do not reject established religion; rather, they maintain its conventional role of providing convents and monasteries as a means of escape when loss and disappointment (particularly romantic) force the characters in their novels to retreat from everyday life. While these eighteenth-century women do not reveal any revolutionary tendencies in their works, they do, McKeown avers, highlight the unhappy marital conditions of many women in their society who are no doubt unable to repair to religious retreats for solace, the way the characters in the novels do. A perspective on love which has developed in France over time is depicted in these novels, in which marriage is seen as more of a contract than a relationship, and where loyalty to the love of one's life, almost always outside of marriage, is viewed as more sacred than the marriage vow. Often forced against her will to enter into a marriage contract, the woman, in particular, operates according to a system of values that makes her extramarital love, her only genuine love, the one to which she must be faithful. Because of its sincerity and unending devotion, this is the relationship that is blessed by God and will last into eternity, in the commonly held perspective adopted by these authors. Therefore, as McKeown reveals, new religious values are created to encourage and sustain the emotional lives of characters suffering from depression, heartbreak, and despair, because of unwanted or unfulfilling marriages imposed on them by society. They find peace and sometimes reconciliation in retreating within themselves in prayer, as does Sophie Cottin's Claire d'Albe, or to a spiritual environment that promises an afterlife, like the lovers in *Les Mémoires du Comte de Comminges* by Madame de Tencin, as opposed to Isabelle de la Charrière's characters who reject all thought of turning to God or to spiritual ideals, and end up desolate and suicidal. Even for the characters who are more religiously inclined, however, the role of the divine in their lives seems minimal, and the spiritual retreat they seek in times of trouble does not allow them to transcend their problems in the world. As McKeown concludes, such a retreat only permits them to distance themselves from their predicaments for a time, believing that in death true comfort will come and that in eternity they will be forever united with their lovers.

In romantic nineteenth-century France, a flight from reality, far from the world's corruption, also provides the means for the female character in George Sand's *Indiana* to find ultimate peace and hope, as well as sexual equality, in a relationship that reflects not only the feminist and revolutionary ideals of the author, but also her desire to portray an authentic, spiritually grounded love relationship. In *Indiana*, Sand produces a plot in which the protagonist's tyrannical husband dies before she enters into a liberating relationship with the ideal romantic figure, Ralph. Sand sidesteps official religion by placing the couple in an exotic island retreat, where on their own they find peace with God and with each other, after much suffering. In the sixth chapter in this volume, Kelsey L. Haskett posits that in *Indiana*, as in those novels discussed by McKeown, a sincere and faithful human love is aligned with divine love and with a truer form of spirituality than that of marriage, which is seen as a mere social convention. The natural religion endorsed by Sand's characters testifies, insists Haskett, not only to their desire for genuine, unfettered love between a man and a woman, but also to their search for an absolute of love which even the structure of the plot suggests is something of another world, unattainable in real life. The ideals espoused, however, do encourage the reader to envision a type of relationship for both men and women beyond the status quo, one based on higher spiritual values.

From Sand's perspective, Haskett observes, the role that religion can play in human affairs is much more active and transformative than that presented by the authors McKeown examined. Both in her first novel, *Indiana*, which is the fruit of her own experience and convictions, and in later works, such as *Le Compagnon du tour de France*, where the influence of various social theorists of her day is evident, Sand portrays God as personally concerned with the plight of the individual and with social values such as justice, equality, liberty, fraternity, and education for all. Combining Enlightenment values and the message of the Gospels, Sand's novels, Haskett argues, reveal a search for social justice and for a higher form of spirituality than that which she sees in society. Indiana decries the religion formed by men while envisioning a God who, Haskett informs us, "raises up the poor, abases the rich," and brings freedom to the oppressed, including women. Pierre, the exemplary Christ-figure in *Le Compagnon du tour de France*, sees himself on a God-given mission to bring social and political equality to his class, the proletariat. Both novels, Haskett claims, depict at some point a kind of "metaphorical paradise on earth," Pierre dreaming of a garden where all classes mingle and walk hand in hand, surrounded by angels. The eventual love between Pierre, the carpenter, and Yseult, the nobleman's daughter, is a pure, idyllic love driven by the cause of social reform which they both embrace, thereby erasing class and gender barriers, as they explicitly attempt to live out the Gospel message. Haskett deduces that through the relationship of Pierre and Yseult, like that of Indiana and Ralph, the author's search for an untainted, exemplary love is revealed, as is her unchanging social idealism. For Haskett, Sand's vision for a new society and her dream of an ideal union between a man and a woman both depend on the spiritual transformation she portrays as essential for social change.

In the twentieth century, although democracy has become a reality, spiritual ideals all but fade in the wake of two world wars fought heavily on French soil, changing belief in human potential and progress into skepticism and despair, while movements such as surrealism and existentialism turn against rationalism and the kind of society that produced these wars. Forging a new meaning for humanity, writers and artists encourage individuals to take charge of their own lives, without recourse to religious values or other prescribed social mores, charting a new course designed to set humanity free from the fetters of the past. The common ground that once provided a framework for a substantial part of society is no longer able to maintain its authoritative role, and secularism accompanied by individualism becomes the new norm. Characterized by a continuous repudiation of the past, accompanied by a less obvious search on the part of French intellectuals for something beyond the material, the twentieth century moves forward in an ever-increasing spiritual vacuum, with lone writers embarking on a quest for God that now resembles more and more a search in the dark.

One of these writers is Simone Weil, whose passion for metaphysics inspired her to undertake "a troubled yet rich spiritual quest," which led her to God, even as she continued to wrestle with spiritual truth(s), as Anne François affirms in the seventh chapter in this volume. George Sand's critique of the Church on a social level is pursued in an intensely theological and philosophical way by Simone Weil, who believed that the intellectual and spiritual realms were intricately interlaced and all encompassing. "Open to religious otherness," Weil chose, as François recalls, to linger on the outer edges of the Christian Church, criticizing facets of Judeo-Christian belief and turning to ancient Greek texts to bridge the gap she perceived between the human and the divine. As François shows, Weil's position concerning God and the Scriptures and her attempt to reconcile her pluralistic perspective with Christianity rendered her beliefs ambivalent. Her mystical ideas, rooted in a mélange of spiritual traditions, also made her a controversial figure. Criticized by both Christians and Jews for her unorthodox beliefs, she rejected both the Jewish religion and culture and distanced herself from her Jewish roots, until she was victimized by the anti-Semitic Vichy government in the 1940s.

No doubt, Weil's writings are often inconsistent in their treatment of religious matters, making it difficult for the reader to reach definitive conclusions about her spiritual vision. However, François is convinced that Weil's treatment of the presence and absence of God, though paradoxical, allows us to grasp one aspect of her thinking also reflected in her life. Through her mystical experiences, Weil senses the presence of God, but sees Him as absent in human suffering, an absence from which the afflicted can spiritually grow if it is properly understood. Love and abandonment occur in tandem for Weil, as do presence and absence, François avers. Weil believes that this paradoxical truth is figured in the crucifixion of Jesus, for example, where God's presence to save is accompanied by his absence at the final moment of his son's death. Weil explores the spiritual growth that could potentially occur through such "*malheur*" or extreme forms of affliction. This kind of thought process led her to use the "discourse of extremes," according to François, and to often go to extreme lengths to show her seriousness toward the causes she held dear. During her early years of social activism she attempted to identify with the lower classes by working in an automobile plant just outside Paris, and then as a farm worker, and during the war, while living in London, she decided to fast to show her solidarity with her people who were dying in Europe, leading to what appears to be her own death by starvation. Half-measures were not part of her life. In Weil, François contends, we encounter a twentieth-century woman confronted with the contradictions of her times, of her sex, and of her Jewish identity in anti-Semitic Europe, in spite of her desire to assimilate into French culture, just as we bear witness to her personal experience with God, despite the intellectual rigor with which she questions both God and religion.

After the war, the notion of the absurd introduced by existentialism and seemingly confirmed by the senseless horrors the world had just endured, paved the way for an anti-literature which was first expressed in the theater of the absurd and then in the New Novel which sought to break away from the traditional novel form. Identified as an early proponent of this type of novel, Marguerite Duras soon became known as an author with her own, very personal style of writing and went on to gain worldwide recognition for her novels, plays, and films. Although for many years her work appeared to be devoid of any trace of spirituality, a gradual turn in literary criticism began to disclose the deeper, metaphysical undercurrents of her work. While spiritual values still stand out by their absence rather than their presence in her writings, the pursuit of a humanly impossible love and the yearning for the eternal nevertheless signal the incessant quest for absolutes that characterizes Duras's female characters. Their desire for transcendence is accompanied, moreover, by a parallel longing for spiritual transformation, as Kelsey L. Haskett explores in the penultimate chapter in this volume. Haskett maintains that both the personal inner void and the outer void of the universe push these characters to desperate and sometimes highly complex measures in an attempt to fill the emptiness of their lives. Nearly always portrayed as victims of solitude, self-rejection, and an extreme lack of self-esteem, their search for inner transformation is manifested in three principal ways, as set forth in

Haskett's chapter: the desire for rebirth, metaphorically speaking, the desire for transformation through sudden death, and the desire to take on the identity of another.

The desire for rebirth, Haskett explains, is most graphically shown in *La Vie tranquille*, where a young woman's encounter with the sea awakens in her a new sense of identity and the feeling of being reborn, as she is expulsed by the waves onto the beach after plunging into the depths of the sea, a symbolic womb where she begins to delight in herself and imagine herself a flower. Her desire for inner change and purification remains unfulfilled in the end, however, as she returns to the language of self-depreciation after her briefly transformative experience in the sea. In the next category, Haskett notes, death through passion is the solution sought after by Anne Desbaresdes in *Moderato cantabile*, in which the stifling atmosphere of a home devoid of marital love and communication pushes Anne to spend her days with a young worker in a café, trying to recapture the emotions of a woman killed in this same café by her lover. The revelation of a passion consummated in death comes to signify, Haskett speculates, the "ultimate experience for Anne, an absolute moment" for which she herself longs as the culmination of her desire for a radical, unchangeable love with no possibility of return. Haskett observes that not only Anne, but a number of Duras's other female characters, live their lives vicariously through the experiences of another woman. Haskett suggests that for some, such as Maria in *Dix heures et demie du soir en été* or Lol in *Le Ravissement de Lol V. Stein*, this idealized woman represents the perfect partner for the lover they have lost to that very woman they allow to replace them. Seeing themselves in terms of total negation, they exchange their identity for that of the ideal woman who becomes a very real substitute for their physical and inner selves, in love affairs in which they try to participate vicariously, either through observation or through their imagination. Abolishing one's own identity in the pursuit of perfection in love constitutes, in fact, another form of spiritual longing, a desire to transcend the limitations of this life by becoming another, although the women who practice this form of self-replacement eventually lose any sense of their own identity or worth. The search for spiritual transformation, Haskett asserts, without "an actual encounter with the Divine" proves to be a destructive if not fatal tendency for the characters of Marguerite Duras.

Although Malika Mokeddem's acknowledged Muslim faith greatly contrasts with the absence of faith on the part of Marguerite Duras, the thematic similarities in their works are striking. The waiting and watching that characterizes the lives of Duras's female characters as they search for love proves to be a key component of Mokeddem's novel *La Nuit de la lézarde*, analysed by Susan Udry in the final chapter in this volume. As Udry demonstrates, the search for a form of absolute love once again becomes the driving force of the main female character, whose waiting for an imaginary lover signifies, in fact, a desire for a form of transcendent love that will enable her to surmount the solitude, pain, and incessant violence she has experienced and which still surrounds her. The breakdown of the family structure, the isolation of women, and their separation from community find parallels in the works of the two novelists. Mokeddem portrays a woman living, like herself, on the margins of Islamic society, having fled after a divorce to a virtually abandoned desert *ksar*, a village made entirely of sand, which Udry believes is emblematic of the desert-like quality of the character's own life. Like Duras's characters who live in their own inner world, Mokeddem's Nour carves out a life for herself in the desert, gardening and selling her produce in a nearby town, but living by her own standards and waiting for a "savior" in the guise of a lover who will fulfill all her needs, as is the case of George Sand's Indiana. Her newfound companion, a blind man, provides company and a source of practical help, but does not touch her inner being, despite his devotion to her, Udry shows.

Interestingly enough, Madame Guyon's desire in the seventeenth century for communication with God based on a relationship of pure love and simply waiting in his presence, finds an echo in Mokeddem's work as well, but unlike Guyon's actual discovery of God's love, Mokeddem's character dies in her desert garden still longing for the arrival of the ever-absent lover. Only in the blind man's dream does she find fulfillment and experience a kind of paradise symbolized by a lake from which she emerges (reminiscent of the new birth theme examined in Duras's novels), dripping with water and physically and spiritually refreshed. Guyon's certainty about God's love, like that of Marguerite de Navarre, stands in contrast to the spiritual aspirations depicted by later authors. The theme of transcendent love in eighteenth- and nineteenth-century works does not so much relate to God as to an idealized human love relationship which only finds fulfillment in death and eternal life, where the lovers are united after failing to realize their relationship in this life, providing some hope based on romantic values. Significantly, in the twentieth century, this desire for a love beyond the reality of our existence does not transcend death; moreover, death itself is the culmination of this quest, in Duras's *Moderato cantabile,* and no hint of the afterlife appears at the end of Mokeddem's novel. No less avid for a spiritual experience, these contemporary authors refuse, nevertheless, to depict what they have not known, such that the indefinable object of their characters' perpetual longing remains unattained and unattainable.

From the concern of our early writers with moral rectitude and virtuous living, as witnessed not only in Christine de Pizan's works but also in Madame de Lafayette's *La Princesse de Clèves*; to authors who seek to instruct their readers in a life of piety and proximity to God, such as Marguerite de Navarre and Madame Guyon; to those for whom true religion implies the reformation of society and the espousal of egalitarian and fraternal values, like George Sand and the philosophical and theological thinker, Simone Weil; to those writers whose lives and works portray an unending search for some form of spiritual reality, whether transcendence, transformation, or ideal love, it is unmistakably clear that women writers of French expression have displayed an unremitting passion for and commitment to the importance of the spiritual in life and literature, whether be it meditational, theological, poetic, or fictional. The impact they have had on the spiritual thinking and experience of countless generations, both in France and Western society as a whole is no doubt impossible to determine, but it is evident that virtually all of the authors examined in this study have played significant roles in their own day and had an influence beyond their time. That they were women authors writing for the most part at times in history when that fact in itself was already a feat is a testimony to their courage, tenacity, and conviction, and speaks to the magnitude of their goals and achievements which have benefited, challenged, and changed our world. That they all incorporate the role of the spiritual into their works distinguishes them, as well, as writers for whom the inner life, in its various transcendent, spiritual, or moral dimensions, proves to be paramount for the fulfillment of the individual, and, in many cases, for the enrichment and betterment of society at large.

Chapter One

"Spiritum nolite extinguere"

Reading Religion in the Works of Christine de Pizan

Holly Faith Nelson and Katharine Bubel

In the last few decades, there has been a resurgence of interest in the life and works of Christine de Pizan (c.1364–c.1430). While she has been hailed by many critics as an articulate proto-feminist, a pioneering political thinker, and a skilled rhetorician, her contribution to the fields of ethics, theology, and ecclesiology has received far less critical attention. The historical tendency to overlook the religious elements of Christine's corpus can primarily be attributed to the belief that she is a secular writer. In this vein, Charity Cannon Willard suggests that "[a] critical overview of Christine de Pizan's writings does not provide an impression of any great piety, and certainly not more than might be expected in any observant medieval woman" since "religious faith was a fundamental aspect of such a life."[1] Willard does acknowledge that "[t]his secular impression must be somewhat modified ... by a few works that are distinctly spiritual in character, even if they are not entirely devoid of worldly overtones."[2] However, she does not address the complex ways that the spiritual and the worldly intersect in Christine's body of works nor does she differentiate between a medieval and modern conception of secularity in her assessment of the worldly in Christine's writings.

The recent religious turn in literary theory, however, has sparked renewed interest in Christine's spiritual thought, to which the research of Josette A. Wiseman, Bonnie A. Birk, Rosalind Brown-Grant, Earl Jeffrey Richards, and Maureen Boulton attest.[3] Their preliminary work in this area suggests that Christine de Pizan's writings on women, politics, and philosophy cannot be fully grasped outside of the authoritative discourse of religion in medieval France. As Mikhail Bakhtin explains in *The Dialogic Imagination*, "[t]he authoritative word demands that we acknowledge it, that we make it our own; it binds us, quite independent of any power it might have to persuade us internally; we encounter it with its authority already fused to it. . . . It is therefore not a question of choosing it from among other possible discourses that are its equal."[4] The language of religion, embedded in the doctrine and discipline of the Catholic Church, was for the medieval writer such an authoritative discourse. Because the identity of Christine de Pizan and her relation to the world were forged in religious terms, as is evident in her autobiographical prose, to remove the spiritual thread from the fabric of her texts is to miss or distort the richness of their vision. This chapter, therefore, seeks to explore the ways in which the language of religion informs and is informed by other aspects of her thought in order to grasp the significance of the spiritual in her writings and to demonstrate, in the words of Paul Ricœur, that "God is in some manner implied by the 'issue' of . . . the world" unfolded in her texts.[5]

MERGING COURTLY AND SCRIPTURAL IDEALS

That Christine's works have been primarily read within a secular context is not an unreasonable practice in light of her association with the literature of the court and the "religion of love" in the period.[6] As she recounts in her autobiographical *Vision*, she began in 1399 to make her living by composing "pretty things . . . of a lighter nature," though, as her study progressed, her books dealt with broader and "nobler subject matter."[7] However, even while composing "lighter" amorous verse, Christine would have found it inconceivable to classify her writing as either secular or religious in modern terms. In medieval Europe, secularity was not, for the most part, viewed as the antithesis of spirituality and the concept rarely signified a lack of concern with matters of Christian belief and faithful practices. Rather, it was a term most commonly applied to the realm of life "in the world"—as the alternative to an existence fully devoted to ecclesiastical service or membership in a religious order or institution.[8] But life in the world was intimately connected with God and the Church, the center around which all of medieval society was oriented. Christine specifies the spiritual purpose of life in the world in *The Treasure of the City of Ladies, or The Book of the Three Virtues*, in which she compares the "two paths that lead to Heaven," the contemplative life and the active life, explaining that the "active life" is simply "another way of serving God."[9] In declaring that "the good and proper active life cannot function without some part of the contemplative" life, Christine discloses her orthodox apprehension of the interdependence of worldly matters and divine purpose.[10] This medieval understanding of secular life led to the close association of ecclesiastical and political formations, which Christine advocates in *The Book of the Body Politic*. In this prose piece, she counsels "the good prince who loves God" to "carefully observe and keep the divine law and holy institutions in everything that is worthy and devout," to "believe firmly that God will guard, defend, and increase him in virtue of soul and body" and, "as vicar of God on earth," to "care with all his heart for the welfare of the church, so that his Creator can be served as his reason demands."[11]

Since secular existence in the medieval period required ordinary men and women as well as political leaders to remain deeply concerned with matters of the spirit, even the most "worldly" literature of the period contains traces of religious language and the values embedded within it. As a result, the "lighter" works of Christine de Pizan bear the impress of her religious convictions or, at the very least, the language of spiritual belief, even when the subject on which she writes is courtly love or earthly desire. In *The God of Love's Letter*, for example, an epistle narrated by Cupid, the "god of lovers," Christine cites Scripture, alludes to the Virgin Mary and "Sweet Jesus," and engages in biblical exegesis to contrast the "great courtliness" displayed by "God on high" "toward women" with the discourteous behavior of David and Solomon.[12] So too, in Christine's pastoral prose work, *The Tale of the Shepherdess*, "courtly lovers all" are asked by a lovesick shepherdess to mimic the posture of the contrite soul—to fall "on naked knees" and don "penitential garb" as they pray that her "valiant" knight will be protected and restored to her.[13] The language of Eros is here and elsewhere in Christine's writings bound up with the language of religion, as is often the case in medieval literature, and her participation in the "courtly religion of love," to borrow a phrase from Nancy M. Frelick, does not necessarily mean that her works erase, elide, or profanely parody religious discourse and values.[14] While, as Sarah Kay maintains, the "religion of love" can be viewed as "sacrilegious" when it is conceived of in sexual (especially adulterous) terms—and is thus placed in tension with religion proper—the secular and the sacred remain in a dialogic and mutually dependent relationship with each other in courtly literature of the period.[15] Indeed, Barbara Altmann asserts that this dialogic and mutually informing relationship is the hinge upon which the "literary diptych" of the *Dit de Poissy* swings.[16] In this "courtly narrative" poem, the realm of courtly love is juxtaposed with the cloister at the Dominican Abbey of Poissy in such a way as to bring to light "unexpected parallels in the codes that regulate these social orders."[17] Moreover, as Prudence Allen and others have shown, Christine not only challenged the "literary tradition upheld by male poets," especially its promotion of adulterous love and its "defamation" and slanderous depictions of virtuous women, but also advocated a reason-based love that would result in "virtuous choices."[18] Courtly love and a virtue undergirded by religious belief, therefore, converge in Christine's works.

This coming together of secular courtly ideals and scripturally informed models of virtue is perhaps most transparent in Christine's *Letter of Othea to Hector*, viewed by Rosalind Brown-Grant and others as a "mirror for princes" whose purpose is to foster the virtue of France's rulers.[19] Here the chivalric tradition is harmonized with the biblical sapiential tradition, the cardinal virtues of Prudence (or Reason), Fortitude, Temperance, and Justice playing a central role. By combining the discourses of classical myth, medieval chivalry, and biblical exegesis in the *Letter*, Christine foregrounds the religious codes and customs inherent in the "knightly system of feudal times," presenting chivalry as a biblical concept.[20] As she writes in the "Prologue to the Allegory,"

> we may call human life virtuous chivalry, as the Scripture says in several places. And as all terrestrial things are fallible, we must have in continual memory the future time which is without end. And in that it is the great and perfect chivalry, and all else is of no comparison, and for which the victorious will be crowned in glory, we will take the manner of speaking of the chivalrous spirit; and this be done for the praise of God principally and for the profit of those who will read this present treatise.[21]

Christine's ability to read classical mythology in this way stems from a medieval analogical perspective, by which the "good knight," and by extension the good prince, can be viewed as analogous to the "good spirit" that is adorned "with [the] virtues" necessary for "glorious victory."[22] Christine does not, therefore, make a distinction in the *Letter of Othea* between a "secular moral code" and a "religious moral code."[23] In fact, she deploys clerical interpretive practices to draw out the religious meaning of apparently secular passages on the gods and goddesses imparted by "Othea, goddess of prudence" to the archetypal chivalrous prince and embodiment of chivalry: Hector of Troy. Each "text" is provided with a moralizing "gloss" and "allegory," supported by scriptural passages and quotations from other authoritative texts.[24] Like the Hebrew sages who composed the Proverbs, Christine adopts this ethical poetic or moralizing aesthetic in order to participate in and positively transform the public sphere by reading provisional worldly realities through the lens of eternal spiritual truths.

READING THE ANCIENTS "IN THE LIGHT OF TRUE FAITH"

As with her attention to courtly love and chivalric ideals, Christine's dedication to philosophy has also been viewed as evidence of her focus on matters of the intellect rather than the spirit—that is, of her interest in the intellectual process of cognition rather than the spiritual process of conversion. For the medieval European writer, however, the philosophical and the theological spheres overlapped, mutually informing each other. As David Knowles has demonstrated, regardless of the growing autonomy of philosophy in the schools, one of the most pronounced aspects of philosophy in this period is its close connection to religion, primarily in service of theology.[25] Knowles explains, "From the age of Augustine to the death of Aquinas there had been a conviction, shared by all the schools, and expressed by all implicitly, if not explicitly, that there existed a single reasoned and intelligible explanation of the universe on the natural level," with the corollary being that "the ancients . . . had said if not the final, at least the most authoritative word in this . . . and that the Christian thinker's task" was to derive and apply this explanation by studying the ancients and bringing the "higher wisdom of the Christian revelation" to bear upon them.[26] For the medieval thinker, the "philosophical universe" was, as Hans Urs von Balthasar argues, "fulfilled . . . in the Christian-theological one," resulting in a unified vision.[27]

Christine repeatedly makes explicit references to the synthesis of pagan and Christian insight, a fusion conceivable because of the medieval extension of the Judaic and Patristic understanding of a universal and, in Ricœur's term, "immemorial" *Sophia* and the Christian *Logos* of God, both of which point to the perfecting of nature by revelation.[28] Like Aquinas, Christine can pattern her ethical theory on Aristotelian moral philosophy as delineated in the *Nicomachean Ethics*, a work she often cites in *The Book of the Body Politic*, to stress the critical place of virtue in "the rule of life."[29] The pagan and the Christian, particularly Aristotle and Augustine, are seamlessly interlaced in her political prose and even more clearly in the *Letter of Othea*. In the gloss to the first "text" of Othea, Christine stresses that though "the ancients" did "not yet" enjoy "the light of true faith," they remained religious and were thus able to pursue wisdom and to build and rule empires effectively.[30] She continues, "[W]e Christians, by the grace of God enlightened with true faith, are able to restore to morality the opinions of the ancients, and on these, many excellent allegories can be made."[31]

The grounds for this assertion can be found in the "Prologue to the Allegory," in which Christine explains, "As by the great knowledge and high power of God all things are created, rationally so must all things lead at the end to him, and because our spirit, which God created in his image, is of the things created the most noble after the angels, an appropriate thing it is and necessary that it be adorned with virtues by means of which it may be guided to the end for which it was fashioned."[32] For a medieval mind such as Christine's, "all things" applies not only to human souls, but also to the exemplary stories of historical and mythical figures and to philosophy. For instance, her gloss on the myth of Pygmalion a little further along in the *Letter of Othea* explains, "To this fable may be set many expositions, and similarly to other such fables . . . because the poets made them so that the understanding of men would be sharpened and made subtle to find there diverse expositions."[33] Christine's interpretive theory accords with the long-held biblical exegetical tradition of the four senses of Scripture (the literal, the allegorical, the tropological or moral, and the anagogical), which led to the practice of finding the same layers of meaning in mythological texts—hence the *Ovide moralisé*, which Renate Blumenfeld-Kosinski identifies as one of the chief sources for the *Letter of Othea*.[34] Christine presents herself as capable and worthy of "translating" the moral knowledge of the ancient world in such a way as to make it meaningful to, and capable of engendering virtue in, those living in late medieval Christendom.

In the figure of Boethius, Christine and many of her contemporaries found an emblem of the unity of the classical and the Christian, the philosophical and the theological.[35] That Christine looked to Boethius as both a literary and spiritual model is evident in her many allusions to the philosopher and his "profitable and celebrated book," *On the Consolation of Philosophy*.[36] In *The Path of Long Study*, a dream vision modeled on the Christian epic of Dante, Christine describes her critical reception of Boethius's treatise, in which she identifies a deeply spiritual purpose, one that is inseparable from moral theology. His chief concern in the *Consolation*, she claims, is to give "good advice" for "the common good" in order to "support righteousness."[37] Boethius is extolled as "an extremely virtuous and valiant man . . . [who] sought no other reward than that given by God to those who try to do His will."[38] This statement of praise connects philosophical reflection with the pursuit of virtue and virtue with submission to the will of God, which is discerned "through rigorous reasoning."[39]

Surrender to the divine will, therefore, is identified by Christine in *The Path of Long Study* as the source of the highest and lasting happiness, a truth stressed in her autobiographical *Vision* by both Lady Philosophy and Lady Theology who, we ultimately discover, are, for Christine, one in the same person.[40] As Prudence Allen explains in her reading of the final chapter of the *Vision*, "Christine takes each field in philosophy and shows how it is integrated into theology: true physics becomes the theology of God as primary cause, ethics leads to the good life in God, logic demonstrates the light and truth of the just soul, and political philosophy is rooted in the common good in a city of people inspired by faith."[41] Christine made ethics her central theological concern in the majority of her writings because she felt she could serve a moral function analogous to that of Lady Prudence or Proverb's Lady Wisdom; she could instruct the public—princes, nobles, knights, and common people—on "the good life in God."[42] This she does, for example, in *The Book of Peace*, where she introduces and anatomizes the exemplary life of King Charles V whose virtue, she instructs, is worthy of veneration by "noble princes." Of this politically inflected virtue, Christine writes, "In spiritual matters, which are the most important, he wanted to be well taught by solemn and worthy theologians . . . and he often heard . . . lessons of wisdom whose teachings he followed so that he could serve God and fear and love Him above all else. Thus he did good works."[43]

David Knowles underscores in *The Evolution of Medieval Thought* M. Etienne Gilson's hermeneutical observation that "every group or school of thinkers has a social or cultural or confessional background," which "leads it to focus its attention upon certain fields of the great area of thought available for development."[44] That Christine's "area of thought" is chiefly moral wisdom or "public forms of virtue" is largely the product of a life defined by the death of loved ones, social marginalization, impoverishment, war, papal schism, and political corruption.[45] Like her contemporary Jean Gerson, Christine wrote during "a period of social unrest, military insecurity, and political instability in France," an environment further destabilized for Christine by the loss of her father and husband and the need to support her mother and children on very limited means, given her difficulty accessing either economic or cultural capital once she was widowed.[46]

DEPLOYING THE DISCURSIVE MODES OF "HOLY SCRIPTURE"

In a world whose foundations were crumbling because Christians were instigators of violence and "consumed" by sin, Christine asserted that ethical behavior built on scriptural principles was essential for her own and the nation's salvation.[47] In *The Path of Long Study*, Christine laments, "It is . . . sad to state that Christians kill each other in deadly wars, because of greed for power or for newly conquered lands. . . . God's Church is injured, more saddened than ever before; her pastors are now wounded, and their scattered and bewildered flocks lose their way, which causes many to be lost."[48] Christine finds in the "Holy Scriptures" and other authoritative texts whose substance accords with biblical truth a linguistic arsenal to combat the intense despondency experienced by witnesses and victims of trauma in periods of unrelenting brutality. She suggests in *The Letter on the Prison of Human Life*, an epistle addressed to a mourning Mary of Berry, that only the authority of Scripture and an unyielding faith can counteract the sorrow that threatens to overwhelm: "Oh, revered lady, shall we not believe the Holy Scriptures and believe in the true God, without which faith no one can please God or be saved, as St. Paul says."[49]

As this Pauline reference suggests, in devising and advancing a program of virtue to treat private and public trauma, Christine depended heavily on various aspects of Scripture—its language, its modes, and its voices. These were necessary elements for a writer who, according to Brown-Grant, conceived of herself as a "teacher or advisor whose task was to provide her readers with much-needed lessons in ethics and morality."[50] That Christine would turn to Scripture to communicate her religious understanding of virtue is predictable, because, in Ricœurian terms, it is through the biblical "modes of discourse" that "the religious faith of a community" "comes to language."[51] Immersed in the Judeo-Christian tradition, Christine is extremely familiar with these "*originary* expressions of a community of faith" evoked by first-order experiences of the sacred; and she relies on them not simply as authoritative proof texts to support her beliefs and propositions, but also as the means by which to bring her ethical vision "to language."[52] Discursive modes in Scripture include, according to Ricœur, historical "narratives, prophecies, legislative texts, proverbs and wisdom sayings, hymns, prayers, and liturgical formulas," traces of which appear in many of Christine's writings, which include allegorized psalms, prophetic hymns, Marian prayers, visionary narratives, moral proverbs, and devout epistles.[53] Some biblical modes were more appealing to Christine than others. Her works show a pronounced interest in the wisdom writings, the Gospels, the Epistles, and prophetic or apocalyptic discourse, which often combine in such a way as to create a sense of movement from a fragile nostalgic vision of cosmic order in the temporal—and temporary—realm to a revelatory future in eternity, mediated by the Incarnate Logos, the embodiment of a transcendent knowledge (Sophia) that directs the faithful heavenward.

DONNING THE AUTHORITY OF THE FEMALE SAGE AND SIBYL

Christine's material allusions to Scripture—quotations from or paraphrases of biblical phrases and verses—reveal her particular reliance on the Judeo-Christian Wisdom tradition. This tradition, as James G. Williams explains, "is dedicated to articulating a sense of order," privileges "discipline and self-control," identifies "folly as disorder" and "tends toward confidence in the dependability and bounty of the world," despite its attention to the disruptive force of language that must be offset by "wise utterance."[54] Following in Barbara Newman's footsteps, Bonnie Birk has recently examined Christine's fascination with the sapiental tradition, as well as her attraction to the "wisdom texts of the Hebrew Scriptures," finding, for example, that nearly 29 percent of the quotations that appear at the end of her allegories in the *Letter of Othea* are from Sirach (or Ecclesiasticus), Proverbs, and the Wisdom of Solomon.[55] This work, like *The Book of the Body Politic,* also includes frequent quotations from the Psalms, the Pauline epistles, and the gospels which are often recast to transmit in a succinct manner a lesson in prudence or wisdom. For example, in the *Letter of Othea to Hector*, Psalm 117:8, "It is good to trust in the Lord, rather than to trust in princes," appears as a wise saying for moral living at the conclusion of the allegorical interpretation of the text,

> If you have a great or busy war,
> Do not trust in the strength
> Of Babylon, for by Ninus
> It was taken; rely on none of them there[,]

just as Matthew 7:1–2, "Judge not, that you may not be judged. For with what judgment you judge, you shall be judged," is quoted as prudent advice in the allegorical reading of the lines

> Do not judge as Paris did,
> For one receives many a hard return
> For approving bad sentences,
> For which many have had bad reward.[56]

The scriptural representation of Sophia or Sapienta as "the ethical wisdom summed up in fear of the Lord, plain speech, honest work, and faithful marriage" as well as "the creatrix 'who came forth from the mouth of the Most High'" certainly bolstered Christine's repeated attempts to redeem the feminine in a misogynist culture, as has been argued elsewhere.[57] However, more broadly, in a world of religious and political disorder, proverbial words of wisdom help Christine to orient and comfort herself and her reader. They give meaning to and transcend the chaotic reality of the society she inhabits.

Yet Christine is deeply attuned to human suffering and turns to the less affirming biblical genre of lamentation in *The Lamentation on the Evils That Have Befallen France*, in which she adopts "the elegiac topos bequeathed to medieval poets" by Jeremiah.[58] She appropriates this mode of prophetic discourse in order to interrogate the consoling pattern of order and harmony encoded in much sapiential literature that overlooks the challenge of evil in its adherence to the totalizing "requirements of logical coherence."[59] Francis Landy explains that Lamentations is a historical biblical book that "marks, with untempered immediacy, the focal calamity of the Bible, the destruction of Jerusalem in 566 B.C.E."[60] In *The Lamentation*, also a clearly historical work, Christine intimates that the fall of Jerusalem is analogous to the prospective fracturing of France by an impending civil war in 1410, which, Christine predicts, will bring about "ruins of cities, destroyed towns and castles, [and] fortresses razed to the ground" in the "very center of France."[61] Here Christine borrows the rhetoric of "barrenness and desolation" from her biblical source text to give voice to the corporate anxiety about the approaching threat to the political and ecclesiastical order of her country of adoption.[62] She, like Jeremiah, is one who "has seen affliction" (Lamentations 3:1) and though she hopes that the salvation of the nation may come about through "the intercession of devout prayers," as it did in Nineveh,[63] she exposes in this work "the fragile balance between the rationality of a providential worldview and the paradoxes of humankind's historicity."[64]

Christine's awareness of the fragility of the beautiful harmony of all things in Wisdom's cosmic order is also recorded in *The Path of Long Study*, where Lamentations and Job are both cited to convey what Ricœur describes (citing Karl Jaspers) as the "limit situations" of life, which include "death, war, disease, crisis and so on"—the unpredictable reversals of Fortune's wheel.[65] As France sinks further beneath the weight of war, in-fighting intensifies among the nobles, and the Church schism remains unsettled, Christine's writing turns more and more to these "limit situations."[66] While these situations were supposedly encompassed by the sovereign order, belief in this sacred harmony was becoming increasingly strained for Christine and many of her contemporaries. As Ricœur maintains, when the discord between order and chaos is felt most acutely, wisdom turns to an Ecclesiastes-like expression of the ambiguity on the margins of proverbial virtue and the synthesizing impulse of the narrative.[67] Such a turn is evident in the rhetorical questions Christine poses at the end of *The Book of the Mutation of Fortune*:

> Considering all that's been said,
> Are [Fortune's] mutations like this so slight?
> What good is it to strive for gain
> When Her caprice will make it wane?
> There's no escape nor surety,
> Just pain and insecurity.[68]

In order to move beyond complaint and cynicism to consolation and renewal, Christine adopts a prophetic or apocalyptic stance in many of her works, as this posture is associated with the potentiality of (virtuous) human existence and the hope for eternal life.[69] Finding hope in the structure of the biblical narrative of Israel's history, Christine integrates "the tragedy of interruption" into the unfolding story of "the Lilies of France" (and, by extension, Christendom) by means of what Ricœur has identified as a prophetic "dialectic of reversal." Therein, the prophecies of misfortune, in response to the wickedness of God's people and the attendant experiences of Fortune's reversals, are met by prophecies of hope anticipating "the reversal of the reversal." Thus, by a "creative repetition" within the narrative, Christine's prophetic utterance "liberates a potential of hope. . . .a surplus of meaning, that, so to speak, lies dreaming in the traditional narrative."[70] So she can say in *The Poem of Joan of Arc*:

> Now hear throughout the world around
> This thing most marvelous of all!
> And see if God, in whom all grace
> Abounds, does not support what's right,

> When all is done. That's notable,
> Considering the case at hand!
> And may this hearten the dismayed,
> The ones whom Fortune's trampled down.[71]

The prominent place assigned revelatory discourse in Christine's works has received a measure of critical attention, especially as it relates to her assignment of prophetic power to female figures. Such is the case in her employment of sibylline references in, for example, *The Path of Long Study*, where the Cumaean sibyl, a female guide, discloses a series of spiritual truths about the operation of the cosmos to Christine, a lover of knowledge. As Willard explains, Christine regarded "the sibyls" as "equivalents of the biblical prophets," and these figures, scattered throughout her writings in various guises, have much in common with Old Testament prophetic types.[72]

Of Old Testament prophetic literature, Herbert Marks writes, the "personification of prophecy" was "erected . . . in the face of rising skepticism and disaffection." Marks makes note of the shift between the conception of "the traditional view of the prophet as messenger against such despair" and "the emergence of a new intermediary figure, the interpreter angel . . . who . . . exercises the traditional prophetic prerogatives of intercession and proclamation."[73] In the medieval period, Marks explains, prophets or prophetic messengers were believed to have access to a "visionary theatre," which permitted them to mediate "the 'overflow' of the divine presence."[74] Individual or trinities of prophetic women—intermediary figures who intercede and proclaim like the "heavenly messenger that guided Ezekiel"—often appear to Christine to reveal divine truths by leading her (as they had Dante) through visionary spectacles.[75] In *The Book of the City of Ladies*, for example, a "ray of light" appears to Christine, after which "three crowned ladies" or daughters of God present her with a spectacular vision of a correlative type of the New Jerusalem: the City of Ladies.[76] While her *City of Ladies*, like Augustine's *City of God*, maps out transcendent spiritual values, so too is it deeply implicated in matters of the world, or in (women's) history, for the prophetic messengers instruct her how to found and erect the City of Ladies inhabited by past and present women who "show forth" specific acts of "virtue" in their daily lives.[77] An instrument of these divine forces, Christine concludes the volume by providing women readers from a range of social stations with detailed instructions on ethical living. Thus, her treatise functions contemporaneously as both a visionary dissertation on moral philosophy and a practical conduct book on moral agency, contributing to what Brown-Grant calls Christine's "universal goal of moral self-edification."[78] Christine's prophetic visions, therefore, become a way to foster, as Bonnie Birk has shown, "justice and righteousness in the earthly realm," and should therefore be identified as a "world-based theology."[79]

This theological perspective is perhaps most evident in Christine's prophetic text, *The Poem of Joan of Arc*, her final work published a year before her death in 1430. Although the prophetic figures that appear to Christine are generally figured as otherworldly beings (and are clearly gendered personifications of abstract ideas), in *The Poem of Joan of Arc*, a contemporary woman appears as the historical fulfillment of past prophecies, which allows Christine to emerge as a prophetess from her "cage" in the "closed abbey" of Poissy, where she had joined her daughter in religious retreat around 1418, into the light of revelation in this world.[80] In the figure of Joan of Arc, the "elected Maid" sent by "[d]ivine commandment" and led "by God's angel" to "the king" of France to "bear the flag / In France's wars," Christine discovers her own prophetic voice, which allows her to speak of hope in this world, since she believes Joan's appearance proves that "God, who stands opposed to wrong, / Upraises those who keep their hope."[81] Of the authorial persona in *The Poem of Joan of Arc*, Kevin Brownlee insightfully observes,

> Christine has become a new, Christian sibyl with regard to Joan. She speaks with the voice of an authoritative—and authentic—female prophet. In the unfolding both of Christine's text and of Joan's life, a kind of continuity is involved here: the sibyl had predicted Joan's arrival and accomplishments up to the historical and textual present: Christine "takes over," in her own voice for the narrative of Joan's future. Past, present, and future converge in Christine's feminist reading of Joan's historico-political significance.[82]

Christine assumes this prophetic biblical identity at the end of her life to establish God's immanent and transcendent nature, to present the divine as a fiercely moral force that regularly intervenes in history to propel his people toward an earthly and spiritual Paradise, which, she believes, will come about through the art of peace.[83] Christine, therefore, relies on her moral authority as God's prophetess to admonish the "[f]oolish inhabitants" of Paris and other towns to "make peace" with their "prince" and to restore the God-ordained political order of Christendom.[84]

THE POLITICS OF RELIGIOUS DEVOTION

Maureen Boulton has shown that Christine's absorption of biblical modes of discourse is sometimes mediated by contemporary religious genres, which also permit her to instruct her readers in living a moral life and persevering in "His holy service."[85] Identifying Christine as "an artist at prayer," Boulton considers how Christine "worked with" and recast in her religious writings familiar devotional resources—"the essential elements of Catholic doctrine, lists of virtues and vices, gifts of the Holy Spirit, works of mercy, the words of the psalter, [and] the meditative program of the Book of Hours."[86] But Christine's most manifestly religious writings are not as private as the phrase "an artist at prayer" suggests, since they are the product of a woman author devoted to her public prophetic role as moral spokesperson for France. Drawing on the work of Raimond Thomassy and Maurice Roy, Willard demonstrates that Christine's most patently spiritual writings appeared in the most tragic period of France's history.[87] Her *Prayers to Our Lady* and *The Hours of Contemplation on the Passion of Our Lord* are filled with references to the victims of France's current turmoil and offer support to particular political figures. *The Hours of Contemplation*, a variation on the Book of Hours, is dedicated to those "who in various ways have been cast down, especially in this kingdom of France, both through the death of friends and through various events, and through other losses,"[88] just as her "Marian prayers," a feature of the late medieval Book of Hours, associate the virtue and authority of the Virgin with the Queen of France, the Dauphin, and the Duke of Orléans.[89] Prayer and politics, the "[m]irror of all virtue" and earthly government, are indivisible in these, as in many other, works by Christine, because she views life in this world as a spiritual exercise.[90] That her final work, *The Poem of Joan of Arc*, was a politically engaged poem composed in a place of religious devotion, the cloister at the Abbey of Poissy, suggests that she maintained the complementarity of the active and contemplative life, of concerns political and religious, even in the face of profound disappointment.

Earl Jeffrey Richards has argued that Christine is, like Dante, a "*poeta theologus*" or "poet theologian." This chapter suggests that there is certainly some merit to his claim. No doubt, the spiritual dimension of her "secular" works reflects an understanding of the operation of the divine.[91] As evidence of his claim, Richards cites Jean Gerson's brief mention in his correspondence of a "little woman" ("*femelete*") whose poor health compelled her to withdraw from the world, granting her the opportunity to "think about God and herself."[92] Although Christine is likely the "*femelete*" referred to by Gerson, even if she were not, her works testify to her frequent encounters with the divine most often achieved through intermediary prophetic figures, real or imagined. However, while Christine's works have a theological dimension, they are rarely concerned with pure or abstract theology. While Christine undertakes a series of epistemological quests in search of higher truths, her inquiries lead her to scripturally based practical moral advice that can be applied by members of all classes, from prince to prostitute.

Christine's focus on the ethical application of spiritual truths to all members of society has led Benjamin Semple to envision her as a kind of religious teacher of the people. In Christine's autobiographical *Vision*, Semple locates a desire to scrutinize and "redefine" medieval theology, arguing that she subverts the religious establishment's "claim to control" spiritual "truth."[93] Semple concludes that Christine "identifies" herself "with the simple person" in order to demonstrate "that the ethical qualities of humility and simplicity are more primary to a spiritual life than are the intricate constructions of theologians, which may appear to bring increased intellectual knowledge of the sacred but which actually lead away from God."[94] Granted, Christine assigns herself, a private laywoman, both ethical authority and agency and she is not interested in producing a systematic theology. Nevertheless, her treatment of spiritual matters is rooted in sophisticated intellectual debates of her time as recorded in a series of patristic and medieval theological texts with which she is familiar. In the *Letter on the Prison of Human Life*, Christine's deference to the knowledge of theologians is evident in her advice to Mary of Berry that she "give credence to the Holy Scriptures and to what the glorious doctors and many wise authors have said" concerning adversity.[95] Christine clearly identifies herself as an educated intellectual qualified to instruct nobles and plebeians alike without diminishing the importance of learned theologians in the religious establishment.[96] This is why she can advise "theologians" in *The Book of the Body Politic* to speak to the prince "about the law of the commandments and what one ought to hold and believe as a Christian" at the same time that she can assert that "any good Christian ought to be" "well informed on" "the law of God."[97] "Noble and godly" "virtue" can be taught, according to Christine, by male theologians or by a "humble" yet learned "[female] creature" "by the grace of God."[98]

As Earl Jeffrey Richards has observed, though the "strong religious element" in Christine's writings "may not appeal to some modern critics . . . it is an historical fact that Christine saw in Christianity a means of overcoming oppression."[99] The authoritative language of religion in medieval France which constrained Christine's thought was also the very medium through which she found the capacity to think more—to impugn the old and envision the new possibilities concerning the dignity of "ladies" of all classes, for example, and, more generally, the future of her nation and, indeed, the world. Were it not for the interpretive resources contained within the prevailing religious discourse, particularly in the modes of wisdom, narrative, and prophecy, Christine could not have imagined or articulated her aspirations for inclusion, dignity, and hope. Her awareness of the dialogic nature of the tradition gave her confidence that "everything comes to a head at a certain point" and that her "little pointed instrument" might prove to be a significant agent of change.[100] It is in this light that Richards is able to credibly compare Christine's "commitment to Christian values" to "that of Martin Luther King."[101] Through her spiritually informed moral aesthetic, the biblical, theological, devotional, and exegetical tradition was translated into a more capacious vessel conveying that "ultimate referent" of supreme wisdom, goodness, and power that has been contemplated "across the expanse of years" under the name of God.[102]

NOTES

1. Christine de Pizan, *The Writings of Christine de Pizan*, ed. Charity Cannon Willard (New York: Persea, 1994), 318.
2. Ibid.
3. See, for example, Bonnie A. Birk, *Christine de Pizan and Biblical Wisdom: A Feminist Theological Point of View* (Milwaukee: Marquette University Press, 2005); Rosalind Brown-Grant, *Christine de Pizan and the Moral Defence of Women: Reading beyond Gender* (Cambridge: Cambridge University Press, 1999); Earl Jeffrey Richards, "Somewhere between Destructive Glosses and Chaos: Christine de Pizan and Medieval Theology," in *Christine de Pizan: A Casebook*, ed. Barbara K. Altmann and Deborah L. McGrady (London: Routledge, 2003); Maureen Boulton, "'Nous deffens de feu, . . . de pestilence, de guerres': Christine de Pizan's Religious Works," in *Christine de Pizan: A Casebook*, ed. Altmann and McGrady; and Josette A. Wiseman, "The Resurrection according to Christine de Pizan," *Religion and the Arts: A Journal from Boston College* 4, no. 3 (2000): 337–58.
4. M. M. Bakhtin, *The Dialogic Imagination: Four Essays*, ed. Michael Holquist, trans. Caryl Emerson and Michael Holquist (Austin: University of Texas Press, 1981), 343.
5. Paul Ricœur, *Figuring the Sacred: Religion, Narrative, and Imagination*, ed. Mark I. Wallace, trans. David Pellauer (Minneapolis: Augsburg Fortress, 1995), 221.
6. C. S. Lewis, *The Allegory of Love: A Study in Medieval Tradition* (1936; repr., Oxford: Oxford University Press, 1977), 12.
7. Christine de Pizan, *The Selected Writings of Christine de Pizan*, ed. Renate Blumenfeld-Kosinski, trans. Renate Blumenfeld-Kosinski and Kevin Brownlee (New York: Norton, 1997), 194.
8. "Secular," *Oxford English Dictionary Online*, 2nd ed. (Oxford University Press, 1989), www.oed.com.
9. Christine de Pizan, *The Treasure of the City of Ladies, or The Book of the Three Virtues*, trans. Sarah Lawson (London: Penguin, 1985), 43–44.
10. Ibid., 60.
11. Christine de Pizan, *The Book of the Body Politic*, ed. and trans. Kate Langdon Forhan (Cambridge: Cambridge University Press, 1994), 15, 12.
12. Christine de Pizan, *Selected Writings,* ed. Blumenfeld-Kosinski, 16, 21, 25, 27.
13. Ibid., 59.
14. Nancy M. Frelick, "Fetishism and Storytelling in *Nouvelle 57* of Marguerite de Navarre's *Heptaméron*," in *Distant Voices Still Heard: Contemporary Readings of French Renaissance Literature*, ed. John O'Brien and Malcolm Quainton (Liverpool: Liverpool University Press, 2000), 140.
15. Sarah Kay, "Courts, Clerks, and Courtly Love," in *The Cambridge Companion to Medieval Romance*, ed. Roberta L. Krueger (Cambridge: Cambridge University Press, 2000), 93. In *The Allegory of Love*, C. S. Lewis claims that courtly love is at odds with religious belief, a position endorsed by Brian Stone in his introduction to *Medieval English Verse* (1964; repr. with revisions, Harmondsworth: Penguin, 1971), in which he claims that "medieval Christian ideas" on love are based in a "system opposite in drift to courtly love, one which, by its very denial of all that the new erotic religion stood for, may have [paradoxically] given strength to it" (21).
16. Barbara K. Altmann, "Diversity and Coherence in Christine De Pizan's *Dit de Poissy*," *French Forum* 12, no. 3 (1987): 263.
17. Ibid., 268.
18. Prudence Allen, *The Concept of Woman: Vol. II: The Early Humanist Reformation, 1250–1500, Part II* (Grand Rapids, MI: William B. Eerdmans, 2002), 560. In *The Tale of the Shepherdess*, Christine highlights that the lady will "never do any harm" to her "honor" nor will the male beloved perform "anything, in word or deed, that would cause . . . [her] to be blamed" (*Selected Writings*, ed. Blumenfeld-Kosinski, 56–57).
19. Brown-Grant, *Christine de Pizan and the Moral Defence of Women*, 216.

20. "Chivalry," *Oxford English Dictionary Online*. So too in *The Book of Deeds of Arms and of Chivalry*, ed. Charity Cannon Willard, trans. Sumner Willard (University Park, PA: Pennsylvania State University Park, 1999), Christine describes chivalric behavior in biblical terms; for example, she defines in Old Testament forensic language the limits of the chivalric prince at war, "For according to God's law it is not proper for man either to seize or to usurp anything belonging to another, or even to covet it. Likewise, vengeance is reserved for God, and in no way does any man have the right to carry it out" (17).

21. Christine de Pizan, *Letter of Othea to Hector*, trans. Jane Chance (1990; repr. Cambridge: D. S. Brewer, 1997), 37–38.

22. Ibid., 37, 41, 43, 37.

23. A. W. Schlegel, quoted in Maike Oergel, *The Return of King Arthur and the Nibelungen: National Myth in Nineteenth-Century English and German Literature* (Berlin: Walter de Gruyter, 1998), 106.

24. Christine de Pizan, *Letter of Othea*, trans. Chance, 35. Birk has recently discussed the theological aspects of the *Letter of Othea* in *Christine de Pizan and Biblical Wisdom* (14). Birk's study attends to Christine's negotiation of the sapiential tradition in this and other works.

25. David Knowles, *The Evolution of Medieval Thought*, 2nd ed. (London: Longman, 1988), 89.

26. Ibid., 335.

27. Hans Urs von Balthasar, *Love Alone Is Credible*, trans. D. C. Schindler (1963; repr., San Francisco: Ignatius, 2004), 18.

28. Ricœur, *Figuring the Sacred*, 177.

29. Anthony Kenny, *An Illustrated Brief History of Western Philosophy*, 2nd ed. (Malden, MA: Blackwell, 2006), 159–63; Christine de Pizan, *Body Politic*, ed. Forhan, 4.

30. Christine de Pizan, *Letter of Othea*, trans. Chance, 36.

31. Ibid., 37.

32. Ibid.

33. Ibid., 58.

34. Christine de Pizan, *Selected Writings*, ed. Blumenfeld-Kosinski, 29.

35. Balthasar, *Love Alone Is Credible*, 17–18.

36. Christine de Pizan, *Selected Writings*, ed. Blumenfeld-Kosinski, 63.

37. Ibid.

38. Ibid.

39. Ibid., 64.

40. *The Vision of Christine de Pizan*, trans. Glenda McLeod and Charity Cannon Willard (Woodbridge: D. S. Brewer, 2005), 132–34. Critics have duly noted Christine's rich reworking, rather than simple imitation, of the Boethian model. Christine reads Boethius through a Pauline lens, for example, at the conclusion of *The Book of the Mutation of Fortune*, a work heavily indebted to *On the Consolation of Philosophy*.

41. Allen, *The Concept of Woman*, 555.

42. These are the socioeconomic categories that Christine uses in *The Book of the Body Politic*.

43. Christine de Pizan, *Selected Writings*, ed. Blumenfeld-Kosinski, 235.

44. Knowles, *The Evolution of Medieval Thought*, 92.

45. Allen, *The Concept of Woman*, 652. Allen assigns this "preoccupation" of Christine to the "middle to late period of her life" (652). We believe that the seeds of her fascination with virtue are evident in her earlier works.

46. Brian Patrick McGuire, introduction to *Jean Gerson: Early Works*, trans. and introd. Brian Patrick McGuire (New York: Paulist Press, 1998), 9.

47. Christine de Pizan, *Selected Writings*, ed. Blumenfeld-Kosinski, 65.

48. Ibid.

49. Ibid., 250.

50. Brown-Grant, *Christine de Pizan and the Moral Defence of Women*, 3.

51. Ricœur, *Figuring the Sacred*, 37.

52. Ibid., 35, 37.

53. Ibid., 37.

54. James G. Williams, "Proverbs and Ecclesiastes," in *The Literary Guide to the Bible*, ed. Robert Alter and Frank Kermode (Cambridge, MA: The Belknap Press of Harvard University Press, 1987), 263–65.
55. Birk, *Christine de Pizan and Biblical Wisdom*, 68.
56. Christine de Pizan, *Letter of Othea*, trans. Chance, 112, 111, 99, 98.
57. Barbara Newman, *God and the Goddesses: Vision, Poetry, and Belief in the Middle Ages* (Philadelphia: University of Pennsylvania Press, 2003), 190–91.The inset quotation is from Ecclesiasticus 24:5. For a discussion of Christine's deployment of the Wisdom tradition for proto-feminist ends, see Newman's *God and the Goddesses* and Birk's *Christine de Pizan and Biblical Wisdom*.
58. Shirley Sharon-Zisser, *Critical Essays on Shakespeare's "A Lover's Complaint": Suffering Ecstasy* (Aldershot: Ashgate, 2006), 19.
59. Ricœur, *Figuring the Sacred*, 249.
60. Francis Landy, "Lamentations," in *The Literary Guide to the Bible*, ed. Alter and Kermode, 329.
61. Christine de Pizan, *Selected Writings*, ed. Blumenfeld-Kosinski, 225.
62. Landy, "Lamentations," 326, 333. Born in Venice, Christine moved to Paris as a young child.
63. Christine de Pizan, *Selected Writings*, ed. Blumenfeld-Kosinski, 227.
64. Ricœur, *Figuring the Sacred*, 238.
65. Ibid., 177.
66. Richard Kearney, *On Paul Ricoeur: The Owl of Minerva* (Aldershot: Ashgate, 2004), 17.
67. Ricœur, *Figuring the Sacred*, 177–78, 238.
68. Christine de Pizan, *Writings*, ed. Willard, 134.
69. Writing about the poetry of Henry Vaughan who, like Christine, lived through a traumatizing civil war, Claude J. Summers observes in "Herrick, Vaughan, and the Poetry of Anglican Survivalism," in *New Perspectives on the Seventeenth-Century English Religious Lyric*, ed. John R. Roberts (Columbia: University of Missouri Press, 1994), "apocalypticism is fundamentally an attempt to escape history by means of an appeal to a vision of eternity and an expression of faith in God's eventual intervention in human affairs" (52). In contrast, Christine's deployment of revelatory or apocalyptic discourse is a way of rendering visible and making sense of the presence of the divine in history.
70. Ricœur, *Figuring the Sacred*, 175–76.
71. Christine de Pizan, *Writings*, ed. Willard, 354.
72. Willard, notes to *Writings*, ed. Willard, 108.
73. Herbert Marks, "The Twelve Prophets," in *The Literary Guide to the Bible*, ed. Alter and Kermode, 213, 215, 217, 221, 227–28.
74. Ibid., 227.
75. Ibid., 228.
76. Christine de Pizan, *The Book of the City of Ladies*, trans. Earl Jeffrey Richards (New York: Persea, 1982), 6, 9. In terms of the City of Ladies as a type of New Jerusalem, Richards argues in "Somewhere between Destructive Glosses and Chaos," that the "virtuous women" that inhabit Christine's city are comparable to "the living stones of the Heavenly Jerusalem" and that Christine "intended" that her City be apprehended "as a rigorous allegory of the Heavenly Jerusalem" (45, 52).
77. *The Book of the City of Ladies*, trans. Richards, 254. In his introduction to his edition of *The Book of the City of Ladies*, Richards considers the relation of Christine's work to Augustine's *City of God*, suggesting that Christine alluded to Augustine's work because she wished "her political vision [to] be understood as participating in a Christian tradition of political philosophy" (xxvix). Richards sees Christine engaged in a new form of revolutionary historiography which is complemented, rather than subverted, by her religious, specifically ethical, commitment (xxviii–vix).
78. Brown-Grant, *Christine de Pizan and the Moral Defence of Women*, 28, 3. Birk, in *Christine de Pizan and Biblical Wisdom*, remarks on Christine's promotion in her *Vision* of "a life dedicated to morality, learning, wisdom, and socially enacted virtue," which Christine

believes is "the way of life desired by God" and thus "the height of human achievement" (105). This moral lesson is inscribed in many of Christine's works, including *The Book of the City of Ladies*, which, Brown-Grant believes, will allow all virtuous women to become, like Christine, moral authorities, despite misogynist claims to the contrary (*Christine de Pizan and the Moral Defence of Women*, 28).

79. Birk, *Christine de Pizan and Biblical Wisdom*, 106.

80. Charity Cannon Willard, "The Dominican Abbey of Poissy in 1400," in *Christine de Pizan 2000: Studies on Christine de Pizan in Honour of Angus J. Kennedy*, ed. John Campbell and Nadia Margolis (Amsterdam: Rodopi, 2000), 218; Christine de Pizan, *Writings*, ed. Willard, 352.

81. Christine de Pizan, *Writings*, ed. Willard, 356, 357, 358, 354.

82. Kevin Brownlee, "Structures of Authority in Christine de Pizan's *Ditié de Jehanne d'Arc*," in *Discourses of Authority in Medieval and Renaissance Literature*, ed. Kevin Brownlee and Walter Stephens (Hanover: Published for Dartmouth College by University Press of New England, 1989), 146.

83. Christine de Pizan, *Writings*, ed. Willard, 361–62.

84. Christine de Pizan, *Selected Writings*, ed. Blumenfeld-Kosinski, 261.

85. Christine de Pizan, *City of Ladies*, ed. Richards, 257.

86. Boulton, "Christine de Pizan's Religious Works," 224.

87. Willard, notes to *Writings*, ed. Willard, 318.

88. Christine de Pizan, *Writings*, ed. Willard, 346.

89. Ibid., 323–24; Boulton, "Christine de Pizan's Religious Works," 217.

90. Christine de Pizan, *Writings*, ed. Willard, 323.

91. Richards, "Somewhere between Destructive Glosses and Chaos," 45.

92. Ibid.

93. Benjamin Semple, "Critique of Knowledge as Power: The Limits of Philosophy and Theology in Christine de Pizan," in *Christine de Pizan and the Categories of Difference*, ed. Marilynn Desmond (Minneapolis: University of Minnesota Press, 1998), 126.

94. Ibid.

95. Christine de Pizan, *Selected Writings*, ed. Blumenfeld-Kosinski, 249.

96. In "Somewhere between Destructive Glosses and Chaos," Richards lists the type of "theological materials" that Christine deployed in her writings, linking her ideas with the theology of Thomas Aquinas (43).

97. Christine de Pizan, *The Book of the Body Politic*, ed. Forhan, 10, 12. Christine also associates the "simple" people with a measure of ignorance in the same volume, although she views them as "most necessary" to the body politic (*Body Politic*, ed. Forhan, 100, 107).

98. Ibid., 3–4.

99. Richards, introduction to *The Book of the City of Ladies*, xxvix.

100. Christine de Pizan, *Selected Writings*, ed. Blumenfeld-Kosinski, 45.

101. Richards, introduction to *The Book of the City of Ladies*, xxix.

102. Christine de Pizan, *Selected Writings*, ed. Blumenfeld-Kosinski, 45.

Chapter Two

Rhetorical and Editorial Strategies of Spreading l'*Évangile* in Marguerite de Navarre's *Le Miroir*

Sinda Vanderpool

Marguerite of Angoulême (1492–1549), later Duchess of Alençon and Queen of Navarre, is one of the most celebrated women leaders of all time. As sister to France's king (Francis I), she became a savvy political negotiator, and the French people looked to her as a chief figurehead upon her brother's frequent absences from court.[1] The siblings partnered to encourage the influx of Italian learning and culture that spawned what we know today as the French Renaissance. Raised with precisely the same education as that of her brother, she was one of the most learned women of the century, an author in her own right and a patron for many of the great poets and intellectuals of her time. Marguerite also gave official, royal credence to one of the lesser-known reformation movements of this era, the *réforme évangélique* that took place in France between the years 1520 and 1534. Its supporters, like other reformers across the European continent, championed the studying of the Scriptures in their original languages and translating them into the vernacular. In combination with the accessibility of the printing press, the Gospel's availability to a wider French-speaking audience fueled the flames of the reform. And, while the movement had an externally focused, evangelical thrust, the philosophical and theological motivation of the movement was the interior life.

The reformers, including Marguerite's spiritual mentor, Guillaume Briçonnet, the Bishop of Meaux, reacted against the tightly guarded walls of the Faculty of Theology at the University of Paris (the Sorbonne) and the emphasis on external works (*bonnes œuvres*) required of the believer in the Roman Catholic Church. Marguerite upheld through her literary works the *philosophia Christi,* a term Erasmus was using concurrently to describe the simple piety of examining one's own soul and imitating the life of Christ.[2] Briçonnet commissioned Marguerite to act as the public figurehead of the spiritual reformation in France; Marguerite promptly accepted this task in the well-known epistolary correspondence between Briçonnet and herself in the 1520s. She agreed that she would grant him her political support (*bons offices*) in courtly circles in exchange for his spiritual guidance (*secours spirituel*).[3] In fact, scholars agree that these letters had a decisive influence on Marguerite's spiritual and scholarly formation.[4] The writings that she began in the late 1520s were thus conceptualized as a form of spiritual leadership of her people. While Marguerite subtly critiqued the corruption that had descended upon the Catholic Church and joined occasionally in conversations with Luther and Calvin, she remained loyal to her Catholic heritage, focusing on how one might reform the Church from within its own walls, diocese by diocese, family by family, individual by individual. Spiritual concerns for her people stood front and center for Marguerite throughout her lifetime.

Of all the works in Marguerite's œuvre, prose and poetry included, *Le Miroir de lame pecheresse* marks her literary début. In 1531, when Simon Du Bois published a small collection of poems by the name *The Mirror of the Sinful Soul* from his Alençon studio, Marguerite's first major work was presented to the greater public. Previously, her poetry had only been distributed to smaller, courtly audiences in the form of hand-written manuscripts. The devotional poem *The Mirror of the Sinful Soul* is composed of approximately 1,400 decasyllabic couplets and appeared in at least twelve printed editions in Marguerite's lifetime, although there are no extant manuscripts of the poem. Retaining a careful and consistent awareness of previous literary traditions that informed her writing, Marguerite asserted a uniquely personal voice whereby inward examination aimed to inspire the reader to follow suit. By reflecting on the sinfulness and transformative process of her own soul, Marguerite desired to stir other hearts to deeper devotion to God. Further, the text's materiality, the way in which the text is physically presented and published, underscores the link between the inner and outer thrusts of the reform movement that Marguerite espoused. In Du Bois's 1531 edition of *Le Miroir*, a range of rhetorical and editorial strategies were deployed to elucidate and endorse Marguerite's reformist vision, and both this vision and Du Bois's strategies are the subject of this essay.

SPIRITUAL AND POETIC PATTERNING

A tripartite ascent pattern undergirds the entire structure of the poem. As with much devotional literature, the central figure (*âme*) is female. The soul's ascension from purgation (*purgatio*), to illumination (*illuminatio*), to perfection (*perfecto*), such as one sees in Bonaventure's work and countless other texts from the history of sacred literature, informs the entire movement of the poem. In *Celestial Ladders*, Paula Sommers provides a perceptive study of Marguerite's utilization of three-fold ascent patterns in her poetry. As the soul (*âme*) recounts her experience in moving toward union with God in three stages, the poet specifically recalls the interpretation that Marguerite's spiritual mentor, Briçonnet, gave of this three-fold pattern in *Celestial Hierarchies* by the Pseudo-Dionysius. Briçonnet indicates to Marguerite in one of his letters that the *purgatio* stage is an initial stage of purification, repentance, and reform; in *illuminatio* the soul gains a higher degree of spiritual insight; and finally, *perfecto* "facilitates contemplation of the beauty and mercy of God and leaves the soul burning with love for the Celestial Spouse."[5]

PARATEXTUAL AND PRINTING CONSIDERATIONS

In printing the spiritually structured poem, Du Bois creates a small prayer book. The publication included this main poem as well as two shorter poems, "Discord estant en l'homme par contrarieté de l'esperit et de la chair" ["The Disharmony in man caused by the contrast between spirit and flesh"] and "Oraison à nostre seigneur Jesus Christ" ["Oration to our savior Jesus Christ"]. The three poems were bound together, forming a devotional prayer book for private use at home. The primary intention of such literature was to "stir their readers to piety and good living, and to expound to them the essentials of right theology."[6] The editor includes a paratextual message on the title page of the first edition, welcoming all with an open and upright heart to read the text: "La Marguerite tresnoble et precieuse s'est preposee a ceulx qui de bon cueur la cerchoient" ["The very noble and precious pearl (Marguerite) offered itself (herself) to those who were looking for it (her) with a sincere heart"] (see figure 2.1).

The reader understands that the pearl of great price from Matthew's Gospel account offers itself to those who seek God's kingdom with a sincere heart. While the wording of this expression was most likely chosen by Du Bois himself, including a reference to the very noble "Marguerite" is certainly also a direct reference to the author. And, one could argue that the paratextual presentation represents a fair picture of the spirit in which Marguerite

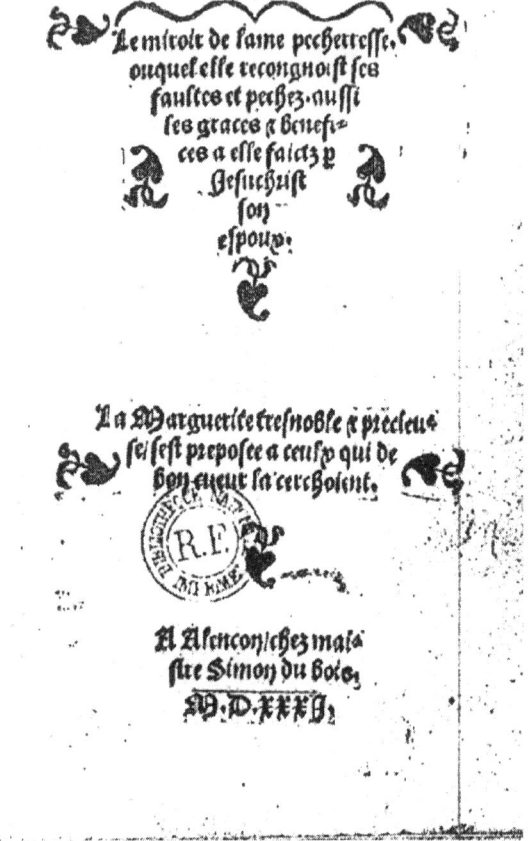

Figure 2.1. Title Page. *Le Miroir de lame pecheresse*. Alençon: Simon Du Bois, 1531. Courtesy of Bibliothèque nationale de France, Rés. Ye-203.

wished to present herself to her audience and is consistent with the meaning conveyed by the poem. The choice of the reflexive verb indicates the willingness Marguerite had to give her efforts fully so that anyone who reads her text with a sincere heart might find Christ.

Marguerite was accustomed to plays on her first name, heavily documented in the epistolary correspondence between Briçonnet and herself in the 1520s. Briçonnet frequently referred to the text of the Vulgate in which *margarita* means "pearl," and the Middle French *marguerite* means "daisy." Sixteen years later, when Jean de Tournes published the largest collection of Marguerite's poetry in her lifetime (*Les Marguerites de la Marguerite des princesses*), the poems in the edition are presented as *marguerites*, directly bearing the same name as their author. In fact, *Le Miroir* becomes one of the "marguerites" in the 1547 collection. Returning to the above 1531 title page, the direct object of the verb *chercher* (la) conflates "Marguerite" with her text that the reader holds. She presents an image of a self that openly invites others to participate actively in her work, offering her reader the very experience that the soul (*âme*) recounts in the poem. Marguerite reaches out and gives freely, willingly revealing her interior experience in order to spawn renewal in others.

While later editions of *Le Miroir* contained Scripture references in the margins, the full Scriptures found in this edition underscore the concept of mirroring. Notice in Figure 2.2 that the Scriptures occupy nearly one-third of the space on the page reproduced from *Le Miroir*. The reader visually observes mirror imagery: the poem is intended as a mirror, reflecting its divine source of inspiration—scripture.

Although a common feature in the works of evangelical Catholics and early Protestants, the mere presence of biblical translation in French was highly controversial at this time. Marguerite was directly implicated in this risky practice on several levels. After Jacques Lefèvre d'Etaples, a leading Christian humanist and champion of the French reform under Marguerite's direct protection, published his 1523 New Testament, the Sorbonne began to condemn biblical translations into French.[7] As persecution became the norm under the watchful eye of the University of Paris, many reformation printers and writers fled France, the majority retreating to Geneva. In 1529, Du Bois moved his atelier from Paris to Alençon under Marguerite de Navarre's protection; in 1530, Marguerite asked her brother if Lefèvre d'Etaples could live under her protection in her territory at Nérac.[8]

Scholars concur that Marguerite revealed a deep knowledge of both the Vulgate and the biblical translations of Jacques Lefèvre d'Etaples in *Le Miroir*. Lefèvre's New Testament text of 1523 and/or complete Bible of 1530 certainly served Marguerite and her editor as partial inspiration for the biblical passages. The two primary editors of *Le Miroir*'s critical editions agree that Marguerite had a hand in selecting the scriptural wording used in the margins. These scholars disagree on how closely Marguerite based the Scriptures in the margins directly on Lefèvre d'Etaples's Bible. Renja Salminen concludes that Marguerite usually had in mind the Vulgate while Joseph Allaire documents that well over half of the marginal verses came directly from Lefèvre's work.[9] Able to commonly recall the Vulgate and the more recent translations from memory,[10] Marguerite and her editor manifest a certain interior processing of the biblical passages for the edification of the reader. As the poem literally reflects the *Évangile*, Marguerite imparts the journey of her soul's transformative experience expressed in Scripture, from sinfulness to divine perfection through grace.

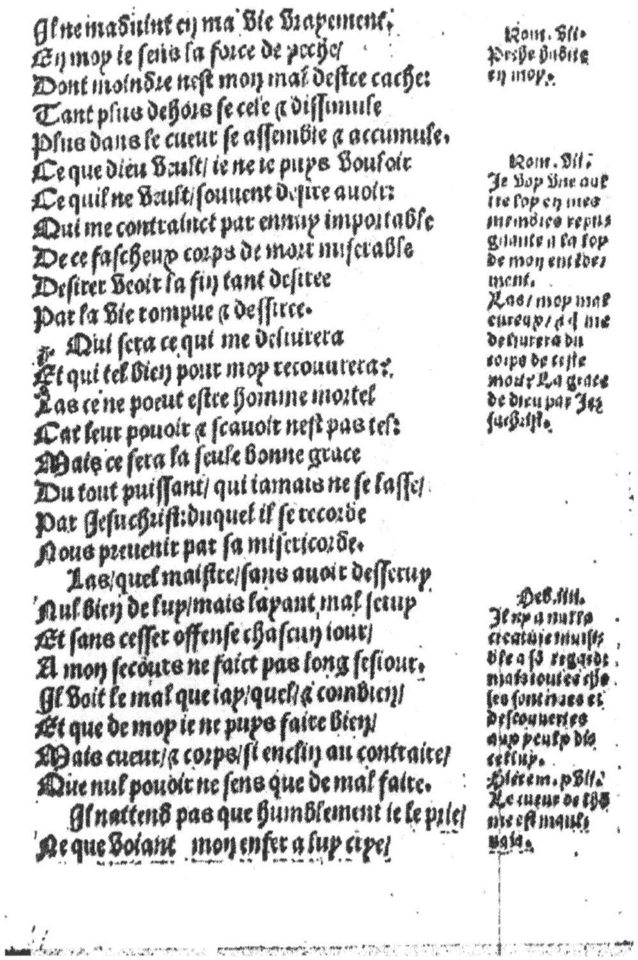
Il ne macquiert en ma vie vrayement,
En moy ie sens la force de peche/
Dont moindre nest mon mal destre cache:
Tant plus dehors se cele & dissimule
Plus dans le cueur se assemble & accumule.
Ce que dieu vault/ ie ne le puys vouloir
Ce quil ne vault/ souuent desire auoir:
Qui me contrainct par ennuy importable
De ce fascheux corps de mort miserable
Desirer veoir la fin tant desiree
Par la vie rompue & dessiree.
Qui sera ce qui me deliurera
Et qui tel bien pour moy recouurera?
Las ce ne peult estre homme mortel
Car leur pouoir & scauoir nest pas tel:
Mais ce sera la seule bonne grace
Du tout puissant/ qui iamais ne se lasse/
Par Iesuchrist: duquel il se recorde
Nous preuenir par sa misericorde.
Las/ quel maistre/ sans auoir desseruy
Nul bien de luy/ mais layant mal seruy
Et sans cesser offense chascun iour/
A mon secours ne faict pas long seiour.
Il voit le mal que iay/ quel/ & combien/
Et que de moy ie ne puys faire bien/
Mais cueur/ & corps/ si enclin au contraire/
Que nul pouoir ne sens que de mal faire.
Il nattend pas que humblement ie le prie/
Ne que voiant mon enfer a luy crye/

Figure 2.2. ***Le Miroir de lame pecheresse*****. Alençon: Simon Du Bois, 1531. Courtesy of Bibliothèque nationale de France, Rés. Ye-203.**

THE MIRROR (OR SPECULUM) LITERARY TRADITION

With Platonic, even biblical roots, mirror or speculum literature arose in the Middle Ages as a tool for teaching. In spite of its varied manifestations, mirror imagery upholds the dual-purpose motif of revealing the world for what it is and pointing out what it should be.[11] Saint Paul's famous passage on charity from his Epistle to the Church in Corinth becomes central to the application of mirror imagery in Christian literature and specifically in Marguerite's work: "For now we see in a mirror dimly, but then face to face.

Now I know in part; then I shall understand fully, even as I have been fully understood" (1 Corinthians 13:12 RSV). Or, as Hugh of Saint Victor states, the Scriptures, by way of reflection, "represent our interior picture, what is beautiful and what is deformed."[12]

Through the French Middle Ages, mirror literature became closely associated with vastly ambitious encyclopedic projects such as Vincent de Beauvais's *speculum majus* of the thirteenth century, which aimed at classifying the entirety of human knowledge. Moreover, in the fifteenth century, French vernacular *miroir* poems such as those of Georges Chastellain, Jean Molinet, and Guillaume Alexis focused on pedantic, moralizing, and didactic ends. A comparison of Chastellain's *Le Miroir de mort* and Marguerite's *Miroir* underscores the sixteenth-century poet's innovative use of this literary form. Chastellain begins his poem ostensibly by reflecting on an experience of earthly love. However, of the ninety-four stanzas of the poem, only the first nine speak at all of this lost love experience. The poet instead utilizes his story as a point of departure for a didactic claim that he will develop throughout the remainder of the poem: the fleeting nature of this world and the weakness of the human being:

> Prenons doncques humilité
> Et laissons ce péchié d'orgueil;
> Pensons à nostre humanité;
> . . . .
> Contemplant nostre povre vie:
> Sage est celuy qui peu s'y fie.[13]
>
> [Let us take on humility
> And leave behind the sin of pride;
> Let us reflect on our humanity,
> . . . .
> Contemplating our pitiable life;
> Wise is he who puts little trust in it.]

In this brief passage, Chastellain emphasizes the weak, fallen nature of human beings or, as Hugh of St. Victor states, what is "deformed" in our interior, present human condition.[14] He asks that the reader join with him through repetitious choruses that reflect on human weakness. In the last ten stanzas of the poem, the eight lines of each stanza begin with the same word. For example in the penultimate stanza, the poet states,

> Mirons enfer et damnement
> Mirons la mort et son tourment
> . . . .
> Mirons nostre fragilité;
> Mirons-nous pour estre saulvé.[15]
>
> [Let us mirror hell and damnation

> Let us mirror death and its torment
> . . . .
> Let us mirror our weakness;
> Let us mirror ourselves in order to be saved.]

Here, the poet encourages a look inward through prayer. However, the prayer resounds with the pedantic repetition of formulaic prayers—the sort that Erasmus and the new humanists of the sixteenth century frequently criticized. Chastellain accentuates sin to invoke guilt in his attempt to convict the reader of the human need for divine intervention.

PERSONALIZING THE MIRROR LITERARY TRADITION

As with the speaker in Chastellain's poem, the lyrical voice in Marguerite's *Miroir* recounts personal experience. Rather than doing so with moralizing authority, the poet turns the focus in on herself in the spirit of Christian humanism. One might recall, for instance, the work *Imitatio Christi*, commonly attributed to Thomas à Kempis and a favorite of Christian humanists, that exhorts, "Look well unto thyself, and beware that thou judge not the doings of others."[16] Erasmus had recently revived the ancient wisdom to "know thyself" in the Christian context where self-examination becomes a means to true Christian virtue. He encourages all Christians: "Let us begin to live the interior life all the more sincerely as we live less exteriorly. . . . [O]utwardly you are a Christian, but in private you are more pagan than the pagans. . . . You venerate the saints, and you take pleasure in touching their relics. But you disregard their greatest legacy, the example of the blameless life."[17]

As with the *Imitatio Christi,* Marguerite's poem promotes a thorough interior self-examination, but unlike Chastellain's poem it does so without a preacherly tone. In fact, just as Du Bois underscores Marguerite's authorship in the paratext, the lyrical voice never ceases to reflect back on the historical person, Marguerite de Navarre, who authored the poem. For instance, the poet expands on images of royalty to describe the divine as she exemplifies her relationship to Him in certain key passages of the text. The lyrical voice uses highly politicized words including throne, seat, war, crown, and empire while describing the divine reign:

> Gracieux lict, *throne* très honorable,
> *Siege* de paix, repoz de toute *guerre*,
> Hauldays d'honneur, separé de la *terre*,
> Recepvez vous ceste indigne personne,
> Me redonnant le *sceptre* et la *couronne*
> De vostre *empire* et *royaume* de gloire? (emphasis mine)[18]

>[Gracious bed, very honorable *throne*,
>*Seat* of peace, repose from all *war*,
>High table of honor, separated from the *earth*,
>Will you receive this unworthy person,
>Giving me back the *scepter* and *crown*
>Of your *empire* and glorious *kingdom*?]

The images of divine reign utilized by the poet are commonplace throughout Scripture and in Christian tradition. In instances where she uses them, the author directly points to herself and to the royal family who, in an effort to promote unity in France, launch a movement in support of the earthly royal family as the terrestrial representation of the divine family whose kingdom is in heaven.[19]

This is not an invention on Marguerite's part. As her mother, Louise de Savoie, anticipated sharing in Francis's power, she consciously constructed the familial royal trinity, consisting of Francis as central and primary, herself as secondary, and Marguerite as the tertiary element. The seamless unity of the three figureheads in relation to the divine becomes a substantial, tangible element in the effort to assert more centralized control over France's disparate territories. This figure is celebrated in poetry such as that of Jehan Marot, who hails the royal trinity as he sings of "[u]ng seul cueur en troys corps" [a "single heart in three bodies"] in one of his *rondeaux*:

>Ung seul cueur en troys corps, aujourduy voy en France,
>Regnant en doulx accords, sans quelque difference,
>D'amour tant enlacez, qu'il semble que nature
>Les formant ayt chassez, dissenssion, murmure,
>Pour nourrir sans discords, amoureuse alliance.[20]

>[A single heart in three bodies, I see today in France,
>Reigning in sweet accord without dissonance,
>So intertwined in love, that it seems that nature
>In creating them, drove out dissention, grumbling,
>To nourish without discord, the loving alliance.]

This three-part *alliance* is also found in prayer books, instructional handbooks, and educational treatises. One such image, for example, includes three smaller hearts with the letters "F," "M," and "L" representing Francis, Marguerite, and Louise, respectively, within a larger heart corresponding to the Divine (see figure 2.3).

Suitably, the soul's ascent from *purgatio* to *illuminatio* and on to *perfecto* involves a pattern of Trinitarian figures within the divine love story as the *âme* of Marguerite's poem aims to become one with the celestial spouse. In addition to the commonplace references between the soul and her holy spouse, the female self becomes in turn mother, daughter, and sister paralleling the divine Trinity of father, son, and spirit. The poet contemplates her

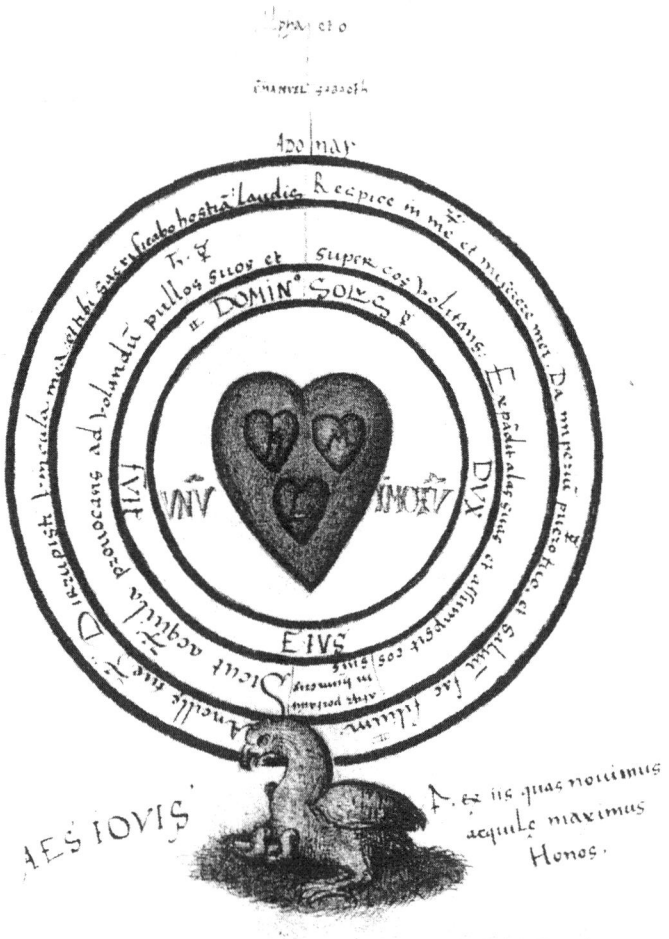

Figure 2.3. MS Lat. 8775, f. 1v. Courtesy of Bibliothèque nationale de France, Rés. Ye-203.

experience with God by living through and becoming the various female, familial figures. As she prepares to develop the relationship between husband and wife (lines 585–86) and reflecting back on the royal bond she shares with her mother and brother, she presents the family roles as interdependent with a cascading effect:

>Si pere a eu de son enfant mercy,
>Si mere a eu de son enfant soucy,
>Si frere à soeur a couvert le peché (lines 581–83)

>[If a father had mercy on his child,

If a mother had concern for her child,
If a brother covered his sister's sin]

Thus, the poem is a profoundly personalized reflection on self, even going so far as to recall the royal reign of power in France and the person of Marguerite of Angoulême as daughter to Louise de Savoie and sister to Francis.

The opening passage of Marguerite's mirror poem provides a prime example of the manner in which she personalizes the speculum tradition. Ironically, the self-reflective poem does not at all begin with the self, but it jolts the reader with horror and terror. In the resounding "Où est l'enfer . . ." ["Where is hell . . ."] of the first line, the poet imparts a sense of alienation in space and place.

Où est l'enfer remply entierement
De tout maleur, travail, peine et torment?
Où est le puitz de malediction
Dont sans fin sort desesperation?
Est il de mal nul si profond abisme
Qui suffisant fust pour punir la disme
De mes pechez? qui sont en si grand nombre
Qu'infinitude rend si obscure l'ombre
Que les compter ne bien veoir je ne puys,
Car trop avant avecques eulx je suis.
Et qui pis est, je n'ay pas la puissance
D'avoir d'ung seul, au vray, la congnoissance.
Bien sens en moy que j'en ay la racine,
Et au dehors ne voy effect ne signe
Qui ne soit tout branche, fleur, fueille, et fruict,
Que tout autour de moy elle produict. (lines 1–16)

[Where is hell, entirely full
Of every misfortune, work, pain, and torment?
Where is the pit of malediction
Out of which comes despair without end?
Is there a deep enough abyss
That is sufficient to punish the weight
Of my sins? Which are so numerous
That infinity creates such a dark shadow
That I cannot see well enough to count them
Because I am so immersed in them.
And, worse yet, I do not have the power
To really have understanding of a single one.
I really feel as though I have their root inside of me,
And outside only see their effect or sign
Such as branches, flowers, leaves, and fruit
That it (the root) produces around me.]

A personal narrative voice reaching out in relation to her reader is nowhere to be found; in fact, the *âme* (personal, universal, or otherwise) exists nowhere in these words. Moreover, in a poem inspired by the *devotio moderna*, it might seem shocking that the poet opens with a resounding question. The author uses the *ubi sunt* rhetorical trope, a question whose principal theme is the transitory nature of all things, such as the famous line from François Villon's "Ballade des dames du temps jadis" with its refrain, "Mais ou sont les neiges d'antan?" ["But where are the snows of yesteryear?"].[21] Rather than situating the self in a familiar world, the reader is confronted with a perilous hell, the unknown non-place of human experience, in order to emphasize a condition as distinct from the self as can be conceptualized. The reader is brought into a state of horror and shock, and made to contemplate a place where God is absent.

The choppy, monosyllabic sounds that open the poem, especially in line five, indicate that a radical shift is about to occur:

> Est il de mal nul si profond abisme,
> Qui suffisant fust pour punir la disme
> De mes pechez? (lines 5–7)

> [Is there a deep enough abyss
> That is sufficient to punish the weight
> Of my sins?]

With the feminine rhyme of *abisme* and *disme,* the couplet is complete; the poet breaks this pattern, extending the object of *disme* onto the next line through its enjambment with *de mes pechez*. The enjambment ushers in a shift from third-person rhetorical questioning to the first-person experience. The metaphysical questioning marks a starting place for self's identity. Following the opening, impersonal lines of the text, the first person voice begins to assert more and more of a presence in the text. In the following ten lines of text, there are seven direct links to the first-person pronoun: *mes pechez, je ne puys, je suis, je n'ay pas, j'en ay, voy, de moy*. Although still uncertain about its place, the self speaks more and more in this first-person voice. The unknown, perilous hell reveals itself as a hell of the soul's own making in this phase of purgation. This reading is directly supported in line 82, where the rhetorical, impersonal "Où est l'enfer" ["Where is hell?"] of line 1 has emphatically become "mon enfer" ["my hell"].

Since the 1531 edition referenced Marguerite as the text's author, contemporary readers would have certainly expected her to adopt a teacherly, superior pose, considering both the French literary precedents in mirror literature and the duchess's royal position. The poet, however, sets up this tone in the beginning of the poem only to personalize it subsequently. Expecting royal and preacherly authority, the reader finds a lost soul, the worst of sinners, confessing sins. Throughout the poem, the authorial voice emphasizes the fact that she is part of the people to whom she speaks. In one instance, she speaks of herself as one among many who used to attend mass only out of custom but confesses that she really only wanted to go about pleasing herself: "A l'eglise n'alloie que par coustume /. . . . / J'aymoie bien mieulx à mon plaisir aller" (lines 676–80) ["I only went to church by habit / . . . . / I preferred going out to please myself"]. This intentional positioning of herself as one with the masses is both a powerful rhetorical strategy and gesture of humility, turning mirror literature toward different ends and new heights of impact.

ACTIVATING THE TRANSFORMATION OF OTHERS

Rather than simply recounting an experience, the lyric voice goes through a transformation and activates it in the language of the poem, emphasizing the fact that telling and doing go hand in hand. J. L. Austin's lectures on speech acts, in which he explores the performative notion of language, aptly pertain to the way in which Marguerite wishes to reach her hearers. Austin argues that a "statement" in language does not always merely "describe" but rather goes in tandem with an action.[22] Emile Benveniste had already identified, in first-person speech, such moments in which utterance corresponds to the act itself. Words become the outward, audible sign that an action is taking place.[23]

Marguerite's poem makes use of such performative utterances in a Christian context, drawing on the biblical understanding of language as both a state of being and an action. In the opening of John's Gospel, we read that from the beginning "the Word was God," and in Genesis the words of God are literally generative: "And God said, 'Let there be light'; and there was light" (Genesis 1:3 RSV). Following the first creation account, the initial command God gives to humans is to participate in originative acts. Significantly, the co-creating process is performed through naming: "So out of the ground the Lord God formed every beast of the field and every bird of the air, and brought them to the man to see what he would call them; and whatever the man called every living creature, that was its name" (Genesis 2:19 RSV).

Likewise, for Marguerite, writing and reading her poem are participatory acts. In the context of remembering her baptism (lines 192–93, 225), the act of naming God calls to consciousness the soul's own identity:

> O quel honneur, quel bien, et quelle gloire
> A ceste ame qui toujours ha memoire
> Qu'elle est de vous fille! et vous nommant
> Pere, elle faict vostre commandement. (lines 215–18)

> [Oh ! What honor, goodness, and glory
> For this soul who always recalls
> That she is your daughter! and by naming you
> Father, she does your will.]

The act of naming God "Father" on one level recalls her spiritual identity, that she is God's daughter through baptism. She layers the personal, lived experience of God with the present writing and reading of the words. Simultaneously, the act of naming God goes in tandem with the present living out of God's will. Contextually, Marguerite is leading up to a reflection on the reciting of the Our Father (*Paternostre* in Middle French):

> Osera bien mon esperit s'avancer
> De vous nommer Pere? Ouy, et nostre,
> Ainsi l'avez dict en la Paternostre" (lines 248–50)

> [Will my spirit dare put itself forward
> To name you Father? Yes, and our,
> As you have said in the Paternoster]

She underscores that, in the actual writing of these words, she is also following God's commands ("faict vostre commandement") in the present instance. The gerund form of the verb "to name" extends the present-ness of the instance, which is further suspended by the use of enjambment since the reader anticipates the object of the clause and must read onto the next line. In the throes of writing the word "nommant," the act of obeying God's "commandement" takes place. The value of rhetoric is the action that occurs as a result of the words. Reading the poem is a participation in the creative act that human beings are called to perform.

As Marguerite's poetic voice emerges in this poem, the teacher, an exemplum, unveils the self in order to link her experiences to that of the reader, hoping to activate the process of the transformation in the other. Like the hospitable invitation included on the title page of this edition, *Le Miroir* urges the reader to experience the words along with the self of the poem and to mirror the process of confession and Scripture reading with her. The poet aims to convince those who hear that these words can be activated for themselves. In so doing, she confesses simultaneously her dependence on the other: the text is dependent upon the reader's activating the words she has written. As the self of this poem was changed by God's *Évangile*, these words, by their performative nature, intend to do the same for their readers and hearers.

In this reflective glance where speaking and doing are one and the same, Marguerite reaches out in a gesture of compassionate humility via an interior, personal reflection. Thus, as with other reformers, Marguerite's goal is to teach and evangelize. As her literary voice emerges in this first major poem, she modifies the traditional form of didactic mirror literature by personalizing the link between reader and author. She utilizes rhetoric of action with an emphasis on the activation and application of her words.

In October 1533, two years after the *Miroir*'s first publication, an unprecedented event took place: the work of Marguerite, a figurehead of the French monarchy, came under scrutiny by the Sorbonne, another sign of the intensifying religious tensions, and eventual wars, in France. Several of those associated with the publication of the *Miroir* were put to death; others were exiled. To make matters worse, a small group of French reformers made a fatal mistake. On the night of October 17, 1534, placards were hung on the walls and doors of public places, including Francis's palace at Blois (this event is now known as the Placard Affair). These contained injurious, biting attacks on central tenets of Catholic orthodoxy. Francis, Marguerite's brother, retaliated by condemning to death dozens of radical reformers as the year 1534 drew to a close. Marguerite could no longer lend outward support to Lefèvre or to Briçonnet's now dissipating dream of internal renewal of the Roman Catholic Church in France. She nevertheless continued to teach and write, albeit with more subtlety, via the convergence of words and living example, and by setting forth a humble posture before all.

NOTES

1. For more on the leadership of Marguerite of Navarre, see Jonathan A. Reid, *King's Sister—Queen of Dissent: Marguerite of Navarre (1492–1549) and Her Evangelical Network*, 2 vols. (Leiden: Brill, 2009).
2. *The Erasmus Reader*, ed. Erika Rummel (Toronto: University of Toronto Press, 1990), 138–54.
3. Guillaume Briçonnet and Marguerite d'Angoulême, *Correspondance 1521–1524*, ed. Christine Martineau, Michel Veissière, and Henry Heller (Geneva: Droz, 1975), 25–29.
4. Henry Heller, "Marguerite de Navarre and the Reformers of Meaux," *Bibliothèque d'Humanisme et Renaissance* 33 (1971): 275.
5. Paula Sommers, *Celestial Ladders: Readings in Marguerite de Navarre's Poetry of Spiritual Ascent* (Genève: Droz, 1989), 13.
6. Gary Ferguson, *Mirroring Belief: Marguerite de Navarre's Devotional Poetry* (Edinburgh: Edinburgh University Press, 1992), xii.
7. Frédéric Delforge, *La Bible en France et dans la francophonie: Histoire, traduction, diffusion* (Paris, Société biblique française, 1991), 57.
8. Ibid., 59.
9. Marguerite de Navarre, *Le Miroir de l'âme pécheresse*, ed. Joseph L. Allaire (Munich: Fink, 1972), 21–22. Marguerite de Navarre, *Le Miroir de l'âme pécheresse*, ed. Renja Salminen (Helsinki: Academia Scientiarum Fennica, 1979), 39–40.
10. *Miroir*, ed. Allaire, 22.
11. Rita Mary Bradley, "Backgrounds of the Title *Speculum* in Medieval Literature," *Speculum* 29 (1954): 102.
12. Ibid., 111; Bradley is actually quoting from *Expositio in Regulam Beati Augustini* (*PL*, clxxvi, 923D–924A).
13. Georges Chastellain, *Œuvres*, ed. Kervyn de Lettenhove, 8 vols. (Brussels, 1863–1866), 6:55.

14. Bradley, "Backgrounds," 111.
15. Chastellain, *Œuvres*, 6:64.
16. Thomas à Kempis, *The Imitation of Christ*, trans. William Benham (London, 1874), 34.
17. *The Erasmus Reader*, 142–44.
18. Marguerite de Navarre, *Le Miroir de l'âme pécheresse*, ed. Allaire, lines 844–49; subsequent references are to this edition and will appear parenthetically in the text by line number.
19. Leah Middlebrook, "'Tout mon office': Body Politics and Family Dynamics in the verse épîtres of Marguerite de Navarre," *Renaissance Quarterly* 54, no. 4 (2001): 1114.
20. Jehan Marot, *Les Deux recueils*, ed. Gérard Defaux and Thierry Mantovani (Genève: Droz, 1999), lines 1–5.
21. François Villon, *Œuvres*, ed. Jean Dufournet and André Mary (Paris: Garnier, 1970), 59.
22. J. L. Austin, *How to Do Things with Words*, ed. J. O. Urmson and Marina Sbisà (Cambridge: Harvard University Press, 1975), 1–6.
23. Emile Benveniste, *Problèmes de linguistique générale* (Paris: Gallimard, 1966), 244, 253.

Chapter Three

Stars, Stones, Ships, and Suckling Children

Guyon's Metaphorical Journeys toward Union with God

Deborah Sullivan-Trainor

In an era when the political, social, and religious power was concentrated in the court at Versailles and around the person of Louis XIV, Jeanne Marie Bouvier de la Motte Guyon (1648–1717) experienced a way of knowing God and, more importantly, of achieving union with Him without the intervention of the Church or its clergy. She asserted that this union comes about through a particular method of prayer and claimed that all believers can undertake this type of prayer and experience union with God. Her conviction that all should be able to pray using her method led Guyon to share it with others both by mentoring fellow believers and by writing a brief prayer guide. Sharing this method embroiled her in one of the great religious debates of the seventeenth century and inextricably linked her name with François de Salignac de la Mothe-Fénelon (1651–1715), for whom she was a spiritual mentor, and Jacques-Bénigne Bossuet (1627–1704), who condemned quietist prayer as heretical and considered Guyon, her method of prayer, and her writings as dangerous. In addition to affecting the spiritual lives of her readers, the text through which Guyon shares her method, *A Short and Easy Method of Prayer* (*Le Moyen court et très facile de faire oraison*),[1] also provides an excellent example of a quietist understanding of ways of experiencing God. The text is also significant for an inclusiveness missing from other quietist prayer manuals and an insistence on the relational experience of the believer with God at a time when the Church and society were increasingly embracing scientific rationalism.[2] Moreover, Guyon's writing itself reflects two essential aspects of her prayer method: the tension between taking action in prayer and passively allowing God to act upon and within the believer and the relational interaction between the believer and God.

The evidence of active/passive tension appears already in the title of Guyon's prayer manual, for it contains a verb that belies the approach to prayer she offers to her reader. While *faire* suggests that the reader will take action, this very action contradicts the essence of Guyon's approach: a passive quietness through which one can join with God in pure love. The tension between the quietist method Guyon proposes in her text and the action evoked by the titular verb is emblematic of the challenge Guyon faces in communicating how to pray using a method of prayer which, in its purest form, consists of doing nothing. Guyon's most effective strategies for meeting this challenge are rhetorical echoes of the accounts of her own experience with prayer and scriptural quotations that are liberally sprinkled throughout her text. Guyon's use of direct address duplicates her frequent references to her own prayer experience, since through her conversations with her readers she speaks as if she is in prayer with them. She puts herself in relationship with her reader in the hopes that, through her method of prayer, they will be able to join her in experiencing union with God. Her scriptural quotations point toward the highly metaphorical language that dominates the text and are the locus of the textual tension with which Guyon contends. A study of Guyon's choice, juxtaposition, and interweaving of metaphors suggests that the essential component of the method of prayer she proposes is that of positive spiritual inertia—an inertia that she presents to her readers through metaphors of journey (stars, stones, and ships) and relationship (suckling children).

Guyon's metaphorical manipulations, the prayer method she practices and proposes, and the union with God she asserts as possible, have drawn and continue to draw others to her person and to her writings. However, since both Guyon's personal story and the context within which she lived and which informed her spiritual journey are unknown to many, a brief foray into her biography will allow the reader to situate the author, her writings, and her prayer method in a distinct historical and cultural landscape and will also contribute to a better understanding of the significance of a spiritual guide, both textual and human, to her spiritual development and her efforts to guide others. A brief introduction to quietism will provide a context for the analysis of Guyon's prayer method and manual.

GUYON'S LIFE

Guyon's upbringing in Montargis was consistent with that of other young aristocratic women in seventeenth-century France. Stays in various convents provided an education that, though not extensive, was sufficient to make her into a fluent and somewhat voracious reader. In addition to reading the entire Bible during a brief convalescence, somewhat unusual in her day, Guyon's reading of François de Sales's *Introduction to the Devout Life* and the writings of Madame de Chantal were foundational to her own future spiritual journey and writings. Though not happy in her twelve-year marriage, Guyon used this time to focus her love on God and sought out those who could guide her spiritually. The concepts and methods Guyon had encountered in de Sales and de Chantal were enlivened by a flesh-and-blood guide, the Duchess de Bethune-Charost, as well as a cousin who had returned from missionary service in China. She observed in him a method of praying that was unlike any that she had previously seen and that profoundly influenced her own approach to prayer: "He prayed without words and without definite thoughts or requests in his mind. His whole being was concentrated in worship, and the power of the divine attention closed his mouth and hushed all process of thought."[3]

Upon being widowed at the age of twenty-eight, Guyon took additional steps, both literally and figuratively, that would have a profound effect on her spiritual practices and beliefs, her writings, and her life. According to Marie-Florine Bruneau, she was at that time "possessed by an apostolic mission she could not as yet define. . . . She searched for her own path, which did not seem to adhere to any of the existing lay roles permitted to women nor to any of the roles that the church reserved for rich widows in the late seventeenth century."[4] Of prime importance during this time was her relocation to Thonon, in Savoy, where she encountered the Barnabite priest, François La Combe, her future confessor who was instrumental in instructing her in interior prayer. Guyon began to immerse herself in prayer, endeavoring to annihilate the self, so that she could experience union with God. She also undertook her first written work, *Spiritual Torrents (Les Torrents spirituels)*. She followed her confessor first to Turin, then to Grenoble, where she wrote *Explanations and Reflections on the Bible (La Sainte Bible avec des explications et réflexions qui regardent la vie intérieure)* and her best-known work and the focus of this study, *A Short and Easy Method of Prayer*. Though a period of prolific writing for Guyon, this was also a time when hostility toward quietism, the movement and doctrine which she espoused, increased, and rumors and gossip about those who practiced this form of prayer and proselytized others mounted. Refused permission by the bishop to reenter Grenoble after a trip abroad, Guyon headed for Paris.

Louis XIV's growing displeasure with any Parisian increase in quietism, jealousies within the various religious orders that influenced Catholic doctrine in France during the seventeenth century, and family greed for Guyon's money resulted in first La Combe and later Guyon being imprisoned. Released after seven months, Guyon returned to the home of the Duchess de Béthune-Charost, where she met Fénelon, the aforementioned abbot with whom she developed a remarkable and intense rapport as she instructed him in the contemplative life. He became not only a devoted disciple but her defender when, in 1693, she was asked to leave the school of Saint Cyr, which Madame de Maintenon, second wife of Louis XIV, founded and oversaw. It was deemed that Guyon, her texts, and practices were having an undue and disruptive influence, and they particularly outraged Godet Desmarais, Bishop of Chartres and Madame de Maintenon's confessor. His charges of heresy led Guyon and her quietiest supporters to call for a reading and judgment of the orthodoxy of her texts. Upon Fénelon's recommendation, Bishop Jacques Bénigne Bossuet, a respected and renowned theologian, was selected to oversee the task and was joined by Noailles, Bishop of Chalon and Tronso, Superior of Saint Sulpice. In the hope of avoiding a second imprisonment, Guyon also sought a judgment of her doctrine and morals.[5] The meetings during which these judgments took place, the Issy Conferences, were characterized by vigorous attacks and defenses of Guyon's person and doctrine and ended in resolutions, known as the Articles of Issy, that, though avoiding complete condemnation of quietism, nonetheless declared that quietist doctrine exceeded the limits of truth.[6] Furthermore, Guyon's works were condemned and she was sent to the diocese of Meaux. Bossuet, who tolerated neither the possibility that Guyon would again have any influence in the capital nor the whisperings that Guyon had defeated him in argument, orchestrated her arrest in 1695.[7] Guyon was first sent to a prison in Vincennes, but was moved to a monastery in Vaugirard upon Madame de Maintenon's request. Two years later, she was transferred to the Bastille where she was held in solitary confinement for four years in conditions that weakened her physically for the rest of her life.[8] The king eventually granted her clemency and allowed her to move to her son's home in Diziers where she stayed under strict supervision for six months. In 1702, perceived to no longer be a threat to the spiritual well being of others, she was banished to Blois with the warning that she would be returned to the Bastille were she to leave the city. Fifteen years later it was there that she died at the age of sixty-nine.[9]

QUIETISM

Though Guyon was not passive in her desire and efforts to share an approach to prayer, passiveness is one of the defining characteristics of quietism. Referred to as both a movement and a doctrine, quietism calls for believers in prayer to "abandon themselves absolutely and entirely to the love of God, in a spirit of total disinterestedness—unconcerned even for the fate of their own souls. Those who succeed in the renunciation of the self through an intense regimen of prayer and devotion would eventually find God actively taking possession of them, bringing about an ecstatic state of 'pure love.'"[10]

In her own era, as well as in the centuries that have followed, Guyon was and continues to be one of the individuals consistently identified as one of quietism's most renowned practitioners and proponents. She shares this notoriety with Michael de Molinos (1628–1697) and Fénelon. However, we can trace the roots of this way of praying, along with some of its theological, spiritual, and moral implications, to a time long before the term quietism is first applied. Similarly, its sources are geographically diverse. In its call for abnegation of the self in the pursuit of unity with God, for example, some see quietist roots in Neo-Platonism. Connections with Augustine's doctrine of grace and the inward focus of Thomas à Kempis and John Hales are also evident.[11]

Because of their belief that closeness to God is brought about by a turning from the world, the mystics of the Counter-Reformation, such as St. John of the Cross and St. Teresa of Avila, are commonly considered as precursors of the quietists.[12] With these mystics, quietists also share an understanding of contemplation as "an absorbed, loving intuition of divine things, a direct spiritual apprehension of God and an adhesion to Him."[13] In this direct apprehension of God, contemplative prayer distinguishes itself from meditative prayer. Neither discursive nor visual, it does not call for active engagement of the imagination, memory, or intellect.[14] Its practitioners seek to abandon their soul to God for Him to act upon it and fill it with pure love. That quietism shares this approach to prayer with so many mystics leads Rufus Jones to suggest that quietism is "the most acute and intense stage of European mysticism . . . [the] result of the normal ripening, the irresistible maturing, of experiences, ideas, and principles that had been profoundly working for a very long period in the religious consciousness of Europe."[15] Likewise, its importance for understanding the history and development of early modern Catholicism leads some scholars to categorize spiritual movements as either pre-quietist or quietist.[16] Yet the terms "quietist" and "quietism" do not become commonly used until Molinos's beliefs are challenged in Rome in 1682. In a letter from the archbishop of Naples to the Pope, denouncing Molinos, we find a declaration that Molinos and others who embrace what he refers to as a heresy, call themselves "quietists."[17] Five years later, in the papal encyclical *Coelestis Pastor*, Pope Innocent XI condemns Molinos for teaching false doctrine "under pretext of the prayer of quiet."[18]

The condemnation and persecution that Molinos and Guyon experience come in part from quietism's implicit theology, one which has been declared by some to be "devoid of any hope of reward and lack[ing] a Christological center of gravity."[19] Claims that spiritual danger and immoral behavior result from the practice of quietist prayer also invigorate the condemnation of quietism as heretical. Equally significant, as can be seen in Guyon's own life story, is the threat to ecclesiastical structures and authorities caused by quietist assertions that union with God can be achieved without rosaries, masses, and the sacraments.

The accusation of quietism as spiritually dangerous most frequently finds it source in its call for the Christian to empty the soul of all things so that it can be open to and ready for union with God. As the soul rests quietly, passively waiting for God to bring it into a divine unity of love, it is said to be vulnerable to Satan, who also seeks unity with the soul for his own purposes.[20] While some see this satanic unity as imperiling the soul and leading the Christian to sin, it is not envisioned as the only source of moral danger for those who pray using the quietist method. For the soul in full union with God, quietism's critics claim, can hardly be expected to control what the body is doing and therefore might unknowingly engage in acts of the flesh. Furthermore, such acts, since they are not undertaken by an individual in control of his or her body, can be construed as sinful acts without moral consequences. Under interrogation by the Inquisition, Molinos gives credence to this claim by confessing to having committed such immoral bodily acts with impunity, claiming that "his higher faculties, in union with God, did not consent [and therefore his acts] were not sinful."[21]

A SHORT AND EASY METHOD

Guyon's prayer guide ignores any mention of these supposed dangers of quietist prayer, insisting instead on the joy, fullness, and ecstasy one can experience through complete union with God in prayer. However, her preface indicates that she is very much aware of the criticism that she and her method provoke, asking "the skilled and the experienced . . . not to decide without first entering into the main design of the Author, which is to induce the world to love God and to serve Him with comfort and success" (3). She guarantees that the "unprejudiced reader may find . . . a secret unction" and that "[n]othing will be found herein to offend, provided it be read in the spirit with which it is written" (3). Guyon calls not just for the reader to approach her text as an unprejudiced seeker with the right spirit, but also insists that only through personal experience can one determine the validity of her claims and the efficacy of her method: "Let them [her critics] not on my testimony alter their opinion, but rather make trial of it, and their own experience will convince them that the reality far exceeds all my representations of it" (4).

In its invitation to all readers to attempt her method of prayer, Guyon's text stands in sharp contrast to Molinos's *Spiritual Guide* (1675), where the author warns: "It is to be taken notice of, that the Doctrine of this Book instructs not all sorts of Persons, but those only who have the Senses and Passions well mortified, who have already advanced and made progress in Prayer, and are called by God to the inward way, who encourages and guides them, freeing them from the obstacles which hinder the course to perfect Contemplation."[22] Guyon, however, insists that "a dreadful delusion hath prevailed over the greater part of mankind, in supposing that they are not called to a state of prayer, whereas we are all called to prayer and are called hereto, as all are called to and capable of salvation" (7).

Essential to understanding why Guyon insists that all are capable of prayer is the distinction between two types of praying, *oraison* and meditative prayer.[23] Molinos shares with Guyon the distinction in types of prayer, and provides a succinct explanation of the differences between these two forms of prayer in his *Spiritual Guide*, referring to them as meditation and contemplation:

> When the Mind considers the Mysteries of our holy Faith with attention, to know the truth of them, reasoning upon the particulars, and weighing the circumstances of the same, for the exciting of affections in the Will; this mental discourse and pious Act is properly called Meditation. When the Soul already knows the truth (either by a habit acquired through reasoning, or because the Lord hath given it particular light) and fixes the eyes of the Mind on the demonstrated truth, beholding it sincerely with quietness and silence, without any necessity of considerations, ratiocinations, or other proofs of conviction, and the will loves it, admiring and delighting itself therein; This properly is called the Prayer of Faith, the Prayer of Rest, Internal Recognition or Contemplation.[24]

The second type of praying of which all are capable, according to Guyon, is *oraison*. It is notable that her affirmation that all are capable of prayer (*oraison*) is immediately followed by a statement that this is not true of meditation: "I grant that mediation is attainable but by few, for few are capable of it; therefore, my beloved brethren who are thirsty for salvation, meditative prayer is not the prayer God requires of you, nor which we would recommend" (6) ["Mais je conviens que tous ne peuvent pas méditer et très peu y sont propres. Aussi n'est-ce pas cette oraison que Dieu demande ni que l'on vous désire" (61)]. However, Molinos does not share with Guyon the same strong confidence that all can or should undertake the quietist prayer to which his texts claim to guide the reader.

If Molinos is explicit in turning away those whom he does not deem ready or appropriate to be guided to contemplative prayer, Guyon is equally explicit in inviting all to join her. Moreover, it is in this invitation that we first encounter the use of metaphors that characterize her writing. In phrasing, including the use of the plural imperative, that mimics Matthew 11:28, "Come unto me, all ye that labor and are heavy laden, and I will give you rest" (AV), Guyon throws open her invitation to all, referring to those she invites as "famishing souls," "poor afflicted ones," "sick," and "poor stray, wandering sheep" (6)—all metaphors found in Scripture. In contrast to these familiar and somewhat endearing metaphors, though, the last line of her invitation, addressed to a specific group, "Come you dull, ignorant, and illiterate" (6), startles the reader with offensive adjectives that disturb the pattern of the phrasing of her invitation as well as any reader lulled into complacency by the repetition of familiar biblical metaphors. By declaring that it is the dull and ignorant who are best adapted to *oraison*, Guyon signals that the intellectual effort required of meditation has no place in *oraison*. Nonetheless, all are called, she states: "Let all without exception come, for Jesus Christ hath called all" (6). But Guyon jars her reader again by appearing to retract the invitation from one group—"let not those come who are without a heart" (6)—a strategy that ultimately allows her to reiterate the capability of all to participate, when she adds, "But who is without a heart? come then give this heart to God, and here learn how to make the donation" (6).

An additional point of divergence between Guyon's and Molinos's guides is the more direct interaction and attempt at connection between author and reader. While direct address is not completely absent from Molinos's text, its use is much less frequent. Particularly notable is the predominant use of the second person in pronoun form or in the imperative verbs encountered in Guyon's first chapter of *A Short and Easy Method of Prayer*. Guyon establishes early that she has experienced the joys of *oraison* herself and that she is inviting others to join her. Guyon places herself as an experienced guide alongside those who read her text. She creates images of the means by which a soul can unite *itself* with God through rich and varied metaphors and writes as if she stands next to her readers before the tableau she has created, inviting them to consider how they might participate in a passive prayer that brings them into union with God and His pure love.

The reader's first encounter with Guyon's metaphorical language comes within the first two paragraphs of her first chapter. As we have seen above, her metaphors often find their source in Scripture. Here we find a complete quotation from the book of Revelation: "I counsel you to buy of me gold tried in the fire, that ye may be rich" (3:18) (6) ["Je vous conseille d'acheter de moi de l'or éprouvé au feu, afin de vous enrichir" (61)], which she uses to invoke not only the value of prayer and the method for prayer that she is about to share with her reader, but also the importance of the fact that her method has been tried (*éprouver*). She plays with the double sense of the word *éprouvé*, which means both to know by experience and to test to determine something's worth or quality. Because she has experienced this prayer and because it proved to be efficacious for her, she considers what she knows to be a precious nugget, one that she offers to her reader. By choosing this particular Scripture with its metaphor of gold and its use of *I* and *me*, Guyon subtly asserts her presence into the text. She stands before her readers and advises them to obtain something precious from *her*, something that has been tried by *her*. She insists on her own experience and wants to engage her readers, to connect with them so that they too can experience life-changing prayer.

Guyon was not alone in her emphasis on personal experience as validation of religious truth. Other spiritual writers in the seventeenth century, like mystics who had preceded them, also asserted the validity of knowledge through experience. Most notable is Marie de l'Incarnation (1599–1672), who in her text *Life* uses "the same vocabulary of sure experimental knowledge . . . in her descriptions of the ecstasy and rapture of marriage with the divine."[25]

Since, for Guyon, experience provides the ultimate validation of her method of prayer, the preponderance of metaphors in her texts should not surprise her readers. For it is through this rhetorical strategy that an author can often effectively render emotions, mental processes, and spiritual experiences real to her readers. Most of Guyon's metaphors are based on one or more of the following domains: the senses, nature, journeys, or the relationship between a mother and child. For many of these, an identical or similar metaphor can be found in Scripture. Common to all is a quotidian quality that refers to experiences or phenomena any reader would have observed or experienced. Moreover, each implies that, despite the passivity essential to her method of prayer, these metaphors also include an action that must be taken, and suggests to Guyon's readers that they must *do* something in order to experience the pure love of God through *oraison*.

The insufficiency of language to communicate adequately the phenomenon of *oraison* is evident as Guyon turns, often in quick succession, from one metaphor to another and from one metaphorical domain to another. In one of the earliest examples in her text, we encounter a metaphor of the senses as the author provides instruction for introducing the soul to *oraison*, which begins by reading a "small portion" of truth (taken from Scripture or from the writings of a saint) and "endeavoring to taste and digest it, to extract the essence and substance thereof and proceed no farther while any savour or relish remains in the passage" (8). She continues to evoke the sense of taste, insisting, though, that because taste is inextricably linked with the action of masticating, the reader must "cease the action and swallow the food" (8). Just as doing otherwise would cause a person who eats to receive no nourishment from the food, failing to stop and allow spiritual food to be taken in will "result in the soul [being] deprived of its nourishment" (8).

Guyon inserts between these two tasting / eating metaphors the metaphor of a bee, which like the humans she has introduced, must extract and ingest. Through the bee, she adds to her admonition to consume only small portions of text, a caution to proceed slowly, telling her reader that "those who read fast reap no more advantage than a bee would by only skimming over the surface of the flower, instead of waiting to penetrate into it and extract its sweets" (8).

While the slowness Guyon calls for with her image of the bee is paradigmatic of her method of prayer, the penetration and extraction of the bee are contrary to the passive images she evokes elsewhere in her text. However, in a gesture that is repeated in multiple places in her text, that of turning an action inside out or in its opposite direction, Guyon asserts that the penetration she speaks of is not that of penetrating a text with intellectual understanding, while at the same time she transforms the pray-er from an active bee into a receptacle:

> When we are thus fully introverted, and warmly penetrated throughout with a lively sense of the Divine Presence, when the senses are all recollected and withdrawn from the circumference to the centre and the soul is sweetly and silently employed on the truths we have read, not in reasoning, but in feeding thereon and animating the will by affection rather than fatiguing the understanding by study . . . we must allow them sweetly to repose and, peacefully, to drink what they have tasted. (8)

Guyon's desire to assist her reader in understanding the role of a pray-er's activity and inactivity in relationship to God's activity is one that drives her repeatedly to metaphors of nature. There is a certain understated motion in many of her nature metaphors. Guyon's first use of the familiar metaphor of light in which she equates God with the sun is not exceptional. However, she adds to this image that of humans who are "stars [that] may be seen directly before the sun rises. . . . As his light advances their rays are gradually absorbed by his and become invisible" (21). Guyon provides her reader with a different way of envisioning humans as *imago dei,* one which posits human bodies as stars that are not without energy (light), but whose energy is appropriately overwhelmed and absorbed into God's light.

Guyon inserts an additional solar metaphor. Just as she turns the pray-er from the penetrating bee to that which is penetrated, Guyon reverses the action of the energy emanating from the sun. In contrast to a sun that rises and overtakes the light of the stars with an outward and upward motion, she offers the image of a more static sun that releases a vapor that "contributes to its exhalation only by its passiveness" (19), a vapor that gently and effortlessly ascends. Like the star / soul that cooperates freely and voluntarily with its absorption into God in the first solar metaphor, the vapor / soul allows itself to be "rarified and rendered pure . . . [as it] cooperates with the attractions of God, by a free and affectionate correspondence" (19).

In a repetition of her gesture of positing opposing actions, Guyon juxtaposes the upward and seemingly weightless motion of the vapor with the metaphor of a natural element that seems to be as unlike a vapor as possible in its mass and in its movement—that of a falling stone. She describes the stone as "by its own weight fall[ing] to the earth as to its center" (19), but this rapid, natural falling will only occur if the stone is first disengaged from a hand and then allowed to continue its path without obstruction. Guyon equates the stone's initial disengagement with a soul's turning toward God, asserting that the pray-er must make an initial effort, that first movement toward God's presence. This first action taken, the pray-er must let the soul plunge toward God, so that "without any other exertion it falls gradually by the weight of Divine Love, into its proper centre" (90). Guyon dismisses any thought of throwing the stone to cause it to arrive more quickly at its destination, insisting that any self effort only serves to impede progress.

Guyon's vapor and stone are, in essence, metaphors of journey, of movement from one location to another, of a trajectory that must first be set in motion and then left to advance unobstructed. Guyon adds to the journeys of the vapor and stone that of a boat, which she portrays as the soul that must be freed to travel toward God: "The cords which withhold [the boat] must be loosed, and then by strong and vigorous efforts it gathers itself inwards, pushing gradually from the old port, and, leaving that at a distance, it proceeds to the interior, the haven to which it wishes to steer" (38). We see again Guyon's insistence on action being required to set things in motion—here it is a strong and vigorous effort—but the reader is cautioned quite strongly to cease effort. Lest they impede the desired movement, "[t]he pilot and the mariners rest from their labours and they repose and leave the vessel to the wind, [so that] they make more way in one hour than they had done in a length of time by all their former efforts: were they even now to attempt using the oar, they would not only fatigue themselves, but retard the vessel by their ill-timed labours" (39).

In her metaphor of the sailors' journey, God becomes the haven to which believers sail and the power by which they move. The port becomes the Self from which the believer must extricate herself. Those who endeavor to experience full union with God must take the initial step of getting the ship underway, but then, as they move away from the port of Self, Guyon tells us, "less difficulty and labour is requisite in moving [the ship] forward" (38). As the stone gathered momentum as it fell, so the ship gathers momentum and "proceeds so swiftly in her course" (38) that the "strong and vigorous efforts" (38) become gentle sailing. In telling her readers that they should be content to "spread the sails and hold the rudder" (38), she reminds them that an initial effort is required, but explains that the purpose of "the rudder is to restrain our hearts from wandering from the true course, recalling it gently and guiding it steadily by the dictates of the Blessed Spirit" (38). Just as the believer is called to take an action to get the ship underway, she is called to take an action to protect the vessel when the ship is threatened by a storm. Guyon identifies this anchor as trust in God. She must hold steady as she awaits "the return of a favourable gale. [We who hope to arrive finally at a full union with God] must be resigned to the Spirit of God, giving ourselves up wholly to His divine guidance" (39).

In addition to her use of metaphors of nature and journeys, Guyon uses an additional significant group of metaphors to communicate her method of prayer: those referring to a child. Consistent with her other metaphors, these find their source in Scripture and also include the reversal of actions we have seen with other metaphors the author uses.

In her metaphor of the ship, Guyon tells the sailors to push out from the port (of Self). There must be an intentional turning, fleeing from Self. In one of her metaphors of the child, she again calls for the believer to turn away: "A little child, on perceiving a monster, does not wait to fight with it and will scarcely turn its eyes toward it, but quickly shrinks into the bosom of its mother, in total confidence of its safety" (30). There is no struggling here, no debating or reasoning, just a simple turning from and turning toward. In this description of her remedy for distraction and temptation, Guyon indicates her awareness of how much believers want to be actors in their spiritual life and recognizes their tendencies to struggle, to work at experiencing God. She calls believers to an abandonment of effort and a quick turning to God, and insists that this turning to the bosom of God happen quickly, as soon as there is any sense of the monster's presence. Those who seek God and full union with Him must not trifle with the monster and, like the child, must not wait to fight with it.

What, though, does one do after turning toward the breast of God? In the passage above where we see the child snuggle against the mother, Guyon speaks of the bosom (*sein*), suggestive of both the emotional and physical comfort offered there. In another passage, however, she focuses initially on the nourishment, by speaking of the child suckling at the breast (*mamelle*) of the nurse maid. As she did earlier when describing adult tasting and swallowing, Guyon emphasizes the importance of the initial effort and then stillness:

"[The child] begins to draw the milk, by moving its little lips, but when the milk starts to flow abundantly, it is content to suspend its suction: by doing otherwise it would only hurt itself, spill the milk and be obligated to quit the breast" (21–22).

Such is prayer for those who desire union with God through *oraison*: effort "exerting the lips of the affections," followed by a stillness that does not disturb the inertia of "the Divine Grace [that] flows freely" (22). Having described the important, but brief, initial action of the lips, Guyon presents a picture of the gentle, continual flow between the mother (God) and the child (the believer), as well as the blissful and transcendent state of the soul in *oraison*:

> But what becometh of the child who thus gently and without motion, drinks the milk? Who would believe that it could thus receive nourishment? The more peacefully it feeds, the better it thrives. What, I say, becomes of this infant? It drops off to sleep on its mother's bosom. So the soul that is tranquil and peaceful in prayer, sinks frequently into a mystic slumber, wherein all its powers are at rest, till it is wholly fitted for that state of which it enjoys these transient anticipations. You see that in this process the soul is led naturally, without effort, art or study. (22)

Guyon's extended metaphor of the child can be singled out as comprehensively and beautifully capturing the spiritual inertia that is the essence of her method for attaining, through *oraison*, the "blessedness [that] consists in union with [God]" (44).

Prayer for Guyon is a relational experience, first with God in prayer, and then, with other believers through her text. She both invites and entices her reader to join her, sometimes quoting Scriptures that can begin the attraction to God and prayer and sometimes using scriptural metaphors and language structures that highlight that all are invited and that she journeys with them. However, paramount for Guyon is providing guidance and instruction for the journey in such a way that her readers do not attempt to travel under their own power. Guyon undertakes this task by using metaphorical language that creates images that all can understand, regardless of education, training, or experience. From stars to stones, ships to suckling children, Guyon's metaphors are designed by their richness, variety, and consistency in the action / inaction they portray to allow her readers to envision a different way of praying, to imagine a journey for which all they must do is take the first step. While other quietist texts assert the essential passivity on the part of the believer that is found in *A Short and Easy Method of Prayer,* Guyon's text stands apart from them for the way in which her relational and metaphorical writing embodies the prayer method she espouses.

NOTES

1. Marie de la Motte Guyon, *A Short and Easy Method of Prayer* (London: Allenson, n.d. [1907]), 3. The English translation of the title and all English citations of Guyon's text, as well as page numbers indicated, are from this translation of *Le Moyen court et très facile de faire oraison*; subsequent references are to this edition and will appear parenthetically in the text by page number. The original French is also cited where necessary, and page numbers in such cases are taken from Jean-Marie de la Motte Guyon, *Le Moyen court et très facile de faire oraison*, ed. Marie-Louise Gondal (Grenoble: Jerôme Millon, 1995).
2. Jan Johnson, *Madame Guyon* (Minneapolis: Bethany House, 1998), 10.
3. Rufus M. Jones, "Quietism," *Harvard Theological Review* 10, no. 1 (1917): 26.
4. Marie-Florine Bruneau, *Women Mystics Confront the Modern World* (Albany: State University of New York Press, 1998), 124.
5. James Herbert Davis, *Fénelon* (Boston: Twayne, 1979), 24.
6. Ibid.
7. E. K. Sanders, *Fénelon: His Friends and His Enemies* (London: Longmans, 1901), 117.
8. Harold Chadwick, introduction to *The Best of Fénelon*, ed. Harold Chadwick (Gainesville, FL: Bridge-Logos, 2002), 2.
9. Ibid.
10. David Bell, *The First Total War* (New York: Houghton Mifflin, 2007), 55–56.
11. Jones, "Quietism," 6.
12. F. Townley Lord, *Great Women in Christian History* (London: Cassell and Company, 1940), 135.
13. James Hastings and John A. Selbie, eds. *Encyclopedia of Religion and Ethics* (New York: Charles Scribner and Sons, 1932), 535.
14. Moshe Sluhovsky, *Believe Not Every Spirit: Possession, Mysticism, and Discernment in Early Modern Catholicism* (Chicago: University of Chicago Press, 2007), 100.
15. Jones, "Quietism," 1–2.
16. Sluhovsky, *Believe Not Every Spirit*, 99.
17. Jacques LeBrun, *La Jouissance et le trouble: Recherches sur la littérature chrétienne de l'âge classique* (Genève: Droz, 2004), 477.
18. Pope Innocent XI, "Coelestis Pastor," Apostolic Constitution issued November 20, 1687, Papal Encyclicals Online, www.papalencyclicals.net/Innoc11/i11coel.htm.
19. Jean-Yves Lacoste, ed. *Encyclopedia of Christian Theology*, vol. 2 (New York: Routledge, 2005), 1330.
20. Sluhovsky, *Believe Not Every Spirit*, 139.
21. Jones, "Quietism," 15.
22. Michael de Molinos, *The Spiritual Guide that Disentangles the Soul and Brings It by the Inward Way to the Getting of Perfect Contemplation and the Rich Treasure of Internal Peace*, translated from the Italian copy, printed at Venice, 1685 (London, 1688), 13, www.adamford.com/molinos/src/s-guide.pdf.
23. The distinction between these two types of prayer is usually lost in English translations of Guyon's text, since the English *orison* is rarely used and would render her text less readable and accessible to Anglophones.
24. Molinos, *The Spiritual Guide*, 19.
25. Patricia Ward, "Madame Guyon and Experiential Theology," *Church History* 67, no. 3 (1998): 488.

Chapter Four

Neither Prude nor Coquette

The Heroine's Spiritual Journey in Lafayette's La Princesse de Clèves

Hadley Wood

From its very first appearance in 1678, *La Princesse de Clèves* has charmed and challenged readers. This tale of unfulfilled love concerns the unassuming Mlle de Chartres, who arrives at the sixteenth-century court of Henri II and, once married to the Prince de Clèves, falls in love with the dashing Duc de Nemours. A virtuous woman, the Princess resists her feelings of illicit love and the lovers never consummate their relationship. Bussy-Rabutin was anxious to read the book, since he had heard it much praised. However, after reading it, he criticized the princess's confession to her husband, her final refusal to marry Nemours, and the court scenes.[1] Fontenelle admits to having read the novel four times, although he criticizes the improbability of the key actions and the uselessness of the lengthy court episodes.[2] Within a year of its publication, both a critique of the novel and a defense of it had appeared in print.[3] Mme de Lafayette (1634–1693) herself admits, *"on est partagé sur ce livre-là, à se manger"* ["people are so divided on this book that they are ready to devour each other"].[4]

Like Mme de Lafayette's contemporaries, subsequent critics and readers have questioned the probability and the motivation of the Princess's confession and refusal. Modern critics have viewed the confession as a step toward feminist self-liberation[5] or as a selfish and vengeful act[6] or even as a compulsive action.[7] As for her refusal of Nemours, some suggest the Princess is afraid of life, cold and prudish, hypocritically using moral language to hide fear.[8] Others have characterized the confession and the refusal as arbitrary, poorly motivated choices[9] or as proof that the Princess's domineering mother controls her daughter.[10] Valincour even quipped that the Princess was "la prude la plus coquette et la coquette la plus prude qu'on ait jamais vue" ["the most flirtatious prude and the most prudish flirt one has ever seen"].[11] As for the court scenes, many see both the lengthy initial description and the inserted episodes as poorly connected since they neither move the plot forward nor impact character development.

THE COURT AS PRINCIPAL ANTAGONIST

The princess's choices and the court episodes make sense once we see the novel not as a love story between two individuals, but rather as the story of a young woman trying to live a morally upright life in a dissolute court. In a letter to a friend, Mme de Lafayette herself characterizes the novel as a perfect portrayal of court life, "une parfaite imitation de la cour et de la manière dont on y vit" ["a perfect imitation of the court and the way people live there"].[12] By displaying the Princess's inability to maintain her moral standards or personal virtue completely uncompromised in the public world of the court, Mme de Lafayette presents a grim picture of the human heart and a far-reaching critique of the court and its values. This novel about the impact of place on the morality of persons chronicles how effortful human virtue is, since, in order to be lived out, it must be enfleshed in individuals and embodied in a social context. The deep tension of the novel, although lived out between the Princess and Nemours, results from the dissonance between the Princess's moral stance and the values of the court, values which Nemours exemplifies to perfection.

Once we see the principal antagonist as the court, its lengthy description at the novel's opening becomes a vital introduction to one of the main characters rather than simply gratuitous local color. Indeed, this description sketches the novel's major motifs and shapes its meaning. The principal characteristics that dominate Mme de Lafayette's interpretive rendering of court life[13] emerge in the very first sentence: "La magnificence et la galanterie n'ont jamais paru en France avec tant d'éclat que dans les dernières années du règne de Henri second" ["Magnificence and courtly love have never appeared in France with so much splendor as during the last years of the reign of Henri II"].[14] "Magnificence" and "galanterie," metonyms for power and love,[15] are the two deep, intertwining impulses that run the court and by placing them at the very beginning of her narrative, Mme de Lafayette suggests that this story will address both the power of love and the love of power. Although *magnificence* and *galanterie* serve as elegantly cloaked references to love and power, they are also external signs of the deeper realities they imply. They thus function like emotional and political promissory notes, but, like all such notes, they can prove empty and worthless—mere surface with nothing beneath.

Through use of the verb *paraître,* meaning either "arise" or "seem" in the novel's first sentence, Mme de Lafayette gestures toward another critical aspect of court life, *la dissimulation. Galanterie* can be mere flirtation covering no real feelings at all, just as *magnificence* can be all show with no underlying power. "Si vous jugez sur les apparences en ce lieu-ci . . . vous serez souvent trompée: ce qui paraît n'est presque jamais la vérité" (265) ["If you judge by appearances in this place . . . you will often be deceived: what appears is almost never the truth"], warns the heroine's mother.[16] Everything at court appears disguised, a coded message for which none are ever assured of possessing the correct key. The devious way by which the Queen tries to discover if the vidame has a love interest typifies the oblique nature of court communication. In addition, love and power so thoroughly intermingle that it is virtually impossible to separate them in order to see events clearly: "l'amour était toujours mêlé aux affaires et les affaires à l'amour" (252) ["love was always mingled with business and business with love"].

This constant mingling of love and power renders court even more dangerous spiritually because love and power generate all-absorbing passions that fixate people in the immediate: "Personne n'était tranquille, ni indifférent; on songeait à s'élever, à plaire, à servir ou à nuire" (256) ["No one was at peace, nor indifferent; people continually thought about getting ahead, pleasing, being of service or harming"]. Being engrossed in the emotional maelstrom of shifting love and power interests leaves little time for thought of eternal matters: "[O]n ne connaissait ni l'ennui, ni l'oisiveté, et on était toujours occupée des plaisirs ou des intrigues" (252) ["People knew neither boredom nor idleness and they were always busy with pleasures or intrigues"].[17] Love (*plaisirs*) and power (*intrigues*) occupy all one's energy.

Within the world of the novel, however, power and love—the very heartbeat of the court—ultimately disappoint because neither truly lasts. One never fully possesses the desired object. The Prince de Clèves possesses his wife's body, not her emotions. The queen appears to have political power, but must hide her emotional hunger, loneliness, and rage. As Diane de Poitiers, Mme d'Etampes, le Connétable, and others discover, a mere instant suffices to undo power, apparently solid and unshakeable, but in reality fragile and unstable. The affections of Nemours, which at first seem so durable because he communicates them with finesse and grace, change frequently, hence his reputation as a faithless lover with "plusieurs galanteries à la fois" (321) ["many love affairs at the same time"].[18]

In opposition to this court culture stands Mlle de Chartres, the future Princess, a gracious young woman with beauty, a cultivated mind, moral integrity, and a sincere love of virtue. In addition, she is very young, a mere sixteen years old (248), and has been raised away from the court and its shifting moral ground.[19] She thus arrives at court innocent and basically ignorant of the ways of the world. Her own moral sense, shaped by her mother's high standards, has developed in a more protected environment than court (247).[20] Mlle de Chartres even lacks the calculating ambition of her mother, who is described as "extrêmement glorieuse" ["extremely prideful"] and "ne trouv[ant] rien digne de sa fille" (248) ["finding nothing worthy of her daughter"].[21] Driven by neither power nor lust, Mlle de Chartres stands out at court by her unselfish nature. She sincerely wishes to harm no one and suffers when her engagement causes the Chevalier de Guise pain. Emotional tenderness, however, does not lead to moral wavering: "[C]ette pitié ne la conduisait pas à d'autres sentiments" (259) ["This pity did not lead her to other feelings"]. As a consequence, perhaps, of her lack of driving desire, she also displays a lack of guile so rare at the court that even her mother admires it (259).[22] Mlle de Chartres thus serves as the ideal foil to a court characterized by insincerity and run by ambition and lust.

THE PRINCESS'S INITIAL STRUGGLE

Mlle de Chartres becomes Mme de Clèves and enters the world of the court with every advantage on her side: a strong sense of moral rectitude; a sincere desire to live a moral life; a close relationship with a mother prepared to defend her daughter's virtue; a loving, generous husband who wants to please her; and, finally, an open nature. She is presented as the very opposite of the guileful, pleasure-seeking court: "[E]lle avait un air qui inspirait un si grand respect et qui paraissait . . . éloigné de la galanterie" (260) ["She had an air about her that inspired such high respect and that seemed . . . distant from flirtatious dalliance"]. Mme de Lafayette thus contrasts the best of human nature with the court and its pleasant, but dangerous, "agitation sans désordre" (253) ["frenzy without disorder"]. However, as Mme de Lafayette ends her initial presentation of the characters, before introducing the Princess to Nemours and beginning the real drama, she warns us that the natural defenses of the Princess may not adequately protect the weak human heart: "Mme de Chartres joignait à la sagesse de sa fille une conduite si exacte pour toutes les bienséances qu'elle achevait de *la faire paraître* une personne où l'on ne pouvait atteindre" (260, emphasis mine) ["Mme de Chartres added to the wisdom of her daughter a conduct so precise in all social amenities that she ended up making her daughter *appear to be* someone that no one could ever reach"]. Mme de Lafayette thus hints at the possible frailty and powerlessness of morality and guilelessness when pitted against the weakness hidden in even the most innocent human heart.

The Princess no sooner meets Nemours than she feels a strong attraction to him (262), an attraction she instinctively hides (262), though not well enough to prevent some others from noticing (263). After repeated contact with him, she starts to lie to herself and others in order to keep her feelings safe from scrutiny (270, 272)[23]; she then rationalizes (272), and wants to show him her feelings (273). These inroads happen before the Princess even recognizes her love. She makes no conscious decision to act on her feelings; everything happens automatically, by instinct: "[S]ans avoir un dessein formé de . . . cacher [ses sentiments à sa mère], elle ne lui en parla point" (270) ["Without having a clear intention of hiding (her feelings from her mother), she simply didn't talk about them"]. Pure of heart and untutored in deception, she nonetheless quickly learns dissimulation.

Mme de Lafayette portrays, in exquisite detail, the slow defeat of the Princess. Without ever consciously purposing to have feelings of love for someone other than her husband, the Princess succumbs to these feelings. Without ever capitulating to love or justifying infidelity, she moves ever closer to the very actions she seeks to avoid. The chronicle of the Princess's long defeat can, in general, be divided into three stages. In the initial phase, discussed above, the Princess's innocence itself aids the development of her impure emotions because she is so slow to realize what is happening. She blunders her way into a love she never intends, naively unaware of her dangerous feelings until they have already taken control, leaving her "*peu maîtresse de ses sentiments*" (279) ["hardly in control of her feelings"].

In the second stage, once she understands the nature of her feelings, she assumes she will prove more capable of defending herself against love. Certainly, her feelings for Nemours horrify her: "[E]lle trouva combien il était honteux [d'avoir des sentiments] pour un autre que pour un mari qui les méritait" (275) ["She felt how shameful it was (to have feelings) for someone other than the husband who deserved them"]. She faces Nemours determined to control her actions, armed with a fierce resolution to resist, a resolution strengthened by her mother's dying exhortation, which she takes to heart: "[E]lle avait fait une forte résolution de s'empêcher de le voir et d'en éviter toutes les occasions qui dépendraient d'elle" (279) ["She had made a firm resolution to prevent herself from seeing him and to avoid any such occasions as were in her power"]. The Princess believes that, fortified with self-awareness, she can prevent any further development of this love. This second stage focuses on her inner conflict, her contradictory desires and divided will. She loves him, yet hates how this passion makes her feel (277). She wants to see him and yet to avoid him. She thinks she should speak to him and should not speak (302).[24] What he says to her pleases and offends her equally.[25] But as the delicate innuendos of Mme de Lafayette's style suggest, the Princess still does not fully recognize the complexity of her own feelings. She mistakes pain for hatred just as she confuses jealousy and remorse with a resolve capable of controlling future actions.[26]

THE PRINCESS'S FUTILE RESISTANCE

When the Princess sees that she cannot prevent her feelings for Nemours, she resolves at least to prevent any expression of these feelings. The Princess does indeed make efforts against this love, but not only do these efforts fail to kill her feelings, the very efforts themselves become a coded expression of her passion that Nemours, the consummate courtier, easily deciphers. At court, where everything is hidden and expressed only in oblique language, the Princess's efforts to avoid Nemours reveal her love (295–96). When she believes the dropped letter belongs to him and proves his infidelity, she refuses to see him (323).[27] When he eventually starts to explain, she still treats him with an icy politeness that she imagines virtuous but that actually proves her love: "L'aigreur que M. de Nemours voyait dans l'esprit de Mme de Clèves lui donnait le plus sensible plaisir" (324) ["The bitterness that M. de Nemours saw in Mme de Clèves's mind gave him the most distinct pleasure"]. Self-awareness cannot control love. Whatever the Princess does, in many small ways she shows her emotions. She becomes an open book that the experienced Nemours has no trouble reading (295).[28] Pitted against experience, innocence works to her disadvantage: "Il avait déjà été aimé tant de fois qu'il était difficile qu'il ne connût pas quand on l'aimait" (298) ["He had already been loved so many times that it was difficult for him not to know when someone loved him"].

Unable to fully control herself in simple day-to-day encounters, the Princess becomes particularly vulnerable when the unexpected happens. Each unforeseen event provokes uncertainty, anxiety, and indecision. In the emotional immobility of these moments, the Princess's passion invariably finds expression. When Nemours steals her portrait she must choose, in an instant, between speaking and drawing attention to his passion for her or remaining silent and tacitly condoning the theft (302). When he falls during the joust, her automatic concern for his health and her obvious relief when he emerges unharmed show the strength of her love (306). Even when fighting to contain her feelings, the Princess has been unable to prevent them from being shown with increasing regularity and force (306). Her willpower fails to suppress the existence or expression of her emotions, and her resolve even begins to erode. As much as she wants to prevent Nemours from knowing of her love, she feels some pleasure when she thinks he has in fact seen it in her unconscious behavior.[29]

She "learns" to distrust her own strength after each misstep, but quickly forgets the lesson learned. When she believes that Nemours is romancing several women, her distress overwhelms her. She imagines herself cured when in reality, says Mme de Lafayette, she suffers from "la jalousie avec toutes les horreurs dont elle peut être accompagnée" (310) ["jealousy with all the horrors that can accompany it"]. She does not recognize, however, this cold anger as just another manifestation of love. Instead, "[t]out ce qui la consolait était de penser au moins, qu'après cette connaissance, elle n'avait plus rien à craindre d'elle-même, et qu'elle serait entièrement guérie de l'inclination qu'elle avait pour ce prince" (311) ["the only thing that consoled her was to think, at least, that after this awareness, she had nothing else to fear from herself and that she was entirely cured of the affection she had for this gentleman"]. This naive conclusion echoes her earlier assumption that knowing her emotions would automatically ensure her control over their outward expression (279, 295, 351).[30] The Princess also lacks any real self-awareness of her own motivations; or, rather, her self-awareness only seems to function in terms of past experience. She has hindsight more than insight or foresight. She can see errors once she has made them, but not before making them. Desire is a practiced liar, even in one so innocent.

FLIGHT TO THE COUNTRYSIDE AND CONFESSION

The third stage in the Princess's moral struggle involves her attempts to support her resolve by some outside, external means, especially by removing herself from Nemours's presence. Betrayed by her will, beyond the reach of reason, a prey to emotions outside her control, the Princess becomes desperate and leaves court for her country home of Coulommiers. She cannot, however, stay indefinitely in the country; eventually she must return to court: "Comme il y avait déjà assez longtemps de la mort de sa mère, il fallait qu'elle commençât à paraître dans le monde et à faire sa cour" (298) ["Because a long time had gone by since the death of her mother, she had to begin to appear in society and to do the work of a courtier"]. The obligation to remain at court means the inability to protect herself from Nemours's pursuit by distance: "[I]l n'y avait de sûreté pour elle qu'en s'éloignant. Mais, comme elle n'était pas maîtresse de s'éloigner, elle se trouvait dans une grande extrémité" (303) ["(T)here was no security for her except in distancing herself (from court). But as she was not free to remain at a distance, she found herself in desperate straits"]. Because it is not a dependable or controllable option for married women, distance cannot combat love effectively.

A seventeenth-century literary convention often employed in popular novels such as *la Diana* and *l'Astrée* and in some important plays such as Tristan l'Hermite's *Amaryllis* and Rotrou's *La Célimène,* the retreat to the countryside involves entering a space in which men and women can meet, talk, flirt, and shift love interests with no real repercussions because in these artificially constructed "private" spaces the real life concerns of social status, parental ambition, financial profit, and male ownership of women have little or no place and never receive authorial approval. Pastoral settings open a morally neutral space where lovers can voice feelings that could not safely be expressed in socially constrained spaces.

When the Princess decides to flee to the country, however, the Edenic retreat she imagines turns out to be a trap. Nemours follows her, enters the garden, and even overhears her conversation with and eventual confession to her husband (332), thus learning what the Princess most wants to keep hidden. The intense social gaze always striving to decode words and gestures (259) exists in the country as well as at court because individuals who embody the court values can go to the country, bringing those values with them. The Princess does not find the solitude she desires and remains subjected to the relentless rule of the gaze. Even after Clèves has died, when Nemours allows the Princess space in which to grieve and recover self-possession, the private garden symbolic of personal space is not inviolate. Mme de Clèves becomes aware that she is being watched (we might even say stalked) and that Nemours's gaze has intruded again on her life.[31] Solitude neither automatically constitutes a safe retreat from others nor is it always an available option.

The Princess's long, fruitless struggle to find effective protection against the seductive and morally destructive world of the court creates the context that clarifies the much-debated confession. Convinced that only removal from the court and from Nemours's presence will allow her to live correctly (329), and forbidden by her husband to leave court, she finally tells him that she needs to distance herself from a man who threatens her marriage (333). The confession certainly surprises the reader by its bold originality, by the moral determination it demonstrates, and by its slight touch of Corneillean *gloire*.[32] However, whether or not we judge it overdone,[33] the novel has well prepared us for this desperate remedy, given the long list of futile solutions tried by the Princess and the set of comments that point to the rationality, and thus advisability, of confession. The Princess's mother plants a seed when she admonishes her daughter to use any possible means to combat illicit love (278). Her husband reinforces the idea when he says that he would assume the role of counselor, not husband, should his wife ever admit to loving another man (284). She has more than once imagined a half-confession, a convenient half-truth that might encourage her husband to let her withdraw from court life (296, 303). She regrets not enlisting his help (311) and begins to recognize the bankruptcy of her will: "Toutes mes résolutions sont inutiles; je pensai hier tout ce que je pense aujourd'hui et je fais aujourd'hui tout le contraire de ce que je résolus hier" (330) ["All my resolutions are useless; I thought yesterday everything I think today and I do today exactly the opposite of what I resolved to do yesterday"].[34] In addition, a confession would fit the Princess's often referenced sincere nature (259, 272, 273, 291, even 327).

Even if the confession does not stretch believability, the fact that Nemours overhears it certainly does. However, this turn of plot emphasizes the inescapability of love and thus the bold wisdom of the confession. Nemours's freedom of movement strengthens our sense that the Princess will find her feelings virtually impossible to escape. Mme de Clèves may withdraw from court, but love can pursue her and invade her retreat. Indeed, as a woman, she remains particularly vulnerable to invasion. The strongly gendered nature of space in the novel gives men a freedom of entrance and egress denied to women.[35] Nemours can visit the Princess's favorite court haunts, drop by her private rooms, stop by her country house unexpectedly, and even enter her property unbidden. The countryside and garden setting of *La Princesse de Clèves* radically differs from the settings of the pastoral, comedy, and sentimental novel. Far from a liberating space where love can be pursued in innocence, the countryside has become one more treacherous spot where the defenseless lover can be ruthlessly followed, observed, and hunted down. Gates can be scaled, forests penetrated, retreats observed, privacy spied upon. The power of the court reigns everywhere.

Eventually Mme de Clèves finds herself unencumbered through her husband's death and free to marry Nemours. The tradition of the sentimental novel would have the Princess and Nemours finally united and leave us with the agreeable fantasy of their eternal happiness. In fact, we believe, for an instant, that the moral tension will resolve itself in a marriage that will give legitimacy to the lovers and allow love and marriage to coexist without conflict. Mme de Lafayette departs from this sentimental paradigm, however, and the Princess refuses Nemours's proposal. As long as we imagine the novel's central conflict as one of individuals, this refusal seems unnecessarily rigorous. But if the central conflict opposes the Princess and the court, the individual soul and a world of corrupt, yet inescapable values, then her refusal makes sense.

PURPOSE OF THE COURT SCENES

Although most of the novel focuses on the love between the Princess and Nemours, he is merely the embodiment of court values. The court episodes scattered throughout the novel serve to refocus our attention on the court and its values as the real antagonist. When the Princess first arrives at court, her mother asks her to admit to all flirtations from men so that she can help her daughter learn how to handle such difficult moments: "Elle lui promit de lui aider à se conduire dans des choses où l'on était souvent embarrassée quand on était jeune" (253) ["She promised to help her behave well in situations which were often messy and complicated for young people"]. Her mother fears the court in general, not just Nemours in particular. Indeed, Nemours is dangerous precisely because he perfectly embodies the values of the court. As focused on the conquest of hearts as the court is on the conquest of power, as flighty as the court is unstable in its alignments, as polished in surface manners yet insistent on his own will, Nemours is the court personified—seductive and perilous.

The periodic appearance of these court episodes refreshes the novel's central thematic concerns and invites the reader to focus on the court at large, rather than on two individuals. The court functions less as a backdrop to help us understand individuals than Nemours and the Princess function as specific cases that illuminate the court and larger spiritual issues. The inserted episodes portray a world that highlights characteristics that the Princess herself displays because of her love of Nemours. As her love continues to develop, despite her efforts, she knows the cruel doubts and worries that accompany love, the relentless agony of jealousy (330), the state of continual inner agitation that both exhausts and engages the individual's energy. These same devastating effects of jealousy appear in her husband (362–63) and she hears of them in the stories of Sancerre, Anne Boleyn, and the vidame de Chartres.

Her own experience with the overlapping political and amorous interests of myriad court figures and her resulting difficulty discerning the truth echoes the complex portrait of the court in the first digressive episode about Henri II and Diane de Poitiers. The story illustrates the coded nature of court language, and the elusive nature of truth in such a deceptive environment. The Princess also experiences the humiliation of having shameful, senseless feelings beyond the reach of all logic or reason, much as Sancerre does when he discovers that he mourns the death of his deceitful lover, Mme de Tournon, with a grief unabated by anger: "J'avoue, à ma honte, que je sens encore plus sa perte que son changement" (287) ["I confess, to my shame, that I feel her loss even more than her betrayal"]. Finally, she sees her mother's direst predictions confirmed by the arguments at home and the tense, suspicious atmosphere that poisons all marital interactions, just as she hears of these same effects in the story of Anne Boleyn. Her mother's account of the dangerous mix of love and ambition, and the devastation they cause,[36] can only increase the Princess's eventual distrust of happiness with Nemours, as does the story of Anne Boleyn, a cautionary tale about the folly of marrying one's mistress that shows the deadly results when great passion and marriage combine. Nemours's assiduous pursuit of her when she was married does not promise much for his possible fidelity as a husband.

Far from digressions, the inserted court episodes provide yet another variation on the novel's central concern over the tension between virtue and the court. Here self-interest, jealousy, suspicion, unbridled passion, deceit, and the chaotic, unstable, ever-shifting rule of emotion sweep aside all moral considerations. The Queen pursues power and love with ruthless guile, the vidame uses deceit to gain both power and the love of three different women, Mme de Tournon deceives three men while assuming an appearance of unassailable virtue, and Diane de Poitiers wields power, through love, with unyielding purpose and a fragile ego. Self-interest and lust rule the court uncontested just as they have invaded the Princess's life uninvited.

The real respite from the court's constant emotional *agitation* becomes the *repos* which Mme de Clèves can only achieve through sustained physical and emotional distance from Nemours and the court. At first, she confuses *repos* with the permanent disappearance of love, experiencing "une suspension à ses sentiments, qui lui faisait croire qu'ils étaient entièrement effacés" (289) ["an interruption of her feelings, that made her believe that they were entirely erased"]. *Agitation* accompanies love so regularly that she mistakes its absence for conquest over love. Although she discovers, when she returns to court after her mother's death, the renewed force of her love, she does not learn to avoid her earlier mistake. She again confuses calm with the absence of love, when she recaptures inner peace after the prolonged separation from the human complexities of court during her husband's illness and after his death. Once more the Princess must learn the fragility of her emotional stability. When she realizes that Nemours has perhaps been observing her from a distance, her whole state of mind changes. Instead of "un certain triste repos" ["a certain sad peacefulness"], she feels "inquiète et agitée" (379) ["anxious and agitated"]. When she thinks she sees him in the woods, her reaction is even stronger: "Quelle passion endormie se ralluma dans son cœur, et avec quelle violence!" (380) ["What sleeping passion was reignited in her heart, and with what violence!"].

The *repos* found in active solitude exists in dynamic contrast to the carefully constructed court context and to the garden or countryside of literary convention. The court represents a constricting hothouse where doubt and desire, duplicity and hope, suspicion and sincerity mix together in doses lethal to the emotional peace that marks inner health and spiritual well-being. As Campbell notes, "*Repos* . . . becomes shorthand for a metaphysical reality beside which the physical world is but empty passion and appearance" (208). Mme de Lafayette's narrative specifically critiques the court's values, the motive forces of self-interest and lust, not the court *per se*. Although the court generates an atmosphere permeated by these two forces, escape from these values demands more than new geography.

The real issue is spiritual not geographical. The court changes those who live in it and they carry those values with them wherever they go. The Princess discovers that as long as court values remain with her, no retreat offers a true haven because love and *repos* are antithetical.[37] Although she finds solitude when Nemours leaves for Reims with the new king, thoughts of him still absorb her and she finds no lasting *repos*. On the contrary, mere physical solitude eventually increases her obsession: "[E]lle trouva une grande peine à penser qu'il n'était plus au pouvoir du hasard de faire qu'elle le rencontrât" (363) ["She was distressed to think that chance no longer had the power to arrange for her to meet him"]. Flight to Coulommiers and the countryside feels calming only because she imagines she can safely indulge her uncensored thoughts. When she overhears a noise and thinks she sees Nemours in the garden, his possible presence instantaneously turns her idyllic garden retreat into a space as charged with danger as the court (367–68).[38] The staking out of any space—either one's inner world or some pastoral retreat—as a private, personal territory where a woman is free and sovereign over self, as a property she herself can control, proves illusory. The *carte de Tendre* and the psychological subtleties of sentimental literature may have wanted to expand the extent of this private, personal world, but Mme de Lafayette shows that these inner complexities simply represent deeper ties to real-world concerns.

THE PRINCESS'S FINAL CHOICE

What of the critique that the Princess simply fears the risks of sex, love, and life? Should she not just marry Nemours and give us a happy ending? Physical attraction, deep respect, implicit promises of enduring affection and devotion, all readily accessible in a man of the court committed to marrying her—could any woman want more? I believe the novel pushes us to say yes. Much of the novel's meaning depends on this issue. The creation of a convincing opposition between the Princess and the court depends on Nemours's inappropriateness as a viable husband. If he offered the Princess a life where love, the court, and moral legitimacy could exist in harmony, then the novel's tension would dissolve (as often happens at the end of sentimental works).

However, as perfect and appealing as Nemours and his offer appear, they are, in fact, only surface. A grimmer reality lies underneath just as deeper messages are inscribed in the novel's coded court language.

By the time the Princess has the chance to marry Nemours, she has learned the value and fragility of *repos* and has experienced the destructive force of jealousy. Most importantly, she has a realistic sense of what the future will probably hold, particularly for her hard-won peace of mind. Marriage to Nemours promises a return to the tumultuous anxiety of suspicion and doubt that she knows all too well. The Princess feels concern that Nemours, once married, will pursue other women as determinedly as he has her. Marriage will change his target, not his character, as happened with Henry VIII. Given his penchant for *galanterie*, marriage to him would bring an endless roller coaster of doubt, suspicion, and tortured emotions: "Vous avez déjà eu plusieurs passions, vous en auriez encore; je ne ferais plus votre bonheur; je vous verrais pour une autre comme vous auriez été pour moi. J'en aurais une douleur mortelle" (387–88) ["You have already had several affairs, you will have more; I would no longer be the source of your happiness; I would see you be for another what you had been for me. It would cause me mortal pain"].

Even laying aside concerns about the patterns established by their premarriage contact, ample evidence from Nemours's behavior suggests poor character and predicts certain unhappiness in marriage. Mme de Lafayette skillfully makes Nemours, and the romantic fulfillment he appears to offer, convincingly attractive while showing the alert reader that he offers no real happiness. In her initial, overwhelmingly positive description of Nemours, she already hints at his character. After a glowing description of the important men at court, Mme de Lafayette ends her list with the Duc de Nemours, "un chef d'œuvre de la nature, . . . l'homme du monde le mieux fait et le plus beau" ["a masterpiece of nature, . . . the best formed and most handsome man in the world"] who displays "une valeur incomparable . . . ; un agrément dans son esprit, dans son visage et dans ses actions; . . . un enjouement qui plaisait . . . , une adresse extraordinaire . . . , une manière de s'habiller . . . , et enfin un air dans toute sa personne qui faisait qu'on ne pouvait regarder que lui dans tous les lieux où il paraissait" (243–44) ["an incomparable worth . . . ; a delightfulness in his wit, on his face and in his actions; . . . a playfulness that charmed . . . , an extraordinary skill . . . , a way of dressing . . . , and finally an air in all his person that meant that you could only look at him everywhere that he appeared"]. Certainly the main characters are all described in glowing terms, but this does not mean that these descriptions are therefore meaningless, only that they are written in the coded, hyperbolic court language where negatives only exist between the lines, in the empty spaces created by genteel praise that occupies too narrow an area. Thus we learn that Nemours is, in fact, ordinary in most things. He apparently lacks the eloquence and religious devotion of the cardinal de Lorraine, the prudent self-control and dignified wisdom of the Prince de Clèves, the valor and nobility of the Duc de Guise, the wit and skill of the Chevalier de Guise, or the bravery and daring of the vidame de Chartres. Distinctive primarily for his physical attractiveness and ability to charm people in general and women in particular, he actually pales by comparison with others.

Although "valeur incomparable" ["incomparable worth"] implies good qualities (243), the term's vagueness also suggests that these qualities lack distinctness and substance. Before launching her initial description of characters, Mme de Lafayette alerts the reader to real differences among the characters: "Ceux que je vais nommer étaient, en des manières différentes, l'ornement et l'admiration de leur siècle" (242) ["Those that I am going to name were, in differing manner, the ornament and admiration of their century"]. In the light of this hint, the description of Nemours seems particularly damning. Having summarized in the brief and potentially ambiguous phrase "valeur incomparable" any solid virtues of character that Nemours might possess, Mme de Lafayette spends nearly a page on his surface qualities, his good looks, his smooth presentation, his practiced art of flirtation and dissimulation. Nemours, like the court in which he shines, offers all surface glitter and little substance.

One could argue that Nemours changes once he has seen Mme de Clèves. He abandons any pretensions to Elizabeth I of England; he no longer flirts or chases women at all, much less many at the same time as previously. He pursues the Princess hesitantly, struggling to maintain a respectful distance; he even waits patiently for her to become available after her husband's death and arranges to see her without harming her reputation. Indeed, Nemours seems to believe that love, devotion, and concern for Mme de Clèves have caused these changes.

The Princess's fear that Nemours's "constancy" stems from the pursuit of a quarry that has proved far more elusive and valuable than his usual prey generates her "certitude de n'être plus aimée de [Nemours]" (387) ["certainty of no longer being loved by (Nemours)"] should they marry. The duke will eventually tire of her once the chase ends because passion is, by its very nature, ephemeral. "Mais les hommes conservent-ils de la passion dans ces engagements éternels?" ["But do men keep their passion in these eternal commitments?"] she wonders (387). Mme de Clèves realizes she would need "un miracle" ["a miracle"] to avoid the end of "cette passion dont je ferais toute ma félicité" (387) ["this passion which I would make all my happiness"]. She even wonders if Monsieur de Clèves's constancy was not itself a devotion to the chase rather than to her herself (387).[39] By the novel's end, the Princess recognizes the flaw in Nemours's character that Mme de Lafayette points out early on—his overwhelming need to charm women and thus his inability to refuse any woman interested in him; she sees the misery it will create for her: "[J]e vous croirais toujours amoureux et aimé et je ne me tromperais pas souvent" (388) ["I would imagine you always loving and loved and I would not often be wrong"].

VALIDITY OF THE PRINCESS'S CONCERNS ABOUT NEMOURS

The text validates the Princess's view. Were Nemours truly concerned with her desires, he would not work against them by following her to her countryside retreat, by wandering onto the grounds, and by listening to her private conversation with her husband. Were he a man of character, he would not talk about her extraordinary confession, work to trouble her marriage by falsely implicating Clèves,[40] or sacrifice a close friend's well-being by flirting rather than providing this friend with a crucial letter. Nemours and Mme de Clèves enjoy several blissful hours of "innocent" fun at the permanent expense of the vidame's reputation with the queen, Catherine de Médicis, who can do him much harm and who, we are told, never forgets or forgives the slight received (329).[41] Were Nemours kind and compassionate, he would not hazard the Princess's reputation and marriage by sneaking two nights in a row unbidden into her garden,[42] by spying on her personal moments, or by penetrating her most private space in a metaphorical rape that wreaks as much personal havoc as a successful seduction might have.[43]

Nemours's behavior to the women he had been interested in when he met Mme de Clèves also reveals his potential for selfishness. He simply abandons them with no word of explanation, dropping them hard, without compassion or sensitivity.[44] His defense, of course, would be the strength of feelings he has for Mme de Clèves. But as the Princess learns, personal feelings are not always the surest moral guide. Nemours's habit of acting unquestioningly on his feelings, leads him to jeopardize Mme de Clèves's honesty when he sneaks into the garden just because the idea presented itself strongly.[45] This same habit leads him to the fatal error of talking with the vidame about the overheard confession because he feels "si rempli de sa passion" (337) ["so filled with his passion"]. Indeed, this habit of using strong feelings as the guide for actions leads Nemours to sneak onto Clèves's country property where he overhears the confession because of "une impatience de la revoir qui ne lui donnait point de repos" (331) ["an impatience to see her again that gave him no rest"]. Although the Princess's decisions are sometimes connected to feelings, the majority of her choices are explained with expressions that imply attempts at reasoned judgment: *trouver, penser, croire, croire devoir, connaître bien, songer, juger, faire réflexion, se souvenir, regarder, prendre la resolution* ["to find, think, believe, believe one must, know well, imagine, judge, reflect on, remember, look, resolve"]. Nemours, by contrast, exists primarily in a state dominated by feelings. His choices are usually preceded by expressions that imply emotion, particularly uncontrolled and unmonitored emotion: *sentir, être rempli de, souhaiter, souhaiter ardemment, ne pouvoir résister, avoir de la douleur, s'abandonner à, sentir un plaisir sensible, être rempli de sa passion* ["to feel, be filled with, wish, desire ardently, be unable to resist, suffer, abandon oneself to, feel a substantial pleasure, be filled with one's emotions"]. Nemours acts on feeling, "sans faire aucune réflexion" (331) ["without having a single thought"], and does not question the validity of these impulses as moral guides. When he reasons, it is usually about the best strategy for seducing the Princess. Rarely does he actually question the good judgment of his actions.[46]

In their final conversation, the Princess herself refers to Nemours's affections and motivation in terms that invite us to think more deeply about them: "Je vous avoue donc, non seulement que je l'ai vu [son attachement pour elle], mais je l'ai vu tel que vous pouvez souhaiter que je l'ai vu" (383) ["I confess to you, thus, not only did I see it (his love), but I saw it as you would have wanted me to see it"]. The Princess's beautifully concise and cryptic expression invites us to realize that Nemours believes his love is more permanent and unchangeable than it would prove in reality. She both recognizes her own blindness in relation to him and hints that she is aware that his love may be less deep and less permanent than he wants (her) to believe.[47]

The Princess, of course, acts on convictions that do not fully correspond to her own feelings: "Mais cette persuasion, qui était un effet de sa raison et de sa vertu, n'entraînait pas son cœur" (381) ["But this conviction, which was an effect of her reason and her virtue, didn't persuade her heart"]. She cannot believe she has turned him down: "Elle fut étonnée de ce qu'elle avait fait; elle s'en repentit; elle en eut de la joie: tous ses sentiments étaient pleins de trouble et de passion" (390) ["She was astonished by what she had done; she repented; she rejoiced over it: all her feelings were full of trouble and passion"]. She succeeds at the end of the novel because she understands that she must live a split existence; her feelings will have a life of their own, but she must be governed by reason for the rest of her life. She recognizes that her feelings will not be changed by any reality but that she must live on the basis of clearly thought-through intentions: "Elle examina encore les raisons de son devoir qui s'opposaient à son bonheur; elle sentit de la douleur de les trouver si fortes" (390–91) ["She examined again the reasons behind her duty that were opposed to her happiness; she felt pained to find them so strong"]. Though her emotions cause her to question the validity of her own rational choices, she stands firm: "Elle eût bien voulu se pouvoir dire qu'elle était mal fondée, et dans ses scrupules du passé, et dans ses craintes de l'avenir" (391) ["She would have really wanted to be able to tell herself that she was ill founded in both her past scruples and her fears for the future"].

In order to live with this difficult decision, she must remind herself that it does not really need to be permanent.[48] Even when asked directly by the vidame, she will not assert that she has made a definitive decision to remove herself from court and from Nemours's presence (394). In addition to these mental gymnastics, she also uses absence from the court and from Nemours as ways of protecting herself from feelings that would sabotage her choice. She refuses to see Nemours (394), and refocuses her mind and her energy: "elle ne pensait plus qu' [aux choses] de l'autre vie" (394) ["she no longer thought of anything other than (of things) of the life beyond"].

We can judge the difference between the Princess and Nemours by what follows their final interview. As she leaves, she tells him, "croyez que les sentiments que j'ai pour vous seront éternels et qu'ils subsisteront également, quoi que je fasse" (389) ["believe that the feelings that I have for you will be eternal and that they will subsist unchanged, whatever I do"]. When she makes herself leave court, knowing that "l'absence seule et l'éloignement pourrait lui donner quelque force" (392) ["only absence and distance could give her some strength"], she falls gravely ill as a result of the intensity of her feelings: "Mme de Clèves, dont l'esprit avait été si agité, tomba dans une maladie violente sitôt qu'elle fut arrivée chez elle" (393) ["Mme de Clèves, whose mind had been so troubled, contracted a violent illness as soon as she returned to her home"]. Nemours, knowing they will be separated, is "affligé" ["distressed"] and feels "une douleur sensible" (392) ["considerable grief"].

We observe the end point of these two paths in the final paragraph of the novel. Nemours's love lasts, from his vantage point, a long time, because it has been "la passion la plus violente, la plus naturelle et la mieux fondée" ["the most violent, natural and best founded passion"]. It lasts "des années entières" (394) ["whole years"]. Mme de Lafayette with dry irony lets us recognize that for Nemours a love that lasts more than two or three full years is an amazing feat: "Enfin, des années entières s'étant passées, le temps et l'absence ralentirent sa douleur et éteignirent sa passion" (394) ["Finally, whole years having gone by, time and absence slowed his pain and extinguished his passion"]. Mme de Clèves, however, never apparently loses her love for Nemours, since she continues the sequestered life established to protect herself from her feelings for him, "et sa vie, qui fut assez courte, laissa des exemples de vertu inimitables" (395) ["and her life, which was fairly short, left examples of inimitable virtue"]. This end offers an enticing and intriguing hint that her life ends early in part because his love, as predicted, eventually fades while hers does not.

By the end of the novel, Mme de Lafayette has increased the contrast between the Princess and the court or its exemplary representative, Nemours. The court remains characterized by *magnificence* and *galanterie* and by the qualities that accompany these: change, instability, passion, deceit, dissimulation, and surface "*éclat*" ["flamboyance"]. As these qualities have played out, they have led to agitation, disorder, jealousy, and a set of destructive feelings and relationships. The path leading away from the court, away from *galanterie* and even from *magnificence*, connected as it is to ego—this harder path—leads to *vertu inimitable* [matchless virtue]. The Princess appears, at the novel's end, as an iconic figure, a sort of female Pilgrim in *Pilgrim's Progress*. But the Princess has made a real-life journey, not an allegorical one, and she has maneuvered around a set of concrete obstacles to attain spiritual well-being.

LA PRINCESSE DE CLÈVES AS A CHRISTIAN NOVEL

It may at first seem extravagant to call *La Princesse de Clèves* a Christian novel when no one mentions religion, Christ, God, the Church, or even sin. However, we should not expect either twentieth-century evangelical language or a religious treatise from a seventeenth-century novel. Although some people question what Levi calls "the uncertainty of [the novel's] moral vision" and the religious nature of the Princess's development,[49] many others see the novel as profoundly Christian.[50] Indeed, language, theme, and plot all point to religious meaning. The words used to describe the Princess's struggle—*devoir, vertu, repos, éternel, sûreté* ["duty, virtue, rest, eternal, certainty"]—all would have clear religious resonance for a seventeenth-century French audience.[51] In addition, her involvement in "des occupations plus saintes" (395) ["holier occupations"] evokes a spiritual life. Likewise, the salutary effects of her prolonged illness clearly suggest a spiritual rather than a worldly perspective: "Cette vue si longue et si prochaine de la mort fit paraître à Mme de Clèves les choses de cette vie de cet œil si différent dont on les voit dans la santé" (393) ["This view of death as so far off and so close made the things of this life appear to Mme de Clèves in a manner very different from how they appear in health"]. As she reflects more and more on what is important, on her reasons for not responding to Nemours, "elle surmonta les restes de cette passion qui était affaiblie par les sentiments que sa maladie lui avait donnés" (393) ["she overcame the remains of that passion which was weakened by the feelings that her illness had given her"]. Indeed, after her illness, she renounces all the fleeting concerns of this world in order to devote herself to "celles de l'autre vie" (394) ["concerns of the life beyond"].[52]

The religious nature of her final position as opposed to Nemours's is captured in the ambiguity of the novel's final paragraph. Nemours holds on to his passion for several years, which from the perspective of one who lives for the moment in a world of change and instability represents a substantial period of time, "des années entières [whole years]." For Mme de Clèves, however, whose eyes remain fixed on eternity, the whole rest of her life, in which she never loses her final resolve, feels "assez courte" (394–95) ["fairly short"]. This final paragraph invites us to recognize that two irreconcilable value systems, two perspectives on life and time, demand our attention and allegiance and that, like Nemours and the Princess, we must choose.

La Princesse de Clevès is, thus, to some extent, an apologetic novel, a novel that works to convince the reader that the way to true salvation does not include the values of court life but rather values diametrically opposed to that life. Not only can a close reading of the text support this thesis, but it is hardly a stretch to imagine Mme de Lafayette, with her well-documented Jansenist sympathies, critiquing the values of the court as she portrays them. Pascal also critiques the *agitation*, the lack of *repos* of the worldly life and sees it as a major obstacle to the peace found in a relationship with God. La Rochefoucauld, another Jansenist and a good friend of Mme de Lafayette, repeats the same concerns about passion as a guide for human action, and its tendency to distract from worthier concerns.

The novel speaks the language of the court, portrays the values of the court, and responds to ideas of the court because it addressed a primarily aristocratic reading public. The novel critiques the cultural currency of a seventeenth-century court audience—the pastoral convention, the *carte de Tendre*, the idealized love plot of sentimental novels and the assumption that inner psychic space represented a private inviolable area where women could love whomever with no real-life repercussions. Although Campbell criticizes Mme de Lafayette for constructing a "moral discourse ... imprisoned within the confines of an austere view of sexual behavior" (189), the sexual nature of the battleground between love and morality is determined by a world obsessed with power and love. When the novel warns us early that "l'ambition et la galanterie étaient l'âme de cette cour" (252) ["ambition and love affairs were the soul of this court"], use of the word *âme* points to the spiritual conflict implicit in court values.

The conflict between sin and virtue, between the world here and the kingdom eternal, plays out in particulars, in the Princess and Nemours, but the message is more general. Jealousy eats at the Prince de Clèves, at Sancerre, at Henry VIII, and even at Catherine de Médicis just as much as it threatens to eat at the Princess. Catherine de Médicis, Sancerre, and Mme de Martigues are victims of dissimulation just as much as the Princess. The vidame, Henri II, Henry VIII, and Mme de Tournon are unable to remain faithful, just like Nemours in the past and, fears the Princess, Nemours in the future. People fall out of love as readily as they fall in love. Nemours loves the reine dauphine until he sees the Princess; before meeting the Princess, Nemours changes women as quickly and as easily as he changes shirts. The vidame loves Mme de Thémines, Mme de Martigues, and the Queen, juggling three women and trying to hide his duplicity from them; François I and later Henri II are far from faithful to the women they claim as mistresses. Mme de Lafayette presents a world that must be radically renounced in order to gain access to a better world, one not driven by lust but rather by real love.

What Mme de Lafayette puts on trial here is the human heart and she finds that heart, be it male or female, guilty of naïveté, of self-imposed ignorance, of self-serving duplicity, of addiction to the intensity of passion and of warped values. The Princess is as horrified to realize that she prefers the shallow, often indiscrete womanizer, Nemours, to her devoted husband who only wants to make her happy (377), as Sancerre is to find that he grieves for a woman who deceived him ruthlessly (287). Mme de Lafayette shows us blind people who are constantly sure that they see things clearly.[53] The picture that Mme de Lafayette paints of human nature is certainly sobering. The Princess begins her journey with every advantage and yet in no time at all, she flounders. As soon as illicit desire takes hold of her heart, she starts a rapid, inner moral decline that her efforts prove useless to resist.

There is no socially or morally neutral space that offers escape or safety. Neither the internal space of the heart and mind that the *précieuses* had mapped out in the *carte de Tendre,* nor the artificially imaginary pastoral space proves to be a real refuge from social constraints. Indeed, the idyllic letter-writing incident proves that these self-indulgent moments when the Princess seems able to enjoy her love in an innocent harmony of personal feeling and social duty are dangerous fantasies with disastrous consequences. The only real retreat from the world of the court is the radical retreat that the Princess practices at the end of the novel. This retreat, focused as it is on her *repos*, aims at the court as much as at Nemours.

REVIEW OF CRITICAL CONCERNS

Why, then, has the novel created such debate? If we are to criticize the author for anything, it should be that the magnetism of Nemours is so strong that the reader wants to ignore the warning signs about his character and the negative messages about the influence of court life. Mme de Lafayette has been too successful in her ability to help us see Nemours through the eyes of the Princess's desire. He is so handsome, so smooth, so polished in his courtship that he triggers our own fantasies about passion. In fact, we believe more easily in Nemours's romantic potential *because* of his vagueness and skill at innuendo. Reality is a powerful antidote to fantasy and Nemours offers very little concrete reality. So we find ourselves *wanting* his love to be real, *wanting* the Princess to marry him at the end and live happily ever after.

Whether we like it or not, religion represents the alternative to fantasies. Mme de Lafayette recognizes the joys and pleasures of love along with its destructiveness and deception. Eternal virtue and reward are the only way to escape the web of love and power. The flight from romantic engagement and a focus on Christian virtue offer the only real solution.[54] The real love in the novel is God's love, the only one that does not change, that does not ultimately falter. Real power lies in the renouncing of power, in a life devoted to helping others. This constitutes the true overturning of the world. As Campbell points out, "[t]o deny the validity of [the Princess's] reasons because they spurn those of the world is to confer on that world a worth which in the novel it does not possess."[55]

We could easily read this novel differently. We need only approach the novel with the firmly rooted conviction that there is no God, that the desire to live a godly life is like milk— only fit for children—and that any desire for spiritual perfection, perhaps even for moral constraint in decision making, represents merely a neurotic smokescreen for deeper (i.e., less religious) motivations. If we approach the novel with these convictions deeply and unquestioningly held, then we will definitely see the Princess differently. If we overlook the nature of the court where these emotional encounters of necessity take place, we will dismiss the Princess's fears as neurotic and ill-founded, rationalizations behind which hides a young woman afraid of her own desire. If we imagine the court not a force to be reckoned with, then we will easily conceive a world where Nemours and the Princess can marry happily. But this ideal world more closely resembles the twenty-first century American reality or at least the Hollywood version of that reality. For the main character of the novel, however, the only way back to an Edenic world of innocence and virtue moves along the arduous path of disciplined service and self-denial.

NOTES

1. Letter from Roger de Rabutin, comte de Bussy, to Mme de Sévigné, June 29, 1678, in *Madame de Sévigné: Correspondance*, ed. Roger Duchêne, 3 vols. (Paris: Gallimard, 1974), 2:617.

2. Fontenelle, quoted in J.-G. Prud'homme, *Vingt chefs d'œuvres jugés par les contemporains (du Cid à Madame Bovary)* (Paris: Librairie Stock, 1930), 62.

3. Jean-Baptiste Trousset de Valincour, *Lettres à Madame la Marquise de **** au sujet de la "Princesse de Clèves"* (1678), ed. Jacques Chupeau (Tours: Université de Tours, 1972); Jean-Antoine, abbé de Charnes, *Conversations sur la critique de la "Princesse de Clèves"* (1679), ed. François Weil et al (Tours: Université de Tours, 1973).

4. John Campbell, *Questions of Interpretation in "La Princesse de Clèves"* (Amsterdam: Rodopi, 1996), 7.

5. Faith E. Beasley, *Revising Memory: Women's Fiction and Memoirs in Seventeenth-Century France* (New Brunswick: Rutgers University Press, 1990), 238; Michael Danahy, *The Feminization of the Novel* (Gainesville: University of Florida Press, 1991), 121.

6. Danielle Haase-Dubosc, "La Filiation maternelle et la femme-sujet au 17ᵉ siècle: lecture plurielle de *La Princesse de Clèves*," *Romanic Review* 78 (1987): 454.
7. J.-M. Delacomptée,"*La Princesse de Clèves": La Mère et le courtisan* (Paris: Presses Universitaires de France, 1990), 46.
8. Serge Doubrovsky, "*La Princesse de Clèves:* Une Interprétation existentielle," *La Table ronde* 138 (1959): 48.
9. Byron R. Wells, "The King, The Court, The Country: Theme and Structure in *La Princesse de Clèves*," *PFSCL* 12 (1985): 548.
10. Campbell, *Questions of Interpretation*, 25
11. Valincour, *Lettres*, 272–73.
12. Beasley, *Revising Memory*, 193.
13. Despite some true historical characters, Mme de Lafayette's description provides a thematically focused interpretation of court life rather than a historically accurate portrait. In *Revising Memory*, Faith Beasley points out that "[t]he historical text . . . [becomes] a literary invention designed . . . to possess meaning in itself" (194).
14. Mme Lafayette, *La Princesse de Clèves*, in *Romans et Nouvelles* (Paris: Editions Garnier, 1961), 241; subsequent references are to this edition and will appear parenthetically in the text by page number.
15. The connection of *magnificence* to power is underscored by the shift from *magnificence et galanterie* to *ambition et galanterie* (252).
16. Certainly this passage echoes the baroque theme of appearance, but as Marie-Paul Laden points out in "Virtue and Civility in *La Princesse de Clèves*," in *Approaches to Teaching Lafayette's "La Princesse de Clèves*," ed. Faith E. Beasley and Katharine Ann Jensen (New York: Modern Language Association, 1998), an even more significant connection is to Castiglione's *The Book of the Courtier* which teaches would-be courtiers how to create the surface appearance of a social figure, primarily through pretense (54).
17. Mme de Lafayette implies that days involve a constant series of amusements that absorb each individual's time: "C'étai[en]t tous les jours des parties de chasse et de paume, des ballets, des courses de bagues, ou de semblables divertissements" (241) ["Every day there were hunting expeditions and handball games, ballets, races for rings, or similar entertainment"].
18. When he is first introduced, Nemours's habit of maintaining several mistresses is mentioned: "Il avait tant de douceur et tant de disposition à la galanterie qu'il ne pouvait refuser quelques soins à celles qui tâchaient de lui plaire: ainsi il avait plusieurs maîtresses, mais il était difficile de deviner celle qu'il aimait véritablement" (244) ["He had so much gentleness and such a disposition toward love affairs that he could not refuse any attention to those who tried to please him: thus he had several mistresses, but it was hard to guess which one he truly loved"].
19. "Après avoir perdu son mari, [Mme de Chartres] avait passé plusieurs années sans revenir à la cour. Pendant cette absence, elle avait donné ses soins à l'éducation de sa fille" (247–48) ["After having lost her husband, (Mme de Chartres) had spent several years without returning to court. During this absence, she had spent her efforts on the upbringing of her daughter"].
20. "Son père était mort jeune, et l'avait laissée sous la conduite de Mme de Chartres, sa femme, dont le bien, la vertu, et le mérite était extraordinaires" (247) ["Her father had died young and had left her under the direction of Mme de Chartres, his wife, whose wealth, virtue, and merit were extraordinary"].
21. One potential suitor is so discouraged by "l'orgueil de Mme de Chartres" ["the pride of Mme de Chartres"] that he does not dare approach her daughter (251, 253).
22. "Mme de Chartres admirait la sincérité de sa fille, et elle l'admirait avec raison, car jamais personne n'en a eu une si grande et si naturelle" (259) ["Mme de Chartres admired the sincerity of her daughter, and she admired it with reason because never did anyone have so extensive and so natural a sincerity"].
23. The Princess lies by commission and by omission. She denies having any idea who Nemours is when she has guessed immediately (262). And she decides not to tell her mother about Nemours and his feelings in order not to have to discuss her interest in him (270).

24. "Elle croyait devoir parler et croyait ne devoir rien dire" (294) ["She believed she was obliged to speak and obliged to say nothing"].
25. "Le discours de M. de Nemours lui plaisait et l'offensait quasi également" (294) ["M. de Nemours's speech pleased and offended her fairly equally"].
26. "Tout ce qui la consolait était de penser au moins, qu'après cette connaissance, elle n'avait plus rien à craindre d'elle-même, et qu'elle serait entièrement guérie de l'inclination qu'elle avait pour ce prince" (311) ["The only thing that consoled her was to think at least, that after this awareness, she had nothing else to fear from herself and that she was entirely cured of the affection she had for this gentleman"].
27. "Ce prince ne fut pas blessé de ce refus: une marque de froideur, dans un temps où elle pouvait avoir de la jalousie, n'était pas un mauvais augure" (323) ["This prince was not hurt by her refusal: a sign of coldness, at a moment when she could be jealous, was not a bad omen"].
28. "Quelque application qu'elle eût à éviter ses regards et à lui parler moins qu'à un autre, il lui échappait de certaines choses qui partaient d'un premier mouvement, qui faisaient juger à ce prince qu'il ne lui était pas indifférent" (298) ["However much effort she put into avoiding his glances and into speaking to him less than to others, certain things still escaped from her that came from her automatic feelings and that made the prince judge that he was not someone of indifference to her"].
29. "Ce lui était une grande douleur de voir qu'elle n'était plus maîtresse de cacher ses sentiments et de les avoir laissés paraître au Chevalier de Guise. Elle en avait aussi beaucoup que M. de Nemours les connût; mais cette dernière douleur n'était pas si entière et elle était mêlée de quelque sorte de douceur" (306) ["She felt great pain because she was no longer in control and able to hide her feelings and had let them be seen by the Chevalier de Guise. She also felt greatly pained that M. de Nemours was aware of her feelings; but the latter pain was not as complete and was mixed with some kind of sweetness"].
30. We see the same lessons not learned when the Princess is removed from Nemours long enough to begin to experience some *repos*. She then assumes she is "cured" of her love, only to learn, again and again that the love is still there (289, 343, 378).
31. Although Danahy sees this as a commentary on the condition of women in particular, the novel itself reminds us, from the beginning, that this is as much a story of power as it is of love and that it especially concentrates on the complex conjunction of these two. Although women seem to be those who are principally occupied with passion and men with power, we should not forget the genuine grief and jealousy of Sancerre or of M. de Clèves. Nor should we overlook the ambition of Catherine de Médicis or of Mme de Chartres herself.
32. Earlier the Princess's good friend remarks, "Il n'y a que vous de femme au monde qui fasse confidence à son mari de toutes les choses qu'elle sait" (327) ["You are the only woman in the world who confides in her husband everything she knows"].
33. Throwing herself at her husband's feet might indeed suggest that she has actually slept with Nemours.
34. This passage clearly echoes Paul's words in Romans 7: 21–23. "When I want to do good, evil is right there with me. For in my inner being I delight in God's law; but I see another law at work in the members of my body, waging war against the law of my mind and making me a prisoner of the law of sin at work within my members" (NIV).
35. Danahy, *The Feminization of the Novel*, 104.
36. Mme d'Etampes, le cardinal de Tournon, le chancelier Olivier, Villeroy, and le comte de Taix all represent the collateral damage of the relationship between Henri II and Diane de Poitiers (267–68), and Mme de Lafayette's audience knows that once Henri II dies, Diane herself along with the Connétable will be destroyed and forever banished from court.
37. Campbell, *Questions of Interpretation,* 202.
38. Conversely, when overwhelmed by more commanding passions, self-interest and love can fade, at least temporarily. The Princess keeps to her rooms when her mother and later her husband sicken. Nemours tries to visit her regularly during her mother's illness (277). Although touched by what she assumes is his kindness, when her mother dies, she becomes so absorbed with her own grief that she imagines her love permanently diminished (289).

39. This cynical view would appear to be the one Mme de Lafayette invites us to adopt since she remarks, toward the beginning of the story, on the role of dissatisfaction in solidifying the Prince's attachment to his wife: "[P]our être son mari, il ne laissa pas d'être son amant, parce qu'il avait toujours quelque chose à souhaiter au-delà de la possession" (260) ["Despite being her husband, he didn't stop being her lover, because he always had something to desire beyond her mere possession"]. Clèves himself appears to admit as much when he remarks to his wife that he has loved her so much that not even possessing her has been able to reduce his love (334). Mme de Lafayette even permits herself a brief authorial speculation that the intensity and duration of Nemours's passion may have been related to the obstacles he encountered: "[P]eut-être que des regards et des paroles obligeantes n'eussent pas tant augmenté l'amour de M. de Nemours que faisait cette conduite austère" (340) ["Perhaps kind looks and words would not have increased M. de Nemours's love as much as this austere conduct did"]. When Nemours overhears the Princess's confession to her husband and realizes that he is the man she is in love with, some of his reaction reveals how much of his personal ego is involved in a challenging "chase": "Il sentit pourtant un plaisir sensible de l'avoir réduite à cette extrémité. Il trouva de la gloire à s'être fait aimer d'une femme si différente de toutes celles de son sexe" (337) ["He felt, however, a considerable pleasure in having driven her to this extremity. He took pride in having made himself loved by a woman so different from all others of her sex"].

40. "Monsieur de Nemours, qui vit les soupçons de Mme de Clèves sur son mari, fut bien aise de les lui confirmer. Il savait que c'était le plus redoutable rival qu'il eût à détruire" (347) ["Monsieur de Nemours, who saw Mme de Clèves's suspicions about her husband, was very content to confirm them for her"]. Ironically, Nemours's lie becomes a prediction of the future: "La jalousie, répondit-il, et la curiosité d'en savoir peut-être davantage que l'on ne lui en a dit, peuvent faire bien des imprudences à un mari" (347) ["Jealousy, he answered, and the inquisitiveness to know more about an issue, can make a husband commit a lot of imprudent actions"].

41. Although the vidame is clear, from the beginning, that this incident could mean his ruin (314), Nemours actually hesitates to help him because he does not want to jeopardize his courtship of the Princess. Self-interest and lust weigh as heavily as the life or death of a close friend: "M. de Nemours avait toujours fort aimé le vidame de Chartres. . . . Néanmoins, il ne pouvait se résoudre à prendre le hasard [que la Princesse] entendît parler de cette lettre comme d'une chose où il avait intérêt" (322) ["M. de Nemours had always cared a lot for the vidame de Chartres. . . . Nonetheless, he couldn't resign himself to taking the chance (that the Princess) would hear talk of this letter as something that concerned him"].

42. The Princess is angry with him, briefly, for one of the rare moments in the novel: "Cette certitude lui donna quelque mouvement de colère, par la hardiesse et l'imprudence qu'elle trouvait dans ce qu'il avait entrepris" (371) ["This certainty made her feel a burst of anger, because of the daring and imprudence she found in what he had undertaken"].

43. Although the Prince de Clèves's dying of jealousy seems far-fetched, it represents the level of damage that can result from Nemours's unbridled passion.

44. "La passion de M. de Nemours . . . lui ôta le gout et même le souvenir de toutes les personnes qu'il avait aimées et avec qui il avait conservé des commerces . . . Il ne prit pas seulement le soin de chercher des prétextes pour rompre avec elles; il ne put se donner la patience pour rompre avec elles" (269) ["M. de Nemours's passion took away his taste for and even his memory of all the persons he had loved and with whom he had kept up contact . . . He didn't even take care to look for pretexts to break with them; he couldn't muster the patience to break with them"].

45. "Ce dessein entra si fortement dans l'esprit de M. de Nemours" (365) ["This plan took such strong hold of M. de Nemours's mind"].

46. Even his regret over having talked about the Princess's startling confession to her husband stems from his unhappiness with the pragmatic consequences of his action not from any clear moral standards.

47. It is possible that she is saying that he has been only pretending to have affection for her. There is nothing, however, to support this view. If she felt he was maliciously fooling her, she would not have spoken to him as she did in the final interview.

48. "Enfin, pour se donner quelque calme, elle pensa qu'il n'était point encore nécessaire qu'elle se fît la violence de prendre des résolutions" (391) ["Finally, in order to attain some measure of calm, she thought it was no longer necessary for her to force herself to make resolutions"].

49. Anthony Levi, "*La Princesse de Clèves* and the Querelle des Anciens et des Modernes," *Journal of European Studies* 10 (1980): 62.

50. Campbell, *Questions of Interpretation*, 198–99.

51. Likewise, the terms used to characterize Nemours and the court (*ambition, passion, agitation, gloire*) (ambition, passion, frenzy, pride) carry negative spiritual overtones and connect to concepts such as *amour-propre* (self-love) and *concupiscence* (lust).

52. Mme de Lafayette does not suggest that we can easily defeat the world. Despite her apparent victory over her passion, the Princess continues to avoid both the court and Nemours as assiduously as ever: "[E]lle connaissait ce que peuvent les occasions sur les résolutions les plus sages . . . [;] elle ne voulut pas s'exposer à détruire les siennes, ni revenir dans les lieux où était celui qu'elle avait aimé" (393) ["She knew how circumstances could affect even the wisest of resolutions . . . ; she didn't want to risk destroying her own resolutions nor to return to places where she could find the man she'd loved"].

53. The Princess is certainly among these. She is constantly sure that she now understands herself and yet she is continually surprised by the tenacious hold that passion has over her.

54. It is not at all clear that this equates with the solution of married love that Mme de Chartres recommends. Perhaps this is one more fantasy that Mme de Lafayette would prefer to hedge, if not deny.

55. Campbell, *Questions of Interpretation*, 196.

Chapter Five

Tempered Witness to the Power of the Soul in Enlightenment France

Four Novels by Charrière, Cottin, and Guérin de Tencin

Joanne M. McKeown

Denis Diderot's *La Religieuse,* written in 1760 but not published until 1796, is among the most shocking novels about institutionalized religion to be written during a period noted for irreverent, scabrous, and provocative literature.[1] In Diderot's fictional hell on earth, the good and innocent Suzanne Simonin seeks God in vain within and beyond monastery walls; in fact, brutally cruel convent experiences steal from Suzanne's life any sense of the sacred. In an ironic twist of fate, she cannot even enjoy the privileges and benefits of a Catholic burial: Suzanne is denied eternal salvation because desperation and hopelessness, fruits chiefly of Church-related ordeals, lead to her suicide. Simply put, Suzanne's faith is powerless against evil. In fact, her belief in God ultimately betrays Suzanne since she is entirely without resources when confronted with the unspeakable horrors set in her path. Suzanne's fate exemplifies Diderot's conviction that dependence on a divine power to combat the forces of evil is pointless because it relies on false assumptions about God. Furthermore, to retreat to a convent for any reason, or to cultivate a spiritual life, is to indulge in fantasies about the soul and to avoid responsibility. Reason, the mind functioning independently of metaphysical forces, is the only source of legitimate and reliable power and truth.

Diderot's virulent attack on forced religious vows and isolation in monasteries and convents is one of many Enlightenment literary efforts to undermine the Catholic Church's authority and raise questions about spirituality and organized religion. Some eighteenth-century female novelists, including Marie-Jeanne Riccoboni and Françoise de Graffigny, address the issue of what Joan Hinde Stewart calls "the narrowness and contradictions of the convent education of girls."[2] Claudine-Alexandrine Guérin de Tencin depicts problems caused by the forced seclusion of women in convents for financial expediency in *Les Malheurs de l'amour* (1786).[3] However, Diderot's depiction of an immoral, perverse convent experience and, by implication, his rejection of the spiritual life it purported to foster, does not find a parallel in novels written by Enlightenment women. In their works, a uniquely feminine perspective on marriage, love, education, and parenting very often includes affirmations of divinely ordered destinies, God, convents, abbeys, and of nuns and other clergy who live there. In fact, convents and similar retreat experiences are popular options and provide important, often life-altering, benefits. Characters faced with deception or trauma in their personal lives typically leave their circumstances in one of the following three ways: by entering an existing monastic dwelling, by creating some kind of spiritual refuge at home that does not compromise existing responsibilities, or by withdrawing mentally and emotionally from obligations and loved ones without actually physically departing. The first two choices are spiritually based; the third is not. What results from these decisions reveals a clear bias on the part of women writers toward choices involving God; only these options bring lasting rewards, including peace.

There are numerous and varied benefits to leaving society for houses of prayer; these include sound ethical or practical advice, solitude, peace, and refuge from family strife and moral ambivalence or decadence. Stéphanie-Félicité de Genlis's Madame de la Vallière in *La Duchesse de la Vallière* (1804) recovers perfect health in the convent where even death can be contemplated without fear: "C'est ici [dans le couvent] . . . qu'il est doux de rêver à la mort"[4] ["It is here (in the convent) . . . that it is pleasing to ponder death"]. In Genlis's *Mathilde* (1820) the title character wants to "s'ensevelir dans un cloître"[5] ["bury herself in a cloister"]. Riccoboni's Fanni Butlerd, in *Lettres de Mistress Fanni Butlerd* (1757), calls the convent "une maison paisible"[6] ["a peaceful home"]. When, in Tencin's *Mémoires du Comte de Comminges* (1786), the Comte de Comminges learns of the death of his lover, Adélaïde, he is anxious to find himself in an abbey where nothing will shield him from his pain. Facing his emotions is necessary to the grieving process: "Je vins sans presque m'arrêter à l'abbaye de la T . . . Je demandai l'habit en arrivant"[7] ["I came directly, practically without stopping, to the Abbey of T . . . I asked for the habit upon arriving"].[8] What was dark and dangerous in Diderot appears intimate and protective in these retreats; what was violent and destructive in his novel is peaceful and restorative here.[9]

The reasons why characters enter the convent or abbey vary, as does the degree of religious incentive for doing so. In fact, some functions of the religious life are overtly secular.[10] In the example above, Comminges states clearly that he has sought out the abbey as a place to indulge his romantic regrets. Later, a chance meeting there with his beloved, believed dead, is an opportunity to affirm their mutual love after years of heartache, separation, and even doubt. The clear and unapologetic coalescence of the secular and religious here occurs in another retreat form replicating the convent experience: some characters seek solitude and healing in a deep spiritual life at home when leaving domestic trials for a new residence is impossible. In Sophie Cottin's *Claire d'Albe* (1798), the title character speaks of consolation found in her own residence through "les élans religieux"[11] ["religious transport"]. Genlis's Madame de la Vallière notes the calming effects of religion experienced at home: "la religion calmera l'agitation cruelle de ce coeur"[12] ["Religion will calm the cruel agitation of this heart"]. Before she retires to a convent Madame de la Vallière has a convent-like cell built in her wing of the palace in an attempt to heal "son coeur égaré et déchiré"[13] ["her wandering and broken heart"], an emotional state resulting from her precarious and equivocal position at court as the King's mistress.

The benefits of home-based spirituality, allowing the characters to experience union with God outside the monastery, do not tempt all those in need of isolation who are unable to leave their families. Instead of contemplating sacred truths through prayer, this final group focuses intensely on difficulties, and experiences negative emotions including anxiety, loneliness, and despair. What ensues, and how the consequences of this response differ from the results of cultivating a life of the soul, are the subjects of this chapter. Two novels by Isabelle de Charrière[14] (1740–1805) and one each by Claudine-Alexandrine Guérin de Tencin (1682–1749) and Sophie Cottin (1770–1807) provide examples of characters enduring serious domestic trials from which they retreat in one of the ways described above. How each character in these four novels thereby copes with personal pain and disappointment emerges as a central theme, and reveals the contrast between novels where characters seek consolation in God and those where they do not. The strong tendency toward the former course of action becomes an indication of the refusal of materialistic Enlightenment thinking by a majority of women authors who do not consider God to be detached from personal life, a claim supported by the other novels briefly referenced in this chapter to demonstrate that rather than being atypical, this type of novel is following a trend. It is evident that these novelists' intimate representations of the eighteenth-century domestic aristocratic universe, or what Vicki Mistacco calls "fine paintings of very distinctive social groups,"[15] differ dramatically from Diderot's portrait of Suzanne Simonin, and provide an alternative way of thinking about convents and, more broadly, about human spirituality.[16]

CLAUDINE-ALEXANDRINE GUÉRIN DE TENCIN: *LES MÉMOIRES DU COMTE DE COMMINGES* (1735)

Tencin's memoir-style novel tells a story of family disputes and forbidden love. The Comte de Comminges loves Adélaïde de Lussan, the only daughter of the Marquis de Lussan, his father's cousin and rival. Comminges deliberately destroys documents that legalize the return of the family fortune to his own father because his lover's family would be ruined if this financial transaction were to occur. A series of events follow, including Comminges's exile and imprisonment, Adélaïde's arranged marriage to Monsieur de Benavides, a duel between Comminges and the same, and a false announcement of Adélaïde's death. This news prompts Comminges to take vows at the Abbey de la T—. A few years later, a dying religious brother—Adélaïde in disguise—admits that her chance arrival at the same abbey after her husband's death has afforded her the unexpected, happy opportunity to be near her lover daily. In her death-bed confession, Adélaïde next reveals that one day she had seen Comminges in the abbey gardens staring adoringly and regretfully at her portrait.[17] At that moment, she realized that they were both in the abbey under false pretenses. Adélaïde admits the sinful nature of this deception to the brothers and monks attending her final hours of life, and asks forgiveness for herself and Comminges:

> Je vins demander à Dieu ma conversion pour obtenir celle de mon amant. Oui, mon Dieu! C'était pour lui que je vous priais, c'était pour lui que je versais des larmes, c'était son intérêt qui m'amenait à vous. Vous eûtes pitié de ma faiblesse, ma prière toute insuffisante, toute profane qu'elle était encore ne fut pas rejetée; votre grâce se fit sentir à mon cœur. Je goûtai dès ce moment la paix d'une âme qui est avec vous et qui ne cherche que vous. (*Mémoires*, 92)

> [I came to ask God for a conversion of heart; the request was for my lover, not for myself. Yes, my God! It was for him that I prayed to you, it was for him that I shed tears, it was his well-being that brought me to you. You took pity on my weakness; you did not reject my pitiful prayer, despite how profane it was. Your grace made its way into my heart. From that moment on, I enjoyed the peace of a soul united with you, who seeks only you.]

Adélaïde's death follows soon thereafter. Despondent, Comminges requests that the head abbot provide him with even greater seclusion in a hermitage. Additionally, the Comte promises not to take his own life despite his suffering, and instead to wait patiently for his soul's salvation through Adélaïde's prayerful intercessions from beyond the grave: "Ma chère Adélaïde obtiendra de Dieu que ma pénitence soit salutaire, et vous, mon père, je vous demande cette dernière grâce, promettez-moi que le même tombeau unira nos cendres. Je vous promettrai à mon tour de ne rien faire pour hâter ce moment qui peut seul mettre fin à mes maux" (*Mémoires*, 94) ["My dear Adélaïde will intercede with God so that my penance is salutary; I ask of you this final grace, Father: allow our ashes to be buried together in the same tomb. In turn, I promise to do nothing to hasten the time of my death, the only moment that can put an end to my suffering"]. The publication of these memoirs, which include this notice, "manuscrit trouvé dans les papiers d'un homme après sa mort" ["manuscript found in a man's papers after his death"], follows Comminges's death.

While the Abbey de la T— is attractive for its secluded location, it becomes the chance scene of reunion for two lovers repeatedly separated since the time of their initial meeting. Brother Don Jérôme, of whose genuine goodness Comminges writes, "Je n'ai jamais vu dans personne plus de vraie bonté" (*Mémoires*, 70) ["I have never seen in anyone else more true goodness"], and the abbot, who promised to bury their ashes together, provide compassion and understanding in scant supply outside the abbey's walls. Finally, after years of doubt and frustration, Comminges knows with certainty that he has been loved all along. The functions of retreat to Tencin's abbey, therefore, are both secular and spiritual: two ill-fated lovers are joined and their love is sanctified. Furthermore, both characters are justified for eternity before God.[18]

SOPHIE COTTIN: *CLAIRE D'ALBE* (1799)

Cottin's Claire d'Albe marries a man chosen for her by her father on the day of his death. Claire honors her father's dying wish, and marries Monsieur d'Albe, a man she does not, and cannot, love. They have one child. Claire eventually falls desperately in love with her husband's adopted son, Frédérick, and he with her. The lovers avoid one another for fear of inflaming their passion, but Claire eventually becomes chronically ill, apparently a consequence of her emotional suffering. Guilt increases Claire's anguish when their love is finally consummated. Indeed, Claire's "forces s'épuisent" ["strength gives out"], and she utters, "la coupe de la vie se retire de moi" (*Claire*, 118) ["the cup of life is withdrawing from me"].

As her body weakens, Claire tends less and less well to her husband and child, withdrawing from the family and focusing increasingly on her emotional suffering. Though a wife and mother, she sees her life as a fruitless void, a desert.[19] Indeed, she avoids her domestic responsibilities, shrinking the boundaries of her physical universe; meanwhile, the boundaries of her mind expand. She confides her desolation to her maidservant, Elise: "Quel désert! Je me perds dans une immensité sans rivage" (*Claire*, 101) ["What a desert! I am lost in an immense expanse without end"]. Claire's enfeebled and sad imagination peoples the wide emptiness that fills her consciousness with shadows and ghosts: "Quel vide! Quel silence! Partout je voyais de lugubres fantômes, chaque objet me paraissait une ombre, chaque son un cri de mort, je ne pouvais ni dormir, ni penser, ni vivre" (*Claire*, 105) ["What a void! What silence! Everywhere, I saw mournful phantoms, every object seemed a shadow to me, every sound a cry of death; I could neither sleep, nor think, nor live"]. Her absorption in thoughts of horror and barrenness reveal the desperate voice of a mind detached from its surroundings, unaware of the outside world. Indeed, no longer functioning in her normal daily activities, Claire has slipped into a dark, mental abyss where ideas of death seem natural, even appealing: "O mon Elise, quand le devoir me lie sur la terre et me commande d'oublier Frédérick, ne puis-je oublier aussi qu'on peut mourir?" (*Claire*, 105) ["Oh my Elise, while duty ties me to life and commands me to forget Frederick, can I also forget the possibility of dying?"].

Thoughts of death are not, in this case, an endpoint in themselves. Instead, they gradually provide Claire with a means of shifting her focus away from her day-to-day suffering. She admits her conviction that "sous la voûte céleste" (*Claire*, 128) ["in heaven"] she will be united with her lover. Her belief in a heavenly place where desires will be filled attests to Claire's spiritual tendencies and to her ability to draw away from the emptiness of mental despair. She reveals to Elise the calming effects of spiritual fervor: "les élans religieux me rendirent la paix. Il me semblait que Dieu venait" (*Claire*, 74) ["religious transport restored peace to me. It seemed to me that God was there"]. Elise explains to Monsieur d'Albe that Claire is a passionate soul who needs nurturing in a way that only God can provide: "les âmes passionnées ont besoin d'aliment, et cherchent toujours leurs ressources . . . dans les idées religieuses ou dans les idées sensibles. Le vide terrible que l'amour y laisse ne peut être remplie que par Dieu même" (*Claire*, 130) ["Passionate souls need nourishment, and constantly seek to be filled . . . through religious thoughts or thoughts of the heart. The terrible void left in their lives by love can be filled only by God himself"]. When Claire is buried, Frédérick prostrates himself on the ground, covers himself in the dirt that was to fill her tomb, and cries out, "A présent je suis libre, tu n'y seras pas longtemps seule" (*Claire*, 142)! ["Now I am free; you will not be alone for long"].

Claire does not enter a convent but withdraws from her normal life because of her physical decline and some degree of mental and emotional dysfunction. Eventually, however, she focuses on the fullness of eternity instead of on the emptiness of her life, and experiences a sense of peace, albeit tinged with sadness. She dies hoping to go to heaven and to be united there with her lover. Her romantic nature, given to flights of imagination and passion, finally finds its rest in God.

ISABELLE DE CHARRIÈRE: *LETTRES DE MISTRESS HENLEY, PUBLIÉES PAR SON AMIE* (1784)

Charrière's Mistress Henley provides an example of a character who, unlike the two preceding protagonists, cannot detach herself from the sadness that results from the painful disappointments of her personal life. Instead, she remains overly preoccupied with them and lives at the mercy of her thoughts and emotions.

Mistress Henley writes six letters to a friend, telling her the circumstances leading to and following her marriage to a thirty-five-year-old widower with a five-year-old daughter. Mistress Henley's reasoned choice of a settled country gentleman ten years her senior came after she had refused several suitors; she thought the choice to be one that even "les anges devaient . . . applauder"[20] ["the angels should applaud"]. Beyond that, her marriage to a stable man of some means freed an aunt from having to forever support what she considered to be her niece's extravagant tastes. Although Mistress Henley enters this union with the best of intentions, she quickly recognizes that she and her husband are incompatible. She feels his cool disdain for her worldly ways; he criticizes the clothing, books, and gifts she chooses for his impressionable daughter. Mistress Henley feels increasingly unworthy and unable to properly fulfill her domestic responsibilities. When her hope that their new baby will unite the couple vanishes, Mistress Henley experiences "un profond abattement" (*Lettres*, 40) ["an abysmal despondency"], and seeks to forget the reality of her wretched existence: "Il fallait sortir de moi-même, m'étourdir, m'oublier, oublier ma situation" (*Lettres*, 41) ["I had to escape from myself, distract myself, forget myself, forget my situation"]. She seeks passing enjoyment in the frivolous lifestyle of fashionable society, "[où] la tête [était] remplie [d']extravagences" (*Lettres*, 41) ["(where) her head (was) filled (with) extravagances"]. Meanwhile, Monsieur Henley decides to refuse a job that would have necessitated a move to London on the grounds that the city would have had a negative influence on his wife and, in his view, on the entire family. In the final letter written by Mistress Henley, she expresses abhorrence at how useless and isolated she feels, and at how completely estranged she is from her husband. Exhausted by her efforts to defend and explain herself and to understand Monsieur Henley's behavior she writes, "ma tête s'est embarrassée; je me suis évanouie. Les soins qu'on a eus de moi ont prévenu les suites que cet accident pouvait avoir; cependant, je n'en suis pas encore bien remise. Mon âme ni mon corps ne sont dans un état naturel" (*Lettres*, 45) ["I felt dizzy; I fainted. The care they took of me changed the dangerous course my condition might have taken; meanwhile, I have not yet completely recovered. Neither my soul nor my body are in a normal state"]. She then speaks of dying at her own hand or of dying from sadness. The final words of her last letter leave the novel open-ended: "Dans un an, dans deux ans, vous apprendrez, je l'espère, que je suis raisonnable et heureuse, ou que je ne suis plus" (*Lettres*, 45) ["In one year, perhaps two, I hope that you will learn that I am sensible and happy, or else that I am no longer alive"].

Mistress Henley's despair is not unlike that felt by Claire d'Albe and Adélaïde. Her initial response, too, is like theirs. All three feel the bitterness, anguish, and unsettlement resulting from the absence of deep, committed married love. They yearn for emotional fulfillment. While Claire and Adélaïde eventually abandon their absorption in despair for thoughts of God, however, Mistress Henley remains mired in her mental and emotional demise, a victim of the ravages of chronic rejection and isolation. Unable to rise above the personal devastation, she cannot entertain hope. Had Charrière imagined a conversion like Adélaïde's whereby Mistress Henley had renounced her preoccupations with her unhappiness and turned her thoughts to God, the character would surely have composed another letter in which she would have reassured her correspondent that a new spiritually grounded outlook was enabling her to accept her circumstances and even to experience some contentment. The absence of another such letter forces the reader to assume that this character chose desolation over hope, and death over life.

ISABELLE DE CHARRIÈRE: *CALISTE, OU SUITE DES LETTRES ÉCRITES DE LAUSANNE* (1787)

Charrière's *Caliste,* told in a series of letters by Caliste's former lover, William, provides another example of individuals who choose to navigate life's challenges in the absence of a spiritual core. William is convinced by his father of the undesirability of a marriage with this one-time actress, whose mother put her on the stage because of her physical beauty and musical gifts: "sa figure, . . . ses talents, et . . . [le] plus beau son de voix qui ait jamais frappé une oreille sensible"[21] ["her face, . . . her talents . . . and . . . (the) most beautiful voice that a discriminating ear has ever heard"]. This talented and beautiful young woman is noticed by the Duke of Cumberland, a man of some means who, "au sortir de la comédie . . . l'alla demander à sa mère, l'acheta pour ainsi dire, et dès le lendemain partit avec elle pour le continent" (*Caliste*, 114) ["at the door of the playhouse . . . asked her mother for her; he acquired her, if you will, and the very next day left with her for the continent"].

Prospects for a respectable reputation for Caliste are dim in light of her childhood experience in the theater and her equivocal status as a dependant and lover of "un homme considerable" (*Caliste,* 114) ["a wealthy man of some social standing"]. The Duke, however, provides Caliste with a good education in an abbey in Paris; the sisters and Caliste's friends there adore her and she excels in her lessons. In fact, William's account contains numerous proofs of Caliste's good character. But William's father is not persuaded that his son should marry Caliste when she is left alone after the death of the Duke. Despite William and Caliste's love for one another, William's father chooses a more socially respectable woman for his son. This arranged marriage to Lady Betty becomes bitterly unhappy; she is unfaithful and eventually William's father admits his own error in judgment. But by then Caliste, too, is married to another. When William learns of Caliste's marriage he becomes "une ombre errante" ["a wandering shadow"] and suffers from nightmares full of ghosts who plague him: "mille fantômes lugubres qui viennent m'assaillir" (*Caliste,* 150) ["a thousand mournful phantoms that beset me"]. Similarly, when she learns of William's marriage to Betty, Caliste reports: "je tombai évanouie, et je fus deux heures sans aucune connaissance" (*Caliste,* 164) ["I fell into a dead faint and remained unconscious for two hours"]. A few days later, Caliste suffers a miscarriage. After other illnesses exacerbate her "chagrin" (*Caliste*, 175) ["grief"], Caliste dies.

William's account is noticeably bereft of references to God or prayer. In their place is a predominantly melancholy, hopeless tone. Neither William nor Caliste sees beyond the immediate circumstances or envisions a better future. References to frightening mental apparitions and sad, prolonged reveries indicate a spiritual void filled by the vagaries of an unstable psyche. William calls himself "l'homme du monde le plus malheureux" (*Caliste,* 179) ["the most unhappy of men"], and he has no strength to bear Caliste's death (180). As in the case of Mistress Henley, the reader is uncertain of William's fate at the end of the novel but is led to believe he may have committed suicide.[22] His servant and a relative keep constant vigil over him, fearing the worst. Indeed, William's deep sense of guilt for having obeyed his father rather than following his heart torments him. And, his sense of culpability and deep regret fail to dissipate in the absence of forgiveness. It is obvious that without confession and pardon for what he sees as his own significant part in his lover's unhappiness and ruin, William will remain miserable and lose the will to live.[23]

On the other hand, a witness to Caliste's death (during a performance of Pergolesi's *Stabat Mater*) notes, "Après avoir eu quelques moments les mains jointes et les yeux levés au ciel, elle s'est enfoncée dans son fauteuil, et a fermé les yeux" (*Caliste*, 185) ["After joining her hands and lifting her eyes to heaven for a few moments, she fell back into her chair and closed her eyes"]. This eye-witness description, evoking what Joan H. Stewart calls "an aura of sainthood,"[24] suggests that, at least in her final moments of life, Caliste's thoughts were with God. A similarly peaceful resolution to William's predicament is unlikely, given his unstable state of mind, and his faithless response to all of the events which finally culminate in Caliste's death.

REASON, SPIRITUALITY, AND THE NOVEL

Two of Charrière's novels have been discussed above because they align most clearly with Enlightenment thinking which precludes the spiritual. In them, personal devastation is evident in the lives of characters who do not seek refuge in their faith. Admittedly, the reference to spirituality as a crucial life force is made indirectly here; it could be said that the subject is simply absent from these two novels and has been inferred for the purposes of the current study. Clearly, the novelist does not take an overtly polemical stand to protest the rational counter-spiritual currents of the time. And, compared to Charrière's last novels and plays, which treat political themes directly, these novels appear quite innocuous on the surface. An anonymous contemporary critic, who disliked Charrière's later output, recommended that she "write novels" rather than get involved in politics: "Faites des romans, Madame."[25] Indeed, novels about love, marriage, motherhood, and the education of girls, traditional material for female writers, seem to lack seriousness and value except for a limited audience. I would argue, however, that the impact Charrière and other female novelists of the period had on contemporaries has long been misunderstood or underestimated.[26] Feminist critics now recognize material in these novels, just beneath the surface, that is discreetly oppositional; it renders them, according to Miller in her study of *Le Comte de Comminges*, "*oblique* fiction of *dissent*" (emphasis mine).[27]

This indirect, dissident feminine vision during the Enlightenment is perhaps best understood in philosophical terms. In "The European Enlightenment," Mark Wallace explains, "Prior to Descartes it was assumed by philosophers that reason gives each person direct access to the visible world of objects and the invisible world of God."[28] Human reason was thought to be "participatory" with divine consciousness. On the other hand, the popular Enlightenment deistic belief posited that God's work was limited to creation, that individuals functioned apart from that God, and that human reason was not participatory, but "autonomous."[29] Accordingly, the *philosophes* (deists and atheists alike) valued the power of the intellect over (or instead of) the power of divine inspiration and the soul, and dismissed prayer and spiritual reflection as an inadequate or futile means of negotiating life's demands and interpreting life's mysteries. Reason alone, using the Cartesian method of observation, analysis, and synthesis of the perceivable material world, was the only reliable means of attaining truth.

In a sense, it is the *philosophes*' public and controversial idea about the primacy of an autonomous reason over a participatory reason that is at work in novels by women of the period. The fictional display of intimate personal struggles provides an opportunity to observe the workings of the thinking and feeling mind (or "autonomous reason") and the praying soul (or "participatory reason"). Clashes between romantic illusions and the realities of love lead characters to respond with all means at their disposal. Eventually, most abandon, in one way or another, their unhappy circumstances. We have seen that convent life, a solution for some, is not always a viable option. An alternative avoidance strategy providing some of the same comforts as the convent is a spiritual life at home, including devotion to prayer. Characters experience some healing when they allow themselves to move away from absorption in personal trials to the contemplation of spiritual promises. This imitation of the convent experience through the development of personal spirituality makes it possible for characters to overpower the disquiet of the heart and mind, heal brokenness, and experience peace. They act not as creatures of reason and emotions alone, but of spiritual impulses, too.[30]

Those characters who choose not to turn away from the material world to experience a spiritual one, as is the case with Charrière's Mistress Henley and William, remain unchanged in any beneficial way. Since the title of the collection of Mistress Henley's letters indicates that her work has been published by her friend, we are led to assume that Mistress Henley did indeed die, either by suicide (although she claims to be incapable of killing herself), or else from a broken heart, which she implied might happen in her last letter: "Je ne suis qu'une femme, je ne m'ôterai pas la vie, je n'en aurai pas le courage; si je deviens mère, je souhaite de n'en avoir jamais la volonté; mais le chagrin tue aussi. Dans un an, dans deux ans, vous apprendrez, je l'espère, que je suis raisonnable et heureuse, ou que je ne suis plus" (*Lettres* 45) ["I am only a woman, I will not take my own life, I won't have the courage to do that. If I become a mother, I hope to never again wish to die that way—but sorrow kills, too. In one year, perhaps two, I hope that you will learn that I am sensible and happy, or else that I am no longer alive"]. Her death, unlike Claire's, Adélaïde's, Comminges's or even Caliste's, does not hold the hope of happiness in eternity with God or of union with her lover. Indeed, she writes nothing in her letters about a faith life. William's fate appears as miserable.

These stories about William and Mistress Henley, when compared to the substance of the other novels, suggest that reason alone, without thought of God and religiously grounded hope, is insufficient to negotiate all of life's difficulties. Without spiritual support the characters lack initiative and practical options. Their romantic disappointments assume an importance that overshadows all else; indeed, their choice of a purely secular mentality means that there *is* nothing else apart from their personal destinies. Consequently, these characters are crushed while others, with a more expansive view of life, are vindicated. For, as certain novels show, the action of the soul, through faith, makes some sense of suffering and enables the believers to see beyond it to God and the afterlife. This bridge between human beings and their Creator allows for a world where some consolation can be found, if only in retreat. Diderot's point that reason should be the only guide for facing life's challenges is clearly refuted in these novels.

CONCLUSION

It is important, finally, to consider the nature of the spirituality experienced by the fictional characters explored in this study: religious truths, valued in so far as they make life's deceptions bearable, are part of a spiritual outlook that is neither mystical nor truly transcendent. Claire d'Albe notes that God alone fills the void left by unhappy love: "le vide terrible que l'amour y [dans les âmes passionnées] laissa ne peut être remplie que par Dieu même" (*Claire*, 130) ["The terrible void left by love (in passionate souls) can be filled only by God"].[31] In the midst of "la triste incertitude" ["sad uncertainty"] during a lover's illness, Riccoboni's Juliette Catesby, in *Lettres de Milady Juliette Catesby à Milady Henriette Campley, son amie* (1759) resorts to "[la] prière"[32] ["prayer"], since God is the source of all good. Riccoboni's Fanni Butlerd, like Claire d'Albe, affirms her intent to turn to God after love's deceptions take their toll: "quand mon cher A... ne m'aimera plus, je me ferai Catholique et j'irai habiter cette maison paisible [le couvent]"[33] ["When my dear A... no longer loves me, I will become a Catholic and will go to live in that peaceful home (the convent)"]. Indeed, her love for A. will survive her death; she imagines her heavenly existence consisting of her weightless, winged soul hovering eternally about him: "Je t'aimerai après ma mort, oui, sans doute, puisque mon âme est immortelle, séparée de mon dépouille terrestre, elle enverra sans cesse autour de toi"[34] ["Yes, I will, without doubt, love you after my death; my immortal soul, detached from my earthly body, will be unceasingly around you"]. Genlis's Mathilde also reflects on union with her lover in heaven: "et dans ce monde si tout nous séparait, dans le ciel tout nous réunira"[35] ["and if in this world everything separated us, in heaven everything will unite us"]. God is significant when a lover is absent; the cloister is desirable when it provides a place to nurse an emotional wound or to contemplate one's realistic options; heaven is attractive because union with a lover is believed possible in the afterlife. The convent and prayer are holy retreats, but, as we have seen, their function is more often practical and secular than not.[36] Divine realities are not valued for themselves, but for their ability to transform everyday reality.[37] One wonders if they would play a role at all in the absence of need.

God's power, then, appears incidental, and the defense of it by women in these novels arguably faint. God and the human soul are, at best, part of a practical solution, a means to a worldly end. Defined in terms of retreat and want, divine influence seems limited. It transforms life, but does not completely transcend it. The unimposing representation of God interfaces with what Janet Whatley has called "the myriad details of everyday existence,"[38] which themselves dominate the narratives. Stewart, likewise, writes of Charrière's "delicate weave of *inconspicuous circumstances and almost infinitesimal occurrences* whose accumulated weight nonetheless determine the heroines' destinies" (emphasis mine).[39] By comparison, the mighty life force of God, moving amid mundane realities, appears domesticated—or tempered. In that sense, the portrayal of spirituality by these women novelists is not completely at odds with the prevailing Enlightenment lionization of human experience.[40]

If realistic details align these writers with the Enlightenment's focus on the material world, elements of Christian spirituality set their novels apart. We have seen that God and the life of the soul, although subtle presences, are real forces in the development of both character and plot in numerous novels by women. Moreover, the apparent causality between a relationship with God on the one hand and the possibility of experiencing happiness on earth and after death on the other, represents a coalescence of the material and the transcendent, and is a compelling affirmation of the spiritual, immortal nature of human destiny. Characters that have recourse to a faith-life, tempered but participatory, are part of a spiritual undercurrent in fiction by women. Their "scattered and timorous voices of manifest protest"—as Stewart refers to their literary impact during the Enlightenment—opposes the louder voice of enlightened eighteenth-century *philosophes* who lashed out at institutionalized religion and championed the exclusive power of autonomous human reason. While more irreverent, radical messages by Diderot and others paved the way for political and spiritual upheaval, the female literary voice, though less politicized and overtly didactic, gives witness to a steady, discreet, enduring faith grounded in the simple—but strong—life of the soul.

NOTES

1. See Robert Darnton's *The Forbidden Best-Sellers of Pre-revolutionary France* (New York: Norton, 1995).
2. Joan Hinde Stewart, "The Novelists and Their Fiction," in *French Women and the Age of Enlightenment* (Bloomington: Indiana University Press, 1984), 202.
3. Claudine-Alexandrine Guérin de Tencin, *Les Malheurs de l'amour* (Paris: Editions Desjonquères, 2001), 92.
4. Madame de Genlis, *La Duchesse de la Vallière* (Paris: Librairie Fontaine, 1983), 38.
5. Madame de Genlis, *Mathilde* (Paris: Imprimerie de P. Gueffier, 1820), 52.
6. Marie-Jeanne Riccoboni, *Lettres de Mistress Fanni Butlerd* (Geneva: Librairie Droz, 1979), 51.
7. Claudine-Alexandrine Guérin de Tencin, *Mémoires du Comte de Comminges* (Paris: Editions Desjonquères, 1996), 86, 87; subsequent references are to this edition and will appear parenthetically in the text by short title (*Mémoires*) and page number.
8. In "Les Romans de Madame de Tencin: Fable et fiction," in *La Littérature des lumières en France et en Pologne: Esthétique, terminologie, échanges* (Wroclaw: Panstwowe Wydawnictwo Naukowe, 1976), Jean Decottignies observes the contrast between Tencin's lived experience and her fictional representation of convent life and of clergy and nuns: "There was even surprise that she would express so little animosity and even considerable moderation in her depiction of religious types, having herself been a victim of these abuses" (259). In "Claudine-Alexandrine Guérin de Tencin (1682–1749)," in *French Women Writers*, ed. Eva Martin Sartori and Dorothy Wynne Zimmerman (Westport, CT: Greenwood, 1991), Sartori notes the same contradiction in Tencin: "[It] is surprising that monks and nuns are portrayed as sympathetic, tolerant, and compassionate . . . and that convents and monasteries are viewed as refuges rather than prisons" (477).
9. See Benedetta Craveri's *The Age of Conversation*, trans. Teresa Waugh (New York: New York Review Books, 2005) for a comprehensive study of seventeenth- and eighteenth-century Parisian salons. Although primarily about salon hostesses and guests, the book also treats the role convents played in a woman's education and also at the end of life.
10. In "Les Romans de Madame de Tencin," Decottignies argues that convents serve the eighteenth-century narrative in ways that are wholly unrelated to religion: time spent in seclusion allows for the germination, so to speak, "d'une nouvelle intrigue" ["of a new storyline"]; retreat, like a marriage or the disappearance of characters, provides a reason to conclude a story (260).
11. Madame de Cottin, *Claire d'Albe* (Paris: Régine Desforges, 1976), 74; subsequent references are to this edition and will appear parenthetically in the text by short title (*Claire*) and page number.
12. Madame de Genlis, *La Duchesse de la Vallière*, 302.
13. Ibid.
14. Although Swiss born, Charrière's thought and work were greatly influenced by French writers. In *Les Femmes et la tradition littéraire: Anthologie du Moyen Age à nos jours. Première Partie: XII–XVIII*̄ *siècles* (New Haven: Yale University Press, 2006), Vicki Mistacco points out, "She feels and is, in fact, French, culturally speaking. Although born in Holland, and a resident of Switzerland once married, she belongs to the tradition of French women writers, in particular the tradition of female novelists who swayed the evolution of the genre, questioning its conventions and leaving traces of their 'uniqueness' as women" (441).
15. Mistacco, *Les Femmes et la tradition littéraire*, 447.
16. In "Women versus Clergy, Women pro Clergy," in *French Women and the Age of Enlightenment*, ed. Samia I. Spencer (Bloomington: Indiana University Press, 1984), Ruth Graham has noted the "feminization of religious life" in France during the eighteenth century. Her socio-historical study of the female Jansenists, the *convulsionnaires de St-Médard,* noble women who influenced hierarchical appointments in the Church and pious women of modest

origins, led her to conclude, "At the beginning of the eighteenth century, men dominated religious life in France; at the end of the century, women were by far the greater number of the faithful" (128).

17. Sartori calls Adélaïde's presence at the Trappist monastery, as well as her loveless marriage, "nothing short of sacrilegious" ("Claudine-Alexandrine Guérin de Tencin," 478). Indeed, Tencin's ending has provoked other similar commentary. Miller notes, "Prévost in his periodical *Le Pour et le Contre*, condemned the scene of the deathbed confession as an offense to plausibility, and in general the ending was criticized for not showing enough repentance and respect for religion" ("1735: The Gender of the Memoir-Novel," 441). These aspects of Tencin's novel, unlike her positive portrayals of religious figures and convents (see note 8), conform better to expectations for Tencin's negative views of institutionalized religion.

18. During the eighteenth century, some considered this novel to be comparable to Mme de Lafayette's *La Princesse de Clèves* (1678). Miller notes that this rapprochement between the two works places Tencin and other female novelists of the eighteenth century in "a strong literary tradition characterized by recognizable narrative poetics" ("1735: The Gender of the Memoir-Novel," 437).

19. In "1799, 10 October: The Ideologists," in *A New History of French Literature*, ed. Hollier, Frank Paul Bowman writes about Cottin's realistic depiction of traditional female roles: "Cottin reformulated the function of the woman novelist as portrayer of the plight of women" (602). As Miller did for Tencin, Bowman aligns this eighteenth-century writer with recognized literary canonical figures, Mme de Lafayette and George Sand. Bowman adds that Cottin foreshadows Jane Austen (602). Others, such as Joan H. Stewart in "Isabelle de Charrière Publishes *Caliste:* Designing Women," in *A New History of French Literature*, ed. Hollier, and Mistacco, in *Les Femmes et la tradition littéraire*, also compare Charrière with Jane Austen.

20. Isabelle de Charrière, *Lettres de Mistress Henley publiées par son amie* (New York: MLA, 1993), 9; subsequent references are to this edition and will appear parenthetically in the text by short title (*Lettres*) and page number.

21. Isabelle de Charrière, *Caliste: Lettres écrites de Lausanne* (Paris: Editions des Femmes, 1979), 114; subsequent references are to this edition and will appear parenthetically in the text by short title (*Caliste*) and page number.

22. See Susan K. Jackson's study, "The Novels of Isabelle de Charrière, or, a Woman's Work Is Never Done," *Studies in Eighteenth-Century Culture* 14 (1995): 299–306, on the inconclusive endings of many novels by women as a metaphor for "l'ouvrage" ["the work"] of women, "a single, interminable process, devoid of product. It cannot count in part because it cannot be counted" (302). Mistacco contends that the novelists chose inconclusive endings, "even if doing so meant suggesting that the heroine's open-ended and uncertain future would likely be uneventful and dull" (*Les Femmes et la tradition littéraire*, 447).

23. See Jean Starobinski's study of William's passivity as an indication of his latent homosexuality: "*Les Lettres écrites de Lausanne* de Madame de Charrière: inhibition psychique et interdit social," in *Roman et lumières au XVIIIe siècle* (Paris: Editions Sociales, 1970).

24. Stewart, "Isabelle de Charrière Publishes *Caliste*," 555.

25. Quoted in Mistacco, *Femmes et la tradition littéraire*, 449.

26. Mistacco develops a detailed analysis of the myth of Procne and Philomela in the opening chapter of her exhaustive anthology of works by women from medieval times through the twenty-first century, already cited several times above. In "Philomèle et les soeurs de Procné," Mistacco shows that Philomela's facial mutilation by her brother-in-law resulting in her inability to ever speak again is a metaphor for the silencing of women writers. During her forced captivity, Philomela uses needlework to secretly communicate the incident to her sister; this manipulation of a traditional feminine activity for a grander purpose shows the eternally relentless creativity and resourcefulness of women who, facing patriarchal obstacles, must transform conventions to serve their needs. Procne's ability to understand the coded message, to free her sister, and to avenge her mutilation show that the value of work produced by women is best understood by women, or else by readers not unduly influenced by the prejudices of traditional literary patriarchal criticism. The myth is particularly helpful when considering the traditional themes (and genres) associated with women, as well as the underlying messages of

those works (1–58). Stewart writes about the masked dissent characteristic of novels by women in "The Novelists and Their Fictions," in *French Women and the Age of Enlightenment*, ed. Spencer: "But protest in the novel is by definition masked and mediated and, hence, in need of interpretation. If, at first glance, the voices of eighteenth-century French women novelists seem less distinctive than, for example, those of the nineteenth century, we must examine the tensions underlying the earlier era's restricted vocabulary and stylized expression" (203). Stewart explains that in their fictions, women writers used conventional words in new ways: "Under the pen especially of women writers of the late century, crucial words such as virtue, reason, and happiness slip from their accustomed places, becoming newly functional and acquiring original nuances that embody specifically female vision and desire" (203).

27. In "1735: The Gender of the Memoir-Novel," when Miller refers to Tencin's *Comte de Comminges* as "an oblique fiction of dissent: a feminist critique of masculine privilege" (438), she is particularly thinking of Tencin's choice of "anonymity by taking a man's name in the title of her memoire" (438).

28. Mark I. Wallace, "The European Enlightenment," in *World Spirituality: An Encyclopedic History of the Religious Quest*, ed. Peter Van Ness, vol. 22 (New York: Crossroad, 1996), 80.

29. Ibid.

30. Some critics attribute to these female writers the pre-romantic tendencies traditionally associated with Rousseau and other male writers of the period. Sartori writes of Tencin, "Her plots announce romantic conventions" ("Claudine-Alexandrine Guérin de Tencin," 479). Bowman writes of Cottin's *Malvina* (1802): "tears, fainting spells, fires, mortal fevers make it very characteristic of the excesses of pre-Romantic sensibility" ("1799, 10 October: The Ideologists," 602).

31. In "Sophie Cottin (1770–1807)," in *French Women Writers*, ed. Samia I. Spencer. Spencer describes the moral strength of Cottin's idealistic female characters. Although, like Claire, they expect happiness only after death, they also "dare to be their own persons and experience the fullness of earthly experience" (96).

32. Marie-Jeanne Riccoboni, *Lettres de Milady Juliette Catesby à Milady Henriette Campley, son amie* (Paris: Desjonquères, 1983), 117.

33. Riccoboni, *Lettres de Mistress Fanni Butlerd*, 51.

34. Ibid., 81.

35. Madame de Genlis, *Mathilde*, 52.

36. In *The Age of Conversation*, Craveri talks about the iconic *La Princesse de Clèves* and the heroine's retreat to a convent in similar terms: "the reasons for the heroine entering a convent are not religious as much as sentimental and moral: the logic that compels her to leave the world is a secular logic" (94–95). On this issue, see the fourth chapter in this volume.

37. In "Sophie Cottin (1770–1807)," Spencer notes the impact of the Enlightenment ideologies on Cottin, specifically with respect to the degree to which her heroines experience life itself to its fullest in all its earthly forms (all the while awaiting complete happiness only after death): "The revolutionary winds of the late eighteenth century . . . have not gone unnoticed [by Cottin]" (96).

38. Janet Whatley, "Isabelle de Charrière (1740–1805)," in *French Women Writers*, ed. Spencer, 36.

39. Stewart, "Isabelle de Charrière Publishes *Caliste*," 554.

40. In "1761, December: What Was Enlightenment?" in *A New History of French Literature*, ed. Hollier, Lionel Gossman contends that the "universality" sought by Enlightenment philosophers, "was not a transcendental universality. It was grounded in and bounded by human experience" (489).

Chapter Six

Spirituality and Social Justice in the Novels of George Sand

Kelsey L. Haskett

George Sand (1804–1876) was both a romanticist and an idealist who dared to portray social reality as it was, while at the same time presenting a vision for change dependant as much on spiritual transformation as on social reform. From her early novels depicting the stifling conditions of women in unhappy marriages to her social novels dealing with the struggles of the lower class, from complex works like *Consuelo*, with its heavy mystical content, to her gentle pastoral novels, where simplicity and purity of heart find their reward in love, the significance of the spiritual is never absent from Sand's writings. And although her feminist and socialist themes have attracted more attention than her spiritual outlook, the former are nevertheless directly linked to her personal religious beliefs.[1] In an attempt to provide insight into the role that spirituality plays in her novels, particularly in shaping her feminist and humanitarian ideals, I will examine two novels chosen from different stages of Sand's career, showing both the evolution and the continuity of her themes.[2]

Echoing the cry of the French Revolution, the notions of liberty, equality, and fraternity are continuously developed in Sand's works. In her first novel, *Indiana*, inequality in marriage is equated with the inequities inherent in a social hierarchy propped up by the Church, but rejected by the main character, whose faith in God is more genuine than that proclaimed by official religion. In *Le Compagnon du tour de France*, written nearly a decade later, inequality permeates a society which excludes the working class from participating in the political process, a wrong which the hero strives to right, certain that God is on his side. In both novels, the depiction of a metaphorical paradise on earth, based on Enlightenment ideals, the message of the Gospels, and Sand's own feminist stance, aptly illustrates the author's ideological response to the social structures responsible for these personal and social injustices.

George Sand's dual Catholic and Enlightenment background, her adherence to nineteenth-century romantic ideals, and her avid pursuit of inner and outer fulfillment, all contribute to her thoughts on the role of religion and the importance of spirituality in her novels. However, beginning in the 1830s, Sand also came into contact with socialist thinking, including various utopian views of society. While she was inspired by the ideas of Lamennais, a priest with republican ideals, Louis Blanc, a utopian socialist, and other social theorists, Pierre Leroux, her most important mentor, made an indelible impression on her thinking.[3] His communist theories included an emphasis on Christian thinking, which appealed to Sand, on various mystical beliefs, which appear in certain of her works, on social solidarity, and on the idea of human perfectibility.[4] Although the influence of these theorists is evident in later works like *Le Compagnon du tour de France* or *Consuelo*, Sand's first novel, which closely mirrors her own life, clearly reflects her own tendency toward social idealism, combined with her personal views on the plight of women in marriage and the role of the spiritual in society.[5] It is Sand's experiences as a woman, portrayed in the lives of her female characters, which allow her to express with conviction her spiritual aspirations and her desire for a form of religion that elevates the downtrodden and brings justice to all. Paul Christophe's study of Sand's spiritual life confirms the relationship between her beliefs and her novels, particularly her female characters: "George Sand's beliefs can, in fact, be discerned through her fictional writings. George Sand produced remarkable female figures that seem to express her own convictions or refusals."[6]

INDIANA

As we begin our exploration of Sand's first novel, *Indiana*, published in 1832, a brief look at her personal and social background is in order. Following her father's death when she was only four, Sand was brought up by her aristocratic grandmother in the family manor in Berry, where she yearned for the love of her lower-class mother living in Paris. A sense of belonging to both classes helped shape her egalitarian view of society and gave her a heart for the common people, as she herself acknowledged: "Je tiens au peuple autant par le sang que par le coeur" ["I hold to the common people as much by my blood ties as by my heart"].[7] Although Voltairian in her views, Sand's grandmother sent her to a Catholic convent school to give her a proper education, but later removed her when she saw that Sand was so touched by the Christian faith that she wanted to become a nun. At age eighteen, Sand married Lieutenant Casimir Dudevant, a hardened military man somewhat older than her; their relationship left her disillusioned about marriage. Separating from him after ten years of profound disappointment, Sand went to Paris where she was able to live independently after the publication of *Indiana*. The novel, like Sand's life, is set in the historical and political context of early nineteenth-century France, where Napoleon's discriminatory Civil Code predetermined a woman's existence. It is also written in the context of the French romantic movement, of which the struggle for democracy and republican values were an integral part. These two influences, both extremely significant in the novel, are woven into the tapestry of the heroine's female aspirations for an enduring love authentic enough to fill her soul and powerful enough to free her from the chains which bind her to an oppressive marriage.[8]

We encounter in Indiana a young woman of fragile frame but determined will, who appears to suffer in silence the imposition of a marriage to a much older, retired colonel of Napoleon's former Grand Army, but whose inner resistance to his absolute authority belies her frail exterior. As she pines away for true love in the midst of a harsh, loveless marriage, she is alternately protected by her phlegmatic cousin Ralph, an insipid young Englishman whose presence in her life poses no threat to the jealous Colonel, and seduced by Raymon de Ramière, a handsome young aristocrat known for his persuasive writing style, matchless eloquence, and feminine conquests. Each of these men stands for the political system which defines his character: Colonel Delmare, who lives in the glories of the past and longs for the return of Napoleonic rule, proves to be the undisputed master of his household, "[un] excellent maître devant qui tout tremblait, femme, serviteurs, chevaux et chiens" ["(an) excellent master before whom everyone trembled, be it his wife, servants, horses, or dogs"][9]; Sir Ralph, having been rejected by his family at an early age and forced to find refuge in nature on Ile Bourbon, where he grew up, defends his dream of a republic which would exclude "tous les abus, tous les préjugés, toutes les injustices" (*Indiana*, 167) ["all abuse, prejudice, injustice"]; Raymon, as convinced of his superiority as Ralph is of his inferiority, attached to the privileges of his class, upholds the restored monarchy, but wisely supports the constitution rather than a return to unpopular absolutism. Indiana, on the other hand, half European, half Indian from the colony of Ile Bourbon, a true flower of nature, exudes simplicity and natural wisdom in her views on society: "Indiana opposait aux intérêts de la civilisation érigés en principes, les idées droites et les lois simples du bon sens et de l'humanité" (*Indiana*, 174) ["Indiana confronted the self-serving interests of civilized society held up as (foundational) principles with upright thinking and the simple laws of good sense and humanity"].

It is into this world of conflicted interests and aspirations that the author draws us, painting a picture of domestic life dominated by male authority, unjust laws, and prejudicial attitudes, where the beleaguered Indiana has no hope but to yearn for a savior to deliver her from the tyranny of marital subjugation. "Like many aspects of Sand's vision, her view of male-female relations is seen above all from the standpoint of personal freedom. Her condemnation of traditional marriage is based on the wife's lack of freedom," remarks Robert Godwin-Jones.[10] Helpless to change the laws, which accord virtually all rights to her husband, even that of the property she has personally inherited, love is Indiana's only avenue of escape. It is this hope which constitutes her inner resistance, both in her childhood, under the tutelage of a neglectful, violent father, and at age nineteen, under the domination of her husband:

> Mais, en voyant le continuel tableau des maux de la servitude . . . elle avait acquis une patience extérieure à toute épreuve, une indulgence et une bonté adorables avec ses inférieurs, mais aussi une volonté de fer, une force de résistance incalculable contre tout ce qui tendait à l'opprimer. En épousant Delmare, elle ne fit que changer de maître; en venant habiter le Lagny, que de changer de prison et de solitude. (*Indiana*, 89)
>
> [But in witnessing the continuous portrayal of the evils of servitude . . . she had acquired an unflinching patience on the outside, and a charming leniency and kindness toward her inferiors, but also a will of iron, an incalculable resistance to everything that tended to oppress her. In marrying Delmare, she had only changed masters; in coming to live at Langy, she had only changed prisons and places of solitude.]

While inwardly defying her oppressors, she waits for life to bring change from the outside, calmly riding out the storms, confident that if some day someone truly loves her, she will give her whole heart in return and thus be set free. However, while persisting in her stoic endurance, she gradually comes to realize that "ce libérateur, ce messie n'[est] pas venu" (*Indiana*, 89) ["this liberator, this messiah, (has) not come"], and she starts to languish both physically and emotionally in the absence of the love she has never known. As a typical romantic heroine, she suffers from an unknown malady, caused not by the vague "mal du siècle" common to male heroes of the period, but rather by an institution to which she is bound by laws over which she has no control.[11]

DECEPTIVE LOVE AND SPIRITUAL AWAKENING

The entry of Raymon de Ramière into Indiana's life marks the first turning point in the novel. Unfortunately, the kind of ethereal love Indiana dreams of is far removed from the earthly passion a lover like Raymon can offer; she longs for a pure, unconditional, absolute love, the very opposite of the self-serving love Raymon tries to bring her. Indiana's romantic and spiritual aspirations are closely intertwined at this point, while her ideas on social change have not yet taken shape. The arrival of Raymon, whose behavior causes one disillusion after the other, sets Indiana on a path of discovery which eventually enables her to define her ideals and counter to some degree the two men who control her life: her husband, who represents the force of the law, and Raymon, whose manipulation of their love relationship represents an even more insidious trap to which women are apt to fall prey.

Although Raymon at first idolizes Indiana as the ideal romantic figure, his selfish nature is so contrary to the image he projects as an adoring lover that in the end he turns her into a broken woman, who all but succumbs to despair and death. As the narrator shows us, never did an egotistical chauvinist meet a more vulnerable young woman. Even after he stops loving her, Raymon still tries to break down Indiana's resistance through clever ploys intended only to build up his own male ego. While Raymon symbolizes all the evils of a corrupt society where love is nothing more than pretense and self gratification, Indiana, the delicate Creole, is a mixture of all that is pure and innocent in nature and all that is refined in civilization, like Chateaubriand's Atala, who is also of mixed race. Atala is both Indian because of her mother, and Christian on account of her Spanish father, exemplifying Rousseau's "noble savage," slightly civilized by true religion. Rousseau's influence can be seen, as well, in Indiana's exotic background and in her name, which is particularly significant at the end. The clash between civilization and nature also evokes the works of Bernardin de Saint-Pierre, whose popular novel *Pierre et Virginie* (1787), set on the island of Mauritius, lauds the virtues of equality and life lived close to nature, while the title of his subsequent novel, *La Chaumière indienne* (1791), is explicitly referred to at the end of Sand's novel.

When Indiana is finally forced by her husband to leave France and return with him to Ile Bourbon—he alone possesses the legal power to make this decision—she daringly runs to Raymon, who, tiring of a platonic relationship, refuses to take her in, supposedly to protect her reputation. Raymon secretly rejoices in his newfound freedom, all the while claiming to be disconsolate. He encourages Indiana in a letter to find solace in God, an exhortation which stirs up her indignation and briefly opens her eyes to his real character: "Partez donc, ma bien-aimée; allez sous un autre ciel recueillir les fruits de la vertu et de la religion. Dieu nous récompensera d'un tel effort; car Dieu est bon" (*Indiana*, 241) ["Depart my beloved; go and pick the fruits of virtue and religion under another sky. God will reward us for our efforts, for God is good"]. This is not the first time Raymon has used the name of God to his own ends, but for once Indiana sees through his duplicity and sends him a letter summing up her thoughts on her own relationship to God and His true nature, which in turn becomes the basis for the social reforms she envisions as her only hope for liberation. Having twice been a victim of enslavement, legally in her marriage and emotionally in her relationship with Raymon, she identifies herself with the slaves in the colonies and cries out for nothing less than a total reversal of the existing social order. It is this vision of a new society that incorporates at once the teaching of the Gospels, the principles of the romantics and revolutionaries, and the author's own desires as a woman, as we shall now see.

After first recognizing in her letter that she has been mistaken about Raymon's love, and after calmly analyzing her failure to foresee how he would let her down at a crucial moment, Indiana only becomes upset when she considers Raymon's injunction to turn to God for comfort. In a powerful condemnation of the religion and society he represents, she spells out the differences between her God and Raymon's God, between her faith and his unbelief. Her ability to see clearly and justly in the midst of hypocrisy is reflected in her articulate defense of a religion which eschews the politics of power and exclusion and hails a much simpler form of faith that is truly egalitarian and compassionate. Raymon's God is "le dieu des hommes" ["the god of men"] (*Indiana*, 249), the king, founder, and supporter of their race. Just as the monarchy and nobility use God to prop up their authority and protect themselves from the people, men like Raymon believe that God has made everything for them, that he is the force that legitimizes their rights and upholds their laws, and gives them the dominant role in society. To him Indiana declares, "Vous vous croyez les maîtres du monde; je crois que vous n'en êtes que les tyrans. Vous pensez que Dieu vous protège et vous autorise à usurper l'empire de la terre; moi, je pense qu'il le souffre pour un peu de temps.... Non, Raymon, vous ne connaissez pas Dieu; ou plutôt... vous ne croyez à rien" (*Indiana*, 249) ["You believe yourselves to be the masters of the world; I believe you are only its tyrants. You think God protects you and authorizes you to usurp the dominion of the earth; I think he is putting up with it for a short while.... No, Raymon, you don't know God; or rather... you believe in nothing"]. Indiana goes on to say that a sense of the existence of God has never penetrated Raymon's heart. It is she, rather, who believes in God, but hers is a personal relationship. She categorically rejects the religion invented by men:

> [L]a religion que vous avez inventée, je la repousse; toute votre morale, tous vos principes, ce sont les intérêts de votre société que vous avez érigés en lois et que vous prétendez faire émaner de Dieu même, comme vos prêtres ont institué les rites du culte pour établir leur puissance et leur richesse sur les nations. Mais tout cela est mensonge et impiété. Moi qui l'invoque, moi qui le comprends, je sais bien qu'il n'y a rien de commun entre lui et vous. (*Indiana*, 249)
>
> [I reject the religion you have invented; all of your morals and principles exist to serve the interests of your (own) society. You have set them up as laws which you claim come from God himself, just as your priests have instituted rituals of worship in order to establish their power and wealth over the nations. But all of that is lies and impiety. I who call upon him, I who understand him, know very well that there is nothing in common between you and him.]

Institutionalized religion has been used to justify the interests of a male-dominated society, but its laws have nothing to do with God.[12] In contrast, Indiana lays out her vision of a society based on God's principles, combining the biblical teaching of "the meek inheriting the earth" with the romantic ideal of equality for all. She insists that God does not want society to oppress the poor or to crush the creatures of His making. In poetic terms reminiscent of the prophet Isaiah's words that "every valley shall be exalted and every mountain and hill . . . made low" (Isaiah 40:4), she paints a picture of a God who raises up the poor and abases the rich, levelling them like the smooth surface of the sea. She imagines God telling the slaves to throw away their chains and flee to the mountains, where he has provided rivers, flowers, and sunshine for them. She pictures him enabling beggars to lie down in comfort by ordering kings to toss them their robes of purple and to descend to the valleys where he has laid out carpets of moss and heather. She realizes that her dreams are all of another life, another world, but she yearns for a place where fleeing from oppression is not a crime and where man can escape from man without the chains of the law ensnaring him and forcing him back again to the feet of his enemy. It is obvious that her own emancipation is bound up in that of the oppressed of society in general and that the spheres of politics and religion are too intertwined for her to imagine the reformation of one without the other. Indiana enjoins Raymon not to speak to her of God, not to use his name to reduce her to silence. She contends that in following her husband her submission is not to God, but to men, but if she were to listen to the voice God has put in her heart, she would escape to the wilderness where she would learn to live alone, without help and without love, a choice favored by many a romantic figure. In concluding her letter on a more realistic note, however, she is forced to concede that no one can live in total isolation, and that this kind of escapism is, in fact, humanly impossible.

At the end of the novel, it should be noted, Indiana's dream of finding a haven in nature from the evils of society actually does come to pass, with the help of the novel's other protagonist, Sir Ralph, who surprisingly turns out to be a romantic hero *par excellence*. But before her ideal is realized, Indiana suffers even further degradation at the hands of her husband and, once again, Raymon, dragging her down to her lowest level. When the jealous Colonel discovers Raymon's letters to Indiana, he physically abuses her in his fury, causing her to flee Ile Bourbon and return to France. Braving the dangers of the stormy seas, the rough sailors, and the ever-present threat of the law for undeclared fugitives, Indiana makes this hazardous trek on the strength of a letter she has received from Raymon, who now gives every indication that he needs her love and care. In reality, Raymon's fortunes rapidly change, and by the time Indiana reaches France, he is advantageously married to the nobly born but adopted daughter of a wealthy industrialist, providing him not only with money and a marriage partner of his class, but also with the political protection now afforded by the bourgeoisie. Caught up in the revolutionary turmoil of 1830 upon her arrival in France, wounded and hospitalized for a time, Indiana despairs to see Raymon alive. Finally making her way to Paris, she returns to the country manor she once owned but which now belongs to Raymon, only to experience the humiliation of discovering that he is living there with another woman, his wife. With no hope for the future and no desire to go on living, Indiana sinks into despair in the miserable room she rents in Paris, allowing the author to enumerate the ills a woman on her own can experience in the impersonal metropolis. Sand, of course, had experienced this transition firsthand, after separating from her husband and going to write in Paris. For her heroine, however, it is the arrival of Sir Ralph that starts to turn the tide, when he rescues the depressed and waning Indiana from a slow but certain death, and informs her of her husband's death on the island.

IDEAL LOVE AND THE PURSUIT OF PERFECTION

Just as Raymon has been a destructive force in her life, Ralph, in his own discreet way, has been a positive factor, having acted all along as her protector, despite Indiana's blindness to his deeply committed love. An awkward, inexpressive man, he has no way with words like Raymon, but has nonetheless remained faithful to his childhood companion and only love throughout her entire life, shielding her from her husband's abuses, while at the same time erecting a thick wall of indifference around himself to keep the Colonel from suspecting his feelings. Having grown up with Indiana on Ile Bourbon, he proves to be a type of Christ, filling the roles of brother, friend, mentor, and guardian angel, and becoming, when she is finally at death's door, her savior. In the romantic tradition, however, he is also a melancholic outsider, a man as despairing of civilization as Raymon is enamoured of it, and who sees the double suicide he eventually proposes to Indiana as a virtuous act. Deeply spiritual, his desire is to leave this vale of tears where sensitive souls live in exile, and return to God their Creator.[13] In accordance with Catholic doctrine, he believes that their earthly baptism of suffering will earn them pardon in the afterlife, but he rejects the Church's teaching on suicide and contends, like Indiana, that misfortune has taught him a religion other than that of men: "Le Dieu que nous adorons, toi et moi, n'a pas destiné l'homme à tant de misères sans lui donner l'instinct de s'y soustraire" (*Indiana*, 305) ["The God we worship, both you and I, has not destined man to so many miseries without giving him the instinct to withdraw himself from them"]. He subscribes to a natural religion, where "l'univers est le temple où nous adorons Dieu" (*Indiana*, 307) ["the universe is the temple where we worship God"]. To consummate their act of suicide, he recommends a return to the sanctuary of nature, to a place untainted by human contact, in the depths of Ile Bourbon's virgin forest. Rejecting, like the romantics, "cette civilisation qui renie Dieu ou le mutile" (*Indiana*, 307) ["this civilization that denies God or mutilates him"], he wants to bring Indiana back to the place of their innocent childhood, and plunge with her to his death in the pure, cleansing waters of a lofty cascade.

The symbolism of their chosen form of death is abundantly clear. It is a kind of baptism, a way to purge themselves not only from civilization's stains but also from their own transgressions. Indiana recalls with sorrow the death of her maid by drowning, a death for which she feels responsible. "Mourir comme elle me sera doux," she confesses, "ce sera l'expiation de sa mort, que j'ai causé" (*Indiana*, 309) ["Dying like her will be comforting to me; it will be the expiation for her death, which I caused"]. To prepare themselves for this solemn act, they use their ocean journey back as a time to detach themselves from the world and draw near to God. Instead of the opposing winds Indiana encountered on her way to France to meet Raymon, a favorable wind speeds them on to their desired destination, implying God's blessing on their enterprise. Refreshed by the tonic sea air and the promise of release from her sorrows, Indiana's heart, soul, and body begin to mend: "Oublieuse de sa vie passée, elle ouvrit son âme aux émotions profondes de l'espérance religieuse" (*Indiana*, 309) ["Forgetful of her past life, she opened up her soul to the deep emotions of religious hope"]. Ralph, as well, sheds his cold outer shell, revealing for the first time his true, stellar character. The blinders come off Indiana's eyes, and before they finally proceed to take their own lives, Ralph explains his life to her in words so sincere and eloquent they totally eclipse Raymon's seductive language, giving Ralph a voice and a new identity. Putting behind her Raymon's perfidious intrusion into her life,

Indiana realizes it is Ralph who has shown her "un amour pur, un amour profond" (*Indiana*, 321), "un amour impérissable" (*Indiana*, 325) ["a pure love, a deep love, an imperishable love"]. Their death together becomes more than a baptism; it is a celestial marriage in which both partners hope to be united in eternal life.

Just as baptism symbolizes not only death but also resurrection, the nuptial couple imagines their death together as a springboard thrusting them into union in the afterlife, a state of bliss beyond the grave where love cannot be altered, an absolute attainable only through death. With Indiana dressed like a bride in white, and using as an altar a rocky shelf above the cataract into which they plan to jump, they both commit themselves to each other in a ceremony that takes place only before God. "C'est moi maintenant qui suis ton frère, ton époux, ton amant pour l'éternité" (*Indiana*, 328) ["It is I who have become your brother, your spouse, your lover for eternity"], proclaims Ralph. Indiana, for him, is the embodiment of heaven: "le ciel, c'est toi, et si j'ai mérité d'être sauvé, j'ai mérité de te posséder" (*Indiana*, 329) ["You are heaven to me, and if I have merited being saved, I have merited possessing you"], he tells her. She responds with equal fervour: "Sois mon époux dans le ciel et sur la terre . . . et que ce baiser me fiance à toi pour l'éternité!" (*Indiana*, 330) ["Be my husband in heaven and on earth . . . and let this kiss join me to you for eternity"]. Her unfulfilled wish for love, for a savior, for a better life, are all incorporated in this dramatic act, which reveals itself to be as much a spiritual longing as a desire for temporal happiness. Ralph becomes the messiah whose unceasing love promises new hope and a new beginning to the awaiting spouse. Indiana becomes the perfect bride, the absolute fulfillment of all his aspirations. It is only in death, however, that such perfection can be realized. Sand aspires to such a lofty ideal of romantic love that it is only in terms of a metaphoric afterlife that she is able to depict her vision of an egalitarian, loving relationship between a man and a woman.[14]

The conclusion of the novel brings about a startling reversal in the plot, which confirms this notion. By an unexplained turn of events, Ralph and Indiana survive their fall, or are divinely prevented from carrying out their suicide (the explanation which Ralph prefers), and are found to be living in the recesses of a wilderness retreat on the island, discovered only by the narrator who emerges in the end. As if they had passed from death to life, from the world of corruption into a paradise on earth, the couple is living out its dream of a perfect relationship in an idyllic setting, close to God and nature, far removed from civilization. Having symbolically "died to self," they treat each other with utter devotion and respect, and are able to live independently from society. Lest they be seen to be exemplifying an egotistical existence, they use their resources to buy and free mistreated slaves, and their servants are their friends. Social and sexual equality are finally realized in this veritable Garden of Eden, where joy comes nonetheless only after suffering. The reformation of society is rejected in the novel in favor of the complete abandonment of society. "Moi, j'ai Indiana" (*Indiana*, 343) ["Me, *I* have Indiana" (emphasis mine)], declares Ralph to the narrator, implying that genuine love is all one needs. He defends his antisocialism by saying that one should bear the chains of society if its laws serve and protect one, but break them if they do not. Indiana and Ralph have given themselves the liberty to cast off the fetters which imprisoned them, but it is clear that for Sand this freedom cannot be purchased without love.

This, in the end, is the message with which we are left. It is not an incitement to reform the laws, which has led feminists to criticize Sand for the novel's lack of political focus. The kind of transformation Sand suggests is rather personal, spiritual, and relational; it begins with the right of a woman to live her life with a man in mutual love and respect, with the man expected to bring a sincere heart into the relationship. Kristina Wingard Vareille maintains that "with Ralph, the young woman will at last know marriage in the fullest and most authentic sense of the word."[15] The spiritual dimension of their life is a prerequisite to true happiness and fulfillment. While Sand strongly opposes institutionalized religion and all the political and legal structures that enslave a woman, her answer is to provide an ideal to strive for, rather than a political agenda to follow.[16] That ideal has emerged from her own aspirations toward unfailing love, along with her desire for purity, equality, and justice, and for freedom that is inner as well as outer. Believing God to be good and just, she portrays him in the novel as the necessary source of social justice. However, it should be noted, it is not his love alone that delivers Indiana in the end, through some kind of personal religious experience, but rather that of the perfect, romantic lover Sand has imagined.[17]

In that sense, Sand's solution in the novel remains unsatisfactory. Human perfection is not of this world, as the very nature of the novel's conclusion suggests. Nor can the love of a couple, however ideal it may be, suffice for all their needs. Perhaps this idealism factored into some of the romantic disappointments in the author's own life, for her pursuits seem to reveal an unending desire for fulfillment in love which she never attains.[18] At the same time, most of her novels reflect her ongoing search for spirituality paired with social justice, including a rethinking of both religion and women's role. *Indiana* presents a vision for change which has not yet been translated into political terms, a vision as spiritual as it is social, calling for an attitudinal transformation to accompany more concrete measures of reform. It is Sand's tragic marital experience, combined with her personal convictions, that provide the framework for this first major work, and it is her own search for independence that motivates her heroine's desire not only for personal freedom but indeed for liberty for all. Sand provides no guidelines for political action, but rather, by contrast and example, portrays not only the kind of absolute love relationship she dreams of for women, but also the need for a complete moral and spiritual reformation of society.

LE COMPAGNON DU TOUR DE FRANCE

By the 1840s, Sand had become sufficiently convinced of the need to incorporate politically engaged themes into her works that she began writing such novels as *Le Compagnon du tour de France*, the first in a series of works that focus on the condition of the common people from a socialist perspective.[19] Encouraged first by republican lawyer Michel de Bourges, and then by Pierre Leroux and other social theorists, Sand placed her art at the service of her revolutionary goals and her desire to portray the working class in a way that would draw respect and admiration rather than disdain. In *Le Compagnon du tour de France*, Sand reveals that she is not only in step with her times, but well out in front in her depiction of social justice and her willingness to counter prejudice in her writings by erasing the class and gender boundaries which still held sway in even the most enlightened circles.[20] The fact that she was radical in her day is clearly evidenced by the backlash of reactions caused by the novel, coming from sometimes unexpected sources and directed against aspects of the novel that might surprise us today, such as her portrayal of a principled, dignified worker whose qualities were considered antithetical to lower class reality by most of the elite reading public. Once again in this novel, Sand's continuous, overt references to Christ and his message of hope for the downtrodden are presented as foundational for social action. Not only her themes but also her character typology draws largely upon Gospel sources, even more so than in earlier works.

A CHRIST-LIKE PROTAGONIST

Set against a background of revolutionary fervour forced underground by the restoration of the monarchy in France after the upheaval of the French Revolution and Napoleon's defeat, the novel depicts as its main character a young carpenter who perfects his training through an itinerant apprenticeship which takes him around the country as a "compagnon," to work under various experts in his field. Although becoming a superior craftsman, Pierre Huguenin remains humble and submits to his father, a master carpenter, after returning to work with him following his four-year "tour de France." In this submission and in every way, he demonstrates all the qualities of a Christ-figure as the novel progresses. Not only does his trade resemble that of Jesus, but his exemplary character and eventual mission as a radical social reformer also take on the aura of the Christ of the Gospels. Identifying himself entirely with the working class, Pierre's main goal in life is to improve its lot through the political and social action needed to bring about true democracy. His female counterpart, the aristocratic Yseult de Villepreux, proves to be equally committed to the cause, and is willing to sacrifice status and public opinion to fight for the oppressed and realize her own dreams of social equality. Together they defy the stereotypes of the rich and poor and demonstrate that a love for others, as commanded in the Bible, requires a commitment to their treatment as equals and the removal of traditional blinders that prevent the classes, both high and low, from mutually accepting each other.

Pierre demonstrates his Christ-like character in both direct and symbolic ways. Not only does he have the vocation of a carpenter, but he is commissioned by the Count de Villepreux, Yseult's grandfather and adoptive father, to repair a medieval chapel adjacent to the nobleman's manor, as it has fallen into disrepair. This work, which Pierre carries on throughout the novel, suggests Christ's role as builder and restorer of the Church.[21] Pierre bears, as well, the name of the great apostle, and indeed is called, at one point, an "apôtre prolétaire" ["proletarian apostle"].[22] His surname, Huguenin, closely resembles that of the early French Protestants, the Huguenots, thereby reinforcing the anticlerical and anti-institutional attitude running throughout the novel, which at the same time elevates personal faith, the teachings of Christ, and the reading of the Bible. George Sand herself was very attracted to Protestantism, suggesting that the association of the hero's surname with the reformed faith was probably intentional. In his carpenters' guild, Pierre becomes a peacemaker who sees beyond the rivalries of the various factions and tries to promote good will and cooperation rather than competition and bitter fighting. For his courageous stand he is eventually rejected by those who want to perpetuate the existing enmity between lodges, but he accepts this opposition with a humility and gentleness akin to those of Christ. His passionate desire for brotherly love and understanding and his persuasive speech win over, nevertheless, a young man who sees in him the example of Christ; he deeply touches, as well, the innkeeper, who believes him to be filled with the Spirit of the Lord ("rempli de l'esprit du Seigneur") (*CTF*, 132) as he addresses his fellow companions in her establishment. Even though his message is not generally accepted, his words fall on fertile soil in a number of hearts, including that of his new "disciple," who thus describes the vision that moved him while Pierre was pleading for peace and reconciliation:

> Je me suis figuré le Christ, ce fils d'un charpentier, pauvre, obscur, errant sur la terre, parlant à de misérables ouvriers comme nous. . . . Je ne veux pas blesser ta modestie, Pierre, en te comparant à celui qu'on appelle Dieu, mais je

me disais: si le Christ revenais sur terre et s'il passait devant cette maison, que ferait-il ? . . . Il entrerait dans la grange, et ne dédaignerait pas de s'asseoir, comme nous, sur une botte de paille, lui qui naquit sur la paille d'une étable; puis il écouterait. Et tout en faisant ce rêve, je me représentais la belle figure de Jésus, attentive et souriant, et ses beaux yeux attachés sur toi avec une expression de douceur et d'attendrissement. Et quand tu eus fini de parler . . . je le vis s'approcher, se pencher sur toi, et te dire en t'imposant les mains ce qu'il disait aux pauvres hommes du peuple dont il faisait ses disciples: "Viens avec moi, quitte tes filets et suis moi; je veux te faire pêcheur d'hommes." Et il me sembla qu'une grande lumière jaillissait du front du Christ, et t'enveloppait dans son rayon. Alors je me dis en moi-même: Pierre est un apôtre, comment ne le savais-je pas? Il prophétise;[23] comment ne l'avais-je pas compris? (*CTF*, 136–37)

[I pictured Christ, the poor, obscure son of a carpenter, wandering on the earth, speaking to miserable workers like us. . . . I don't want to hurt your modesty, Pierre, by comparing you to the one we call God, but I said to myself, if Christ came back to earth and if he passed by this house, what would he do? . . . He would enter the barn and wouldn't be disdainful of sitting, like us, on bales of hay, he who was born on the straw of a stable; and he would listen. And while I was dreaming, I imagined the beautiful face of Jesus, attentive and smiling, and his beautiful eyes fixed on you with an expression of gentleness and tenderness. And when you finished speaking . . . I saw him draw near and lean over you, and tell you, while imposing his hands on you, what he said to the poor working men who became his disciples, "Come with me, leave your nets and follow me; I want to make you a fisher of men." And it seemed to me that a great light shone from the face of Christ, and enveloped you in its rays. So I said to myself, Pierre is an apostle, how could I not have known it; he prophesizes, how could I not have understood it?]

Thus, the novel's egalitarian, democratic values are fully assimilated with the gospel message of peace and brotherly love conveyed through the person and message of Pierre Huguenin, a model Christ-figure.[24]

EQUALITY THROUGH EDUCATION

Pierre's heart for his fellow workers and his Christ-like character are complemented by his noble bearing, his physical beauty and strength, and an appearance which could well recall the portraits of Christ painted by old European masters. Unaware of his good looks, he is modest, hard-working, compassionate, and highly intelligent. Having been raised by a father for whom social justice ended with the failure of the French Revolution to achieve its ends, he sets out on his apprenticeship journey through France with the desire to learn about society while mastering his trade, and returns home full of idealism. When given the contract with his father to restore the old Villepreux chapel, he applies himself diligently to the task, drawing satisfaction both from his labour and the aesthetic side of his work.[25] He soon discovers, however, the more rarefied pleasures of the mind when he clandestinely gains access to the study of Mademoiselle de Villepreux adjoining the chapel, having removed the door of her study to repair it while the Villepreux family is in Paris. Metaphorically, he has opened the door to a whole new world, the realm of books and learning, which is strictly the domain of the upper classes, and begins to devour the volumes in Yseult's study whenever he can, after his work. He reads the great writers of the Enlightenment, the tragedies of Racine, Plato's *Republic*, and much more, while his soul burns with the desire to cultivate his mind. He realizes that this is the key to changing not only his own condition, but that of his entire class, and feels while he is reading that inside the skin of the worker lies another man, sensitive to beauty and exalted by the discoveries afforded by literature.[26]

Education for the people is certainly one of the major themes in the novel, where it is shown to be a necessary condition for the freedom, dignity, and equality of the lower classes.[27] It is because of his reading, added to his matchless character and deep desire for social justice, that Pierre is able to rise above the forces of society which want to constrain him, and command respect from those above him who still believe that the common people are not ready for democracy, that they are too brutish to take on the responsibilities of intelligent participation in the political process, and that considerable time is needed before they can ever hope to become equal partners in society. He knows that all that separates him from the well-educated man is the time and means to study, a luxury one class possesses and another has been denied. He is articulate enough to be able to share his thoughts with Yseult de Villepreux, when circumstances bring them together, and is able to win her heart and mind to the cause of the people in a way that goes beyond her previous understanding. Not only does the author break taboos by having the daughter of a nobleman converse regularly with a worker, but also by endowing that worker with enough wisdom and intelligence to help enlighten a learned and thoughtful young noblewoman, who secretly falls in love with him. Pierre's refined qualities are certainly exceptional for a lower-class laborer, but Sand has based her character on the life and writings of a real worker and "compagnon," Agricole Perdiguier, an educated man with a social vision who, as Sand acknowledges, provided the model for her main character.[28]

IDEALIZING THE PROLETARIAT

It is precisely because of her portrait of Pierre Huguenin that Sand was severely criticized. Neither friends nor critics could admit that a worker could be intelligent, morally upright, sensitive, and endowed with a kind of ideal beauty reserved only for the nobility, in their own minds. For Sand, however, Pierre embodies the new nobility, that of the working classes and of the future. Perdiguier himself responds to some of the criticism, which includes an article published in *Le National,* a republican paper generally favorable to liberalism, but which denies that Pierre could be "un vrai prolétaire" ["a true proletarian"] because he is so well spoken. While he may not typify his class, Perdiguier asserts, he himself is nonetheless real, and just as able to express himself as some of the noblemen who have criticized him.[29] In his own book, *Le Livre du Compagnonnage,* he exhorts his fellow companions to exemplify moral behavior, and to see themselves as equal to other men: "Considérez que nous ne sommes pas d'une substance moins délicate, moins pure que les riches; que notre esprit, que notre sang, que notre conformation n'ont rien de différent de ce qu'on voit en eux" ["Consider that we are not made of a substance less delicate or less pure than the rich, that our minds, our blood, and our makeup are no different than that which we see in them"].[30] The critiques of Sand's novel, however, were consistently and resoundingly negative. One of her good friends, Marie d'Agoult, wrote an article in *La Presse,* condemning "tout cet échafaudage d'invraisemblance" ["all this unrealistic (plot) build up"] and claiming that "[l]'intérêt [du livre] est nul; je ne sais quoi de contraint et de faux se fait sentir. Pas la moindre sympathie ne s'éveille dans l'esprit pour les personnages ainsi faits" ["(the book) is of absolutely no interest; one feels something forced and false in it. No feeling of empathy is stirred up for characters created like these"].[31] She concludes by strongly advising the author to give up her plans for a sequel, stating that "jamais le développement d'un caractère aussi faux à son point de départ ne pourra produire une œuvre durable" ["the development of a character so false at its outset will never be able to produce a lasting work"].[32] Finally, Balzac sums up the criticism by bluntly remarking, "On ne veut plus nulle part de George Sand: *Le Compagnon* l'a tuée" ["Nobody anywhere wants to have anything more to do with George Sand: *Le Compagnon* has killed her"].[33]

In the *Notice* of the 1851 edition, Sand explains her purpose in writing the novel and justifies its contents, acknowledging a certain amount of idealism on her part, which she defends: "Pourquoi, en supposant que mon type fût trop idéalisé, n'aurais-je eu le droit de faire pour les hommes du peuple ce qu'on m'avait permis de faire pour ceux des autres classes? Pourquoi n'aurais-je tracé un portrait, le plus agréable et le plus sérieux possible, pour que tous les ouvriers intelligents et bons eussent le désir de lui ressembler?" (*CTF*, 31) ["Supposing that my character was too idealized, why shouldn't I have the right to do for working class men what I have been permitted to do for the other classes? Why wouldn't I have painted the most agreeable and serious portrait possible, so that good and intelligent workers might have the desire to be like him?"].[34] She affirms that Perdiguier was at least as intelligent and well read as Pierre Huguenin, and declares, "Un ouvrier est un homme tout pareil à un autre homme, un *monsieur* tout pareil à un autre *monsieur*, et je m'étonne beaucoup à ce que cela étonne encore quelqu'un" (*CTF*, 32) ["A worker is a man the same as any other man, a *monsieur* like any other *monsieur*, and I am astonished that this still astonishes anyone"]. Both women and workers with intelligence and a strong will are able to learn quickly at a mature age, she insists, adding, "Enfin, cette prétendue infériorité de race ou de sexe est un préjugé qui n'a même plus l'excuse aujourd'hui d'être soutenue de bonne foi" (*CTF*, 32) ["Finally, this supposed inferiority of breed or sex is a form of prejudice that no longer has the excuse of being upheld in good faith"]. Lastly, recalling the virulent attacks on her book by the nobility, the bourgeoisie, and even the clergy, she concludes, "Voilà comment un certain monde et une certaine religion accueillent les tentatives de moralisation, et comment un livre dont l'idée évangélique était le but bien déclaré, fut reçu par les conservateurs de la morale et les ministres de l'Évangile" (*CTF*, 33) ["This is how a certain class of people and a certain religion welcome attempts at moral writing, and how a book whose declared goal was to reflect the thinking of the Gospels was received by the keepers of morality and the ministers of the Gospel"].

AN EGALITARIAN RELATIONSHIP

In a class society, the relationship between Pierre Huguenin and Yseult de Villepreux represents, of course, another subject of contention. Even Yseult, in the novel, cannot admit she is actually having a culturally relevant conversation with Pierre when her cousin bursts in on their first exchange, which happens to develop while he is installing her study door. When her cousin hastily excuses herself by saying she expected to see Yseult alone, the embarrassed Yseult retorts, "Eh bien, ne suis-je pas seule?" (*CTF*, 205) ["What, am I not alone?"]. Her implication, of course, that Pierre does not count as a man because he is only a worker, translates the utter disdain of the nobility for the working class, but the genuinely repentant young woman eventually manages to repair the cruel wound she has inflicted on Pierre by asking and receiving forgiveness. The two go on to develop a relationship of mutual respect which evolves as they share their lofty ideals of justice and their dreams of transforming society.

Although they belong to different classes, the relationship between Pierre and Yseult is founded on a deep admiration for the other's ideas, character, values, and moral qualities, combined with the mysterious attraction of a love that transcends social barriers, even though they have no thought of ever transgressing that invisible line that permanently divides them. Their platonic love is based first and foremost *not* on a love for each other, but on the great ideals of equality, fraternity, and a fairer distribution of wealth, for which they are both willing to sacrifice. These ideals stem not only from their Enlightenment readings, but also from the Bible, which constitute the cornerstone of their thinking. "Ne sentez-vous pas qu'il y a au fond de mon cœur une soif inextinguible de justice et d'égalité?" (*CTF*, 295) ["Don't you sense that at the bottom of my heart I have an unquenchable thirst for justice and equality?"], Yseult inquires of Pierre, as she tries to persuade him of her sincerity. She continues, "Quelle brute perverse serais-je donc si j'avais pu lire Jean-Jacques et Franklin sans être pénétrée de la vérité? . . . Et d'ailleurs, croyez-vous que je n'ai tiré du Christianisme aucun enseignement?" (*CTF*, 295) ["What kind of perverse brute would I be if I had been able to read Jean-Jacques (Rousseau) and (Benjamin) Franklin without being penetrated by the truth? . . . And on top of that, do you think that I have learned nothing from Christianity?"]. Like Indiana in the previous novel, she insists that her faith is more authentic and more radical than that of the established Church: "Si je m'éloigne de l'Eglise c'est que les prêtres, en se faisant les ministres du pouvoir temporel et les serviteurs du despotisme, ont trahi la pensée de leur maître et altéré l'esprit de sa doctrine. Mais moi, je me sens prête à la pratiquer à la lettre. Aucune souffrance, aucune misère, aucun travail ne me rebutera, s'il faut que je partage les douleurs du peuple" (*CTF*, 295–96) ["If I distance myself from the Church it is because the priests, by making themselves ministers of temporal power and servants of despotism, have betrayed the thought of their Master and changed the spirit of his doctrine. But I feel ready to practice it to the letter. No suffering, no misery, no work will discourage me if I have to share the suffering of the people"].

Pierre, for his part, is caught up in the same revolutionary spirit as Yseult, trusting that God himself, not man, will give him counsel. He uses his faith to uphold the rights of his class when talking with men like Achille Lefort, who tries his best to win him over to his secret society, "la Charbonnerie," which is conspiring to overthrow the monarchy. Countering the interests of the bourgeoisie upheld by this underground movement, Pierre defends the working class as having an equal place in God's creation. As a premonition of things to come, Pierre's arguments seem to foreshadow the workers' failure to gain a voice in government after the insurrection of 1830, which occurred seven years after the happenings in the novel, set in 1823. At the time Sand was writing the novel, the lower class was still suppressed by the bourgeoisie, which controlled the monarchy from 1830 until the revolution of 1848, when full democracy was briefly won. In the novel, Pierre is convinced that the common people can take their destiny into their own hands, without the help of the bourgeoisie, by counting on themselves and Providence. He also assures a fellow worker that a change in their condition is bound to happen, because, as he says, "Dieu est trop juste pour abandonner l'humanité" (*CTF*, 366) ["God is too just to abandon humanity"].

AN IDEAL SOCIETY: HEAVEN ON EARTH

Pierre's dreams of future equality are equated with the vision of heaven which comes to illumine his democratic and evangelical goals. Following his reconciliation with Yseult, which reveals her true heart and motives, he falls asleep on the wood shavings in the chapel he is restoring and dreams of a heavenly paradise which poignantly depicts his longings for a better world. This moment of revelation is attributed by the narrator to the working of God's Spirit, "cet *esprit du Seigneur* qui, bien réellement, plane sur toutes les âmes" (*CTF*, 255) ["this *spirit of the Lord* that truly hovers over all souls"]. As the heavens open and his soul soars into the realms of an ideal world, he is carried into an exquisite setting, in which the beauties of art and nature grace a perfect garden; all around him are peace and joy, as he hears an angel say, "Vous voici enfin dans le ciel que vous avez tant désirez posséder" (*CTF*, 256) ["Here you are at last in the heaven that you have so much wanted to possess"]. Suddenly, he finds that the angel is Yseult, that the garden is none other than the grounds surrounding the Villepreux manor, but totally transformed. He sees his own father, the carpenter, and Yseult's father, the nobleman, walking arm in arm, while other characters in the novel from different classes mingle in perfect harmony and love, accompanied by angels.[35] Again he hears Yseult's voice murmur, "Ne vois-tu pas que nous sommes tous frères, tous riches et tous égaux? La terre est redevenue ciel . . . parce que nous avons effacé toutes les distinctions et abjuré tous les ressentiments" (*CTF*, 256) ["Don't you see that we are all brothers, all rich, and all equal? Earth has once again become heaven . . . because we have wiped away all distinctions and renounced all resentment"].

Sadly, this magnificent dream is followed, when he awakens, by a talk with Yseult's grandfather, which reveals that despite the lip service the Count pays to republican values, he is, in fact, a fatalist, who does not believe in social progress. Yseult, on the other hand, is convinced that her grandfather is as devoted to reform as she is, a belief which leads to the final crisis and dénouement of the novel. As Pierre completes his major project in the chapel, a beautifully sculpted staircase winding from the ground floor up to the tribunal located just outside Yseult's study door, Yseult has reason to believe that her grandfather would not be opposed to her marrying Pierre if he knew she loved him, a fallacious belief which serves to destroy her dream. The staircase is truly a labor of love for Pierre; he puts all his skill and craftsmanship into this *chef d'œuvre*, which takes on symbolic proportions as the novel comes to an end. Just as Pierre is in the process of striving for equality in society, he is also building a staircase reaching up to the study of a noble young woman, the place not only of their first significant encounter, but more importantly, a sanctuary of learning and culture. In line with Sand's convictions regarding education, it now appears that through reading her books and dialoguing with Yseult, Pierre has risen to her level, just as he symbolically rises to her level by working on the staircase, which reaches her study through the chapel he has restored.[36] This passageway through the chapel can be seen as a metaphor not only for the spiritual dimension of their relationship but also for the significant contribution of the biblical message of brotherhood and unity, which the restoration of the chapel suggests. As Pierre arrives at the top of his newly completed staircase, Yseult also arrives at that moment to open the door and declare her love for him for the first time, just as he declares, "Mon escalier est fini" (*CTF*, 368) ["My staircase is finished"]. His words are almost an echo of Christ's final words on the cross, "It is finished." The two classes have finally met and merged, the barriers have been broken, the dream of equality has become a personal reality, for Yseult graciously asks the dumbstruck Pierre if he loves her enough to marry her.

    Like the perfect love which emerges between Indiana and Ralph, Yseult's love is an exalted, virtuous love, as pure as the souls of the two young people involved. It contrasts greatly with the passion her cousin in the novel has had for a handsome worker, leading them into a stormy love affair that leaves her broken and debased, rather than edified as Yseult is by Pierre. However, the thought of his cherished granddaughter marrying a man of the lowest caste is too much for the Count, who succumbs to a sudden stroke, and would certainly have refused the marriage upon regaining consciousness, had Pierre not told him first that he does not intend to marry his granddaughter. Through a painful night of soul-searching, essentially his own Gethsemane, Pierre has come to the decision to remain true to his class, in order to better fight for its rights, even if it means sacrificing his love for Yseult. In a manner resembling Christ's choice to come to earth to identify with lowly humanity, by shedding his glory to become one with our kind, Pierre renounces the thought of taking on Yseult's lifestyle, wealth, and station in life, thereby losing his identification with the common people. Despite her protests, he remains firm in his resolve, while Yseult leaves him in the end and returns to Paris with her family, promising to wait as long as she must for them to be able to be united in marriage.

Thus, in the end, the novel falls short of actually erasing class barriers through marriage, although the author's intentions are very clear. Using both Yseult and Pierre as her mouthpiece, Sand preaches equality and reconciliation between the classes, basing her arguments largely on the Gospel message of brotherly love, forgiveness, and equality before God. That her novel was so strongly rejected by the critics and even the Church is evidence of the degree to which class attitudes were still entrenched. The fact that Sand did not continue her story in a second novel, as she intended to do, gives us a probable indication of the vehemence of the attacks against her. Seeds were sown, nevertheless, by this woman who dared to confront society, and Sand herself came to be known as "la bonne dame de Nohant" ["the good lady of Nohant"] by the class she sought to include and elevate in her novels. Although greatly influenced by the utopian social theorists of her day, Sand brought their theories to life by creating a world where romantic imagination and biblical principles intertwine to produce a convincing and relevant story, at least for those who have the privilege of living on this side of history. It is a potent reminder of a time in France when democracy was still an ideal to fight for and a distant dream to cherish. It is no doubt only in more recent times that readers have been able to fully appreciate Sand's radical vision, with the hindsight of those who have reaped the benefits of the avowed "mission évangélique" (*CTF*, 40) ["evangelical mission"] that both the author and her characters represent.

CONCLUSION

The evolution of Sand's thinking and writing plainly comes to light through the study of the two novels examined in this chapter. From a novel born out of the personal struggles of the author in marriage to one which argues for the political and social rights of the proletariat, Sand has come a long way in understanding what it means to take up the cause of the oppressed. From a time when the best solution she could envision for a woman suffering from an abusive marriage was the arrival of a "knight in shining armour," so to speak, advocating the total withdrawal of the couple from society, to the political aims she is finally willing to defend in her novels, Sand has become much more overt in her political convictions. That these are still not clearly defined in terms of specific action, but remain steeped in a certain philosophical idealism, does not diminish the courage she displays in including these ideas in her works.[37] In *Indiana*, the heroine and her "messiah" Ralph remain isolated in the end, whereas Pierre Huguenin preaches the value of fraternity or solidarity as strongly as the ideals of liberty and equality.[38] He faces the challenges of social reform with courage and sacrifice and the knowledge that he is not alone, but on a God-given mission to change society.

While Sand's social and political goals show considerable growth and transformation during the period between the two novels, thanks to the impact of her mentors, her spiritual aspirations remain constant. The strength of her original beliefs is borne out by the contents of the long letter Indiana writes in the first novel, where she defiantly condemns the entire social order, including the oppressive role played by organized religion, and calls for an egalitarian society founded on a much higher level of spiritual understanding, which she claims to possess. "Often the first work of an author contains her whole message," Pierre Vermeylen declares in reference to Sand.[39] Indeed, the author's ideals, as expressed in her first novel, are the same as those of Pierre Huguenin, her mouthpiece in the latter novel, and are heavily based on biblical notions which permeate the two works. Both the quest for a form of pure, absolute love between a man and a woman, and the pursuit of social justice for every class of society testify not only to the social and literary influences of the period in which Sand lived, but even more so to her deep-seated convictions as a woman and her search for a higher, truer, more relevant kind of spirituality. It is these convictions, passed on to her readers through the imaginary world of her novels, that made a difference in her own time and finally gained for Sand a significant place among the democratically minded writers of nineteenth-century France, and a unique place in their midst as a woman writer.[40]

NOTES

1. While critical studies on the theme of spirituality in Sand's works are not abundant, several authors have written on her spiritual life. Paul Christophe's *George Sand et Jésus: une inlassable recherche spirituelle* (Paris: Les Éditions du Cerf, 2003) is an excellent examination of the evolution of Sand's spiritual perspective throughout her life, particularly in relation to both the Church and the person of Jesus. Bernard Hamon's *George Sand face aux Églises* (Paris: L'Harmattan, 2005) looks not only at Sand's position in regard to Catholicism and Protestantism, but also at her interaction with social/religious thinkers like Lamennais and Pierre Leroux. In addition, Pierre Vermeylen's *Les Idées politiques et sociales de George Sand* (Bruxelles: Université de Bruxelles, 1984) presents a comprehensive study of Sand's social views, including a chapter on the role of religion in her life and thinking.

2. Part of the introduction to this chapter and the section on *Indiana* have been adapted, with permission, from the following article: Kelsey L. Haskett, "Spirituality and Feminism in George Sand's *Indiana*," *Journal of Christianity and Foreign Languages* 8 (Spring 2007): 47–60.

3. Leroux's influence on Sand's life is thus described by Christophe: "In 1836, George Sand was converted to the idea of progress. The influence of Pierre Leroux, a Saint-Simonian philosopher who planned to create a new encyclopedia and who taught the religious philosophy of progress, prevailed over that of Lamennais. He became her counselor and intellectual men-

tor" (*George Sand et Jésus*, 59). Leroux's influence extended to her family as well as to her works, as Christophe points out: "Pierre Leroux became not only the pedagogical guide for Sand's children, he influenced part of her work for a considerable period of time" (*George Sand et Jésus*, 62).

4. See chapter 7 of Pierre Vermeylen's study for a description of Sand's relationship to the social theorists of her day, including an explanation of the ideas of Pierre Leroux. Bruno Viard notes in his article on human perfectibility, "Leroux and Sand clearly adhere to this notion and belong, with Hugo, to the family of historical optimists, as opposed to the great pessimists such as Baudelaire, Flaubert, and even Balzac" (Bruno Viard, "Sand et Leroux devant la question de la perfectibilité," in "*Le Compagnon du tour de France de George Sand*," ed. Martine Watrelo and Michèle Hecquet [Lille: Presses de l'Université Charles de Gaulle—Lille 3, 2009], 59). In *George Sand: le parti du people* (Sury en Vaux: A à Z Patrimoine, 2004), Jean-Claude Sandrier reveals the influence of Freemasonry on Sand's thinking, stemming from the teaching of Leroux, a Freemason, and from her own research (153–55). In *George Sand mythographe* (Clermont-Ferrand: Presses Universitaires de Blaise Pascal, 2007), Isabelle Naginski indicates that Sand's library contained an impressive array of esoteric works (102–3), although she maintains that Jules Michelet's Christian perspective particularly influenced her: "It remains that the vision of a tolerant and generous early church, spread by Michelet and other romantic thinkers, could only appeal to Sand" (104).

5. In *Romantic Vision: The Novels of George Sand* (Birmingham, AL: Summa, 1995), Robert Godwin-Jones states, "Few would claim for Sand the status of having been a profound and original thinker. Yet she was far from being the slavish follower of Lamennais, Leroux or others that even today she is portrayed as. The revelation that many of the ideas supposedly borrowed from others appear in Sand's earliest fiction—before her relationships with Leroux or even Michel de Bourges—counteracts this image of servile imitation. Kristina Wingård, in her perceptive study of Sand's early novels, rightly points out that it was largely because Sand was a woman that she has been denied credit for original and independent thought (*Socialité* 4)" (3).

6. Christophe, *George Sand et Jésus*, 13.

7. Quoted in Hélène Sabbah et al., *Itinéraires littéraires: XIXe siècle* (Paris: Hatier, 1988), 221.

8. In *Socialité, sexualité et les impasses de l'histoire* (Uppsala: Université d'Uppsala, 1987), Wingård Vareille remarks, "We know that this institution requires the total submission of the wife: forever a minor, unable to make any important decisions without the consent of her husband (whether it be about the future of her children, her place of residence, the management of her goods . . .), she finds herself truly in the position of an employee (for life!) in relation to her husband, her employer. The husband is responsible for maintaining his wife, who, in turn, owes him passive obedience and the duties of housekeeper" (28).

9. George Sand, *Indiana* (Paris: Gallimard, 1984), 49; subsequent references are to this edition and will appear parenthetically in the text by title and page number.

10. Godwin-Jones, *Romantic Vision*, 296.

11. Christophe underscores Sand's opposition in the novel to France's marital laws: "*Indiana* denounced the hardship of women in marriage and society because of the injustice and barbarity of the laws" (*George Sand et Jésus*, 47).

12. According to Christophe, "George Sand broke with Catholicism because she believed the Church incapable of reform" (*George Sand et Jésus*, 71). He adds that when questioned about her supposed rejection of Christianity, Sand replies in a long letter, in which "she concedes that the sublime moral doctrine of the Gospels will always live on, but affirms we have changed Christ's doctrine through false interpretations" (73). Moreover, "St. John's Gospel retains Jesus' highest doctrine in Sand's eyes because it insists the most on universal love and especially on compassion for the little ones" (75–76). Nevertheless, in the end, Sand does not accept that Jesus was the Son of God, as Christophe indicates (79), but sees him as "the revealer of equality, the one who has come to redeem the poverty and misery of the human condition" (80).

13. Christophe notes, "Faith in God and in eternal life—outside of a brief period of depression—never left George Sand's heart" (*George Sand et Jésus*, 91).

14. On the one hand, for Vermeylen, Sand's feminism in *Indiana* can be seen as "an act of accusation against marriage, as instituted by the Civil Code. The wife being the slave, love is banished" (*Les Idées politiques et sociales*, 9). On the other hand, her ideal is expressed here, for "only the love of two perfectly equal beings can give their union the seal of eternity" (9).

15. Wingård Vareille, *Socialité, sexualité, et les impasses de l'histoire*, 63.

16. Flora Tristan, a contemporary of Sand's who embodied a much more political form of activism, disagreed with Sand's belief in the role played by literature as opposed to politics in women's struggle for reform.

17. Christophe contends that "George Sand's religion becomes a search for love through God, just as her life was a search for love through human beings. "Love," she wrote, "is all that we know and it is still the greatest and the most ennobling thing" (*Corr.* II, 825)" (*George Sand et Jésus*, 55).

18. Vermeylen asserts, "The need of an absolute that inhabits her and her spiritual honesty cause her to break her love ties as soon as the impulses [feelings] that overwhelmed her have left her" (*Les Idées politiques et sociales*, 355).

19. In noting that her novels from 1840 to 1845 "incorporate even more explicitly the social and political ideas George Sand was beginning to embrace with more vigor," Godwin-Jones ironically remarks that "[i]f critics of Sand's earliest novels complained they offer no solutions to the problems raised, they now voiced their opposition to the extent to which Sand elaborated in her fiction a new social model which would resolve the fundamental problems of French society" (*Romantic Vision*, 6–7).

20. In chapter 5 of *George Sand* (Boston: Twayne, 1990), David Powell briefly reviews some of Sand's earlier novels that use love relationships to overcome class barriers, including the mixed-class relationship in *Valentine*, Sand's second novel. He mentions, however, that "Sand does not discuss in these early novels a need to pull down social class markers, just the need to be able to cross them" (66). He regards *Simon* (1836) as Sand's "first conscious effort at socialist theory in literature" (66), but indicates that "*Le Compagnon du tour de France* (1840) stands as Sand's first successful insertion of socialist theories into narrative form, and is far superior to *Simon* in this respect" (67).

21. It is true, as revealed by Claudine Grossir's study of the chapel ("Une chapelle en restauration," in "*Le Compagnon du tour de France*" *de George Sand*, ed. Martine Watrelo and Michèle Hecquet [Lille: Presses de l'Université Charles-de-Gaulle—Lille 3, 2009]), that after having been used for numerous purposes throughout its long history, the chapel is to become both a museum of family treasures and objects of art for the Villepreux family, and a studio for aspiring artists, thus redefining its usage. However, it will still keep its original "sacred" character, rather than being turned into a theatre or some other "secular" space, as was the fate of many repaired churches after the Revolution, because it is being *restored* to its original state as a medieval chapel, and not merely repaired (144). The loving work of the craftsmen with their creative skills and the goal of using the chapel for artistic purposes reinforce the spiritual meaning of the chapel for Sand.

22. George Sand, *Le Compagnon du tour de France* (Grenoble: Presses de l'Université de Grenoble, 1988), 255; subsequent references are to this edition and will appear parenthetically in the text by the acronym *CTF* and page number.

23. In "Poésie du peuple, poétique sandienne dans *Le Compagnon du tour de France*," in "*Le Compagnon du tour de France*" *de George Sand*, ed. Watrelo and Hecquet, Nathalie Vincent-Munnia comments that "the common people, for Sand and working-class poets, are both anchored in their poetic nature and prophets of social emancipation; they are at the origin of humanity and vector of its progress, these two poles having the specificity in the novel of being incarnated in a character representing the whole, the poet-thinker Pierre, and showing their tensions in the unfolding plot" (124).

24. Godwin-Jones claims that Sand was trying to accomplish two goals through Pierre's speech: "She wanted to convey her views on the organization of society and demonstrate that the common man, when inspired like Pierre, has the ability to serve as a guiding beacon to his class and an ideal to society as a whole. In the process she created a figure who surpasses

human dimensions (e.g., his frequent comparison to Jesus). The narrator exceeds the limits of verisimilitude in emphasizing Pierre's virtues. In fact, Pierre is something other than a conventional fictional character. He comes to embody all earthly wisdom" (*Romantic Vision*, 97).

25. The aesthetic side of this work is virtually inseparable from its spiritual significance for Sand, whose reverence for art is closely related to her concept of the spiritual, as Pierre's first visit to the chapel attests. "Une joie sainte" (56) ["A holy joy"] illumines his face as he discovers the beauty of its craftsmanship, a point highlighted by Claudine Grossir: "His knowledge allows Pierre Huguenin to appreciate the quality of the chapel's ornamentation, and it is the esthetic pleasure he feels during this first visit that restores the sacredness of the place. Religious sentiment, whose loss Victor Hugo deplores, regains its strength here, borne by the aesthetic experience which will be prolonged in the work" (150–51).

26. According to Godwin-Jones, Pierre's love of learning "was an important function which Sand incorporated into the figure of Pierre: to serve as a symbol for the great potential of the working class" (*Romantic Vision*, 96).

27. Vermeylen affirms, "George Sand always attached a high importance to education. She saw it as the most effective tool for the emancipation of women and the common people. The gradual spreading of knowledge would avoid the clashes of social transformation that was too rapid; instead of revolution, she preferred the benefits of a slow maturation process, a necessary condition for progress" (*Les Idées politiques et sociales*, 97).

28. Hamon describes how Perdiguier was a perfect fit for Sand's novel: "The novelist could only be attracted by the character and ideas of the man she met at an important juncture in her life. Perdiguier, indisputably a man of the common people, knowing his milieu perfectly, a convinced republican, non-violent but able to make himself respected, anticlerical but believing in God, also thought man perfectible by reason, example, and education" (*George Sand*, 119). Sand even engaged in helping him on a new "Tour de France," with the purpose of convincing the various guilds to give up their rivalries.

29. Perdiguier, quoted in René Bourgeois, introduction to *Le Compagnon du tour de France*, by George Sand (Grenoble: Presses de l'Université de Grenoble, 1988), 11.

30. Ibid., 6.

31. Marie d'Agoult, quoted in Bourgeois, introduction to *Le Compagnon du tour de France*, 14.

32. Ibid., 14.

33. Ibid., 15.

34. In *George Sand: Indiana, Mauprat* (Glasgow: University of Glasgow French and German Publications, 2000), Janet Hiddleston notes that Sand also reveals her literary aims in her autobiography, "stressing the combination of realism and sentiment in all her works, 'l'idéalisation du sentiment . . . dans un cadre de réalité assez sensible pour le faire ressortir' (*Vie*, p. 161)" (44).

35. While critics often refer to Sand's "utopian" views, in *Le Musée imaginaire de George Sand: l'ouverture et la médiation* (Saint Genouph: Librairie Nizet, 2005), Gérard Peylet emphasizes her double vision, which looks back to the Garden of Eden and forward to the utopian ideal of harmony and social equality, while attempting to unite the two: "Pierre and Yseult's meeting allows Sand to include in the same utopian dream the emancipation of the worker and of women and to affirm Leroux's new social Gospel through the harmony this couple creates. The novel setting removes some of the didacticism of Leroux's philosophy and allows for a synthesis of the myth of human origins and the ideas on human progress which undergird the novel" (219).

36. Naginski's study, *George Sand mythographe*, confirms this interpretation: "The masterpiece of the journeyman-carpenter in the novel is, as we know, the design and construction in the Villepreux manor of a spiral staircase which joins a former chapel, rebuilt as a museum and situated on the main floor, to the upper storey, which opens onto Yseult's study. Sand uses a powerful image to express the ability of the so-called lower classes to liberate themselves and rise to the heights of a project of social reconstruction. Pierre's staircase is the perfect reflection of this whole enterprise of self-liberation" (161–62).

37. In reference to *Le Compagnon* and similar novels, Godwin-Jones states that although Sand "expresses open concern for the welfare of the working class, she does not advocate that class conflict be resolved through violent means. The solution is instead symbolized in the projected union of a working-class man with an aristocratic woman. In place of revolution, social harmony can be achieved through mutual understanding and cooperation between the social classes" (*Romantic Vision*, 7). Bruno Viard reveals that the political philosophy of Sand's mentor, Leroux, is "pacifist and evolutionary" ("Sand et Leroux," 59), while Vermeylen recognizes Sand's aversion to violence, but stresses her unchanging resolve, for "from her writings and her actions emerges the unity of thought of a lucid revolutionary, always fearful that violence born of impatience will compromise the ideal being pursued" (*Les Idées politiques*, 97).

38. Nathalie Vincent-Munnia maintains that "in *le Compagnon*, fraternization is at the heart of the fictional work, symbolized by the utopia of social and gender integration, represented by the story of Pierre and Yseult" (122).

39. Vermeylen, *Les Idées politiques et sociales*, 10.

40. In celebrating Sand's life and work in *George Sand à Nohant* (Paris: Christian Pirot, 2000), Pierre de Boisdeffre highlights the significant role she played for women in her day: "George Sand's work would not have the same importance to us if its author had not preached with such courage women's freedom, in love as well as in politics, and women's ability to engage in the struggles of their century. She was the prophet and one of the great actors of women's liberation" (20).

Chapter Seven

Simone Weil

Ambivalence in Search of God

Anne M. François

As one of the great mystics of the last century, the Franco-Jewish philosopher theologian Simone Weil (1909–1943) situated herself in an ambivalent theological and philosophical position concerning God and the Scriptures. Weil's passion for metaphysics led her to a troubled yet rich spiritual quest. As revealed in her intense and numerous writings, including *Autobiographie spirituelle* (1942), *Attente de Dieu* (1942), *Formes de l'amour implicite de Dieu* (1942), *Lettres à un religieux* (1942), and *L'Enracinement* (1943), she appears to have found God despite her struggles with Christianity, and yet the question of God remained deeply challenging and problematic to her. Torn between the idea of a Jewish God from the Old Testament and that of a "different" Christian God from the New Testament, Weil seems to have created a third plural space—open to religious otherness, disparate beliefs, and polyphonic voices—that could arguably be a privileged location from a postmodern point of view. This position, however, full of paradoxes and contradictions is considered ambivalent from an orthodox Christian perspective. Religious syncretism apparently caused some internal tension in Weil as well, as she sought to construct a spiritual life based on her studies of Christian teachings, Eastern religions, and Greek philosophy. Nevertheless, Weil's passionate spiritual quest and her exegetical talents as revealed in her writings are inspiring for anyone searching for spiritual meaning and truth.

Readers familiar with Weil's work are aware that she always seemed to challenge and surpass herself, whether analyzing academic, social, political, philosophical, or theological topics, as her fifteen volumes of posthumously published writings demonstrate. As the daughter of a medical doctor and sister of André Weil (1906–1998), a well-known and gifted mathematician,

Weil adopted from an early age a rigorous attitude toward the search for knowledge and a passion for the absolute. This passion and the restless search for truth turned her into an "intellectual bulimi[c]," according to Francine du Plessix Gray.[1] She remained in constant motion throughout her turbulent and difficult short life. Her concerns with issues of social justice, violence and peace took her to many places. She traveled extensively across France and Western Europe. In 1934 and 1935, she spent some time working in the Renault auto plant outside Paris alongside the workers. This experience of incessant manual labor allowed her to record her own alienation as well as that of her coworkers from a Marxist perspective. She later labored as a farm worker in the region of Cher. In 1936, she briefly joined the anti-Franco red troops in the Spanish Civil War. She also visited Assisi in Italy (which had inspired St. Francis) where she reported having her first mystical experience in the Santa Maria degli Angeli chapel. Escaping from Nazi-occupied France in 1943, she fled to England. While in London, she participated briefly in the French Resistance movement. She died at Ashford in Kent in August 1943 after a brief stay in the United States. During her short life span, she produced a great number of works in a rather somber historical period.

As her biographers reveal, Weil clearly distanced herself from her bourgeois milieu on the Left Bank in Paris to embrace a life of social and political activism, and, most importantly, to reflect on the significance of the spiritual in her life, studies, and writings. Raised as an agnostic by atheist Jewish parents, Weil's interest in Christianity began in early adolescence. Her fascination with metaphysical questions started to develop at the Lycée Henri IV, where her thinking was much influenced by Emile Alain (1868–1951), an eminent philosopher well-versed in Christian, Gnostic, and Manichean doctrines.[2] Alain, whose real name was Emile Auguste Chartier, introduced Weil to the works of Plato, Hegel, and Kant, among others.

RESURRECTING WEIL

In considering how Weil's theological reflections have impacted a number of religious thinkers and groups, the philosopher Heinz Abosch highlights the fact that her posthumous fame did not come about until after World War II.[3] Even after this war, however, few of her works were translated for publication in North America, and Weil is still not widely known in academic circles despite her critical importance as a philosopher and religious thinker. In the editorial preface to *Discussions of Simone Weil*, D. Z. Phillips remarks that "[t]he work of Simone Weil (1909–1943) has not been given the attention it deserves by philosophers in Anglo-American philosophical traditions,"[4] and, indeed, most academics in British and North American colleges and universities know little about Weil, though scholarship is available on her thought.

Interestingly, her works are not only omitted from the majority of American philosophical anthologies, but also from their French counterparts.[5] This is likely because Weil's theoretical approach to spiritual matters differs from that of other French philosophers interested in the question of God. Her distinct combination of mystical and metaphysical traditions apparently marginalizes her work within the French philosophical canon. As Miklos Vetö points out,

> Weil surely occupies a special place in the history of French thought, where religious reflection has always shown great restraint in matters of speculation. Mystics, protected by the solid walls of theology and scholastic philosophy, devoted their writings to the "practical" problems of prayer, contemplation, and moral conduct; philosophers interested in religious questions wrote armed with the conceptual instruments of metaphysics and epistemology, or were content to meditate on God and humanity without claiming to construct a system. Weil's way of thinking, in which metaphysics and mysticism support each other and merge, that penetrating gaze before which moral actions and religious acts are transposed into ontological perspectives, is not a familiar one in the French tradition.[6]

Of both the French and American lack of interest in her work due to its idiosyncratic nature, the Weil scholar Rush Rhees also remarks,

> It is hard to see, or formulate, what it is one can *learn* from what Simone Weil writes.... Her work is so foreign to the habits of thinking of most people there [America]. I was going to speak of a provincialism, parochialism in our thinking, but these are not the right expressions. The fact that she is French is part of what makes it hard for people to fit her into their pockets. But I would bet that there are many philosophers in France who show the same kind of impatience, the same sort of misunderstanding, the same objection to having to *try* to follow what she says.[7]

Weil is not popular in many Christian circles either, as her philosophical and religious speculations, as this chapter shows, typically stand in stark opposition to orthodox Christian doctrine. However, Weil remains for many a religious visionary because of her unrelenting search for transcendent truth, her exposure of the social ills of her time, her passion for social justice, her altruistic activities, and her spiritual enlightenment. Though her detractors are often enraged by her provocative narrative on spiritual matters, her admirers hail her work with great enthusiasm, many philosophers, theologians, and sociologists acknowledging they have been appreciably influenced by her polyphonic writings, which convey a deep sense of humanity. Despite the conflicted ideas and controversies to which her work gives rise, famous twentieth-century thinkers such as Albert Camus, T. S. Eliot, and Flannery O'Connor, as well as Popes John XXIII and Paul VII, have reported being inspired by Weil's mystical thought. A great admirer of Weil, Camus characterized her as "the only great spirit of our time."[8] Most recently, she has been acclaimed by a number of scholars for her radical thinking and advocacy of social change and justice in *The Relevance of the Radical: Simone Weil 100 Years Later*. In this collection, Sarah K. Pinnock writes, "Since her death she has become a prophetic voice challenging hierarchies in religion and society. In short, her remarkable life evidences feminist attributes because she broke societal limits on women to pursue her intellectual, political, and humanitarian goals."[9]

WEIL AND RELIGIOUS TRADITION

A major paradox in Weil's religious writings is her apparent faith, which has a decidedly Christian character in some respects, despite her ongoing spiritual questioning of, and skepticism toward, Christianity, the Bible, and God's existence. Weil's faith was not rooted in any specific religious tradition. In her writings, she expressed great admiration for Eastern religions while exalting at the same time the beauty and the power of Christianity. She gives equal attention to her study of the Bible, the Upanishads, and Catharism.[10] Weil was, however, generally suspicious of any organized religion, whether Judaism, Catholicism, or Protestantism, because she associated it with the misuse of power. Like Voltaire, Weil denounced what she believed were the Church's crimes, including its excessive authority: "Tout se passe comme si avec le temps on avait regardé non plus Jésus, mais l'Église comme étant Dieu incarné ici-bas" ["With the passing of time it seems it is no longer Jesus but the Church that has been looked upon as the incarnation of God on earth"].[11] Therefore, although influenced by Christianity, or more precisely Catholic mysticism, in her lifelong search for truth, Weil chose to remain on "the threshold of the church" as she willingly and proudly proclaimed on more than one occasion.[12] She refused baptism despite the encouragement from and insistence on it by Joseph-Marie Perrin, a Dominican priest who was her spiritual counselor. More importantly, in her philosophical and theological musings, she criticized and rejected the Judeo-Christian religion more than any other.[13] Weil articulates her position in relation to the Catholic Church in a long letter to Perrin, in which she identifies one of the chief reasons she feels more comfortable on the edges of that institution: "Je voudrais appeler votre attention sur un point. C'est qu'il y a un obstacle absolument infranchissable à l'incarnation du christianisme. C'est l'usage de deux petits mots[,] *anathema sit*. Non pas leur existence, mais l'usage qu'on en a fait jusqu'ici. C'est cela aussi qui m'empêche de franchir le seuil de l'Église"[14] ["I would like to bring your attention to the following. There is an absolutely impossible obstacle to the incarnation of Christianity. It is the use of two little words, *anathema sit*.[15] It is not their existence but the way they have been used up to now that also prevents me from belonging to any church"].

Weil's attitude toward the Church is not always to be taken literally. Rather, it sheds light on her personal approach to engaging such a powerful topic while keeping a critical distance. She tends to protect the intellectual self from compromising itself as she develops an ambivalent love-and-hate relationship with Christianity. Rejecting the Thomist conception of faith, which only recognizes as genuine or efficacious a faith exercised within total submission to the Church, she might have considered herself a Christian outside the Church, as she experiences as much attraction as repulsion toward it.[16]

Adopting a tone of personal authority in focusing on her individual spiritual quest, Weil sought to establish her own theological system. Her syncretic tendencies led her to rely heavily on Greek philosophy which holds an abstract idea of God. Her sources of inspiration were Platonism and the Greek drama of Homer, Aeschylus, and Sophocles. Other philosophers writing long before Weil argued for an affinity between early Greek culture and Christianity.[17] For Weil, however, classical Greek culture constitutes the key to bridging the gap between God and humanity.[18] Her admiration for Greek thought is evident in her approach to interpreting the Scriptures and reflecting on the question of God. Considering Plato "an authentic mystic" and "the father of Western mysticism," she uses Greek philosophy to broaden her understanding of Christian spirituality. In her study *L'Iliade ou le poème de force* (1940), for example, she points out similarities between the *Iliad* and the New Testament on the law of retribution and punishment of abusive force; and in *Commentaires de textes pythagoriciens* (1942), she borrows Plato's formula "God is a perpetual geometer" to conclude, "En somme, l'apparition de la géométrie en Grèce est la plus éclatante parmi toutes les prophéties qui ont annoncé le Christ"[19] ["Overall, the emergence of geometry in Greece is among all prophecies the most brilliant one to announce the coming of Christ"]. Weil goes even further in emphasizing the link between Hellenism and the Gospels in her *Commentaires*, in which she proceeds from the Pythagorean theory that all knowledge is reduced to numbers to illustrate the existence of God: "On sait que chez les Pythagoriciens un est le symbole de Dieu"[20] ["We know that among the Pythagoricians, the number one is the symbol of God"]. Since numbers exist as abstract entities, God's existence and greatness may be compared to them in a mystical way. The number one is considered a just and perfect number as Weil tries to understand the mysterious unity between God and his son Jesus: "Quand le Fils de Dieu est dans une créature raisonnable comme le Père est dans le Fils, cette créature est parfaitement juste"[21] ["When the son of God is in a just creature as the Father is in the Son, this creature is perfectly just"]. Using mathematical notions for theological speculations is Weil's attempt to grasp God's reality and to reflect on his perfect and just nature.

With this kind of speculation, Weil seems to have found some insight into God's impenetrable mysteries. In spite of her eagerness to understand these mysteries, however, Weil places herself in an ambivalent position. While she establishes the link between Greek thought and the Gospels in her interpretation of the Christian faith, she overemphasizes the Greek source of Christianity, from an orthodox Christian point of view. Weil does not trust the Bible—the core of Christian beliefs—to be a sufficient and reliable source for revealing the true nature of God. As a result, she does not differentiate between the Egyptian god Osiris and Jesus, and does not hesitate to put them in the same divine category. She further asserts that early accounts of Osiris are more accurate than those of Jesus, "Si Osiris n'est pas un homme ayant vécu sur terre tout en étant Dieu, de la même manière que le Christ, alors du moins l'histoire d'Osiris est une prophétie infiniment plus claire, plus complète et plus proche de la vérité que tout ce qu'on nomme de ce nom dans l'Ancien Testament"[22] ["If Osiris is not a man who lived on earth while being God, in the same manner as Christ, then at least the story of Osiris is a prophecy infinitely clearer, more comprehensive and closer to the truth than everything called by that name in the Old Testament"]. Weil disregards the notion of the Bible as the infallible word of God and rather puts her unassailable faith in Greek philosophy. Throughout history, of course, philosophy has always addressed the question of God, although, according to Origen of Alexandria (185–254 C.E.), an early Christian thinker, philosophy, for all its benefits, cannot lead to a true and proper knowledge of God since it is contaminated with false and erroneous teaching.[23] Origen also addressed the intellectual credibility of faith within a Hellenistic setting, maintaining that Christians could study Greek philosophy and borrow from pagan cultures to help them grasp the reality of God. However, even this approach, with no cautionary advice, could understandably cause some concern to an orthodox Christian reader for whom the practice of closely associating Christian spirituality with the values of Greek philosophy may seem contradictory. Taking these ideas much farther, as we have seen, Weil unapologetically stresses the affinity between the sacred and the profane by mixing without any distinction the Christian God, Osiris, myths, and folklore.

An orthodox Christian reader may be startled when considering such posthumously published works as Weil's *Autobiographie spirituelle* or *L'Enracinement* in which she professes her found faith, while at the same time claiming the position of a skeptic. Commenting on Weil's conception of

Christianity, Jacques Cabaud, in *Simone Weil: A Fellowship in Love*, underscores this contradiction: "At the same time as Simone Weil was analyzing her reflections on the *Iliad*, she was also to speak of God, of grace, of the supernatural, and of Christianity with an assurance that may appear surprising."[24] While Weil's religious writings reflect an affirmation of a rich spiritual experience that is often Christian in nature, they also virulently reject at times—with a tone bordering on hatred—established doctrines of both the Catholic and Protestant churches. George A. Panichas explains,

> One must not expect to derive lessons in orthodoxy or in doctrinal sustenance from Simone Weil's writings. Her religious thought, even as it enabled her to reach the apogee of spiritual life, is rife with heterodoxy. Her religious experience is one of intensity and not of systematic coherence. Paradox and contradiction pervade genuine and basically Christian testimony in its uprightness, purity, and humility. Read in the special light of catholic theology as dogmas as a whole, her faith shows deficiencies, defections, imperfection, as theologians have been wont to point out.[25]

As suggested above, Panichas is hardly alone in accusing Weil of heterodoxy in her spiritual writings. It is well known that she does not follow any particular religious system of thought, reflected in the ideas scattered throughout her notebooks.

Weil's heterodoxy is attributable to more than her dedication to Hellenic sources in her spiritual quest and questioning of Christianity. It is also rooted in her application of a Gnostic interpretive framework to Christian texts. In her studies of the Bible in 1938, she developed her own exegetical approach to the Old Testament, arguing that the avenging Jewish God, in certain passages of the Old Testament, could not be the same God in the New Testament. Her judgment of the Old Testament as "un tissu d'horreurs" ["a fabric of horrors"], woven with errors, echoes that of her spiritual guru Alain.[26] Espousing the Gnostic doctrine of a demigod creating an evil world, Weil seems to put God on trial for His alleged "irrational" actions in the Old Testament. Weil's rationalist stance on God is similar to that of other French philosophers such as Rousseau and Voltaire, who also reject the Old Testament figure of God whose actions puzzle them. The Christian theologian Lesslie Newbigin, who rejects this line of thought, admits nevertheless, "There is the religious difficulty of believing in a God whose ways appear to be arbitrary and irrational; there is the philosophical difficulty of assigning meaning to the very idea of God acting in history if his actions are defined this way."[27]

Furthermore, a vein of Gnostic anti-Judaism runs through Weil's writings. She attempts to dismiss the Hebraic origin of the Old Testament or Christianity *per se* by asserting, "Je pense que les 11 premiers chapitres de la Genèse (jusqu'à Abraham) ne peuvent être qu'une traduction déformée et remaniée d'un livre égyptien; qu'Abel, Hénoch et Noé sont des dieux et que Noé est identique à Osiris, Dionysos, et Prométhée"[28] ["I think that the first eleven chapters of Genesis (up to Abraham) can only be a translation, distorted and recast, of Egyptian origin, that Abel, Enoch and Noah are gods, and that Noah is identical to Osiris, Dionysus, and Prometheus"]. Weil's most virulent rejection of the Old Testament is found in an epistolary essay, *Lettre à un religieux*, in which she contests the Christian conception of history in reference to God's purpose in announcing the arrival of the Messiah. Such statements from Weil have given rise to severe criticism in orthodox Christian circles. Theologian and philosopher Francis Schaeffer in his lengthy study on the Christian worldview discusses modern writers such as Weil for whom "[biblical] material is simply a Jewish myth, having no more historical validity for modern man than the Epic of Gilgamesh or the stories of Zeus.... Without a proper understanding of these chapters [Genesis 1–11] we have no answer to the problems of metaphysics, morals or epistemology, and furthermore, the work of Christ becomes one more upper-story 'religious' answer."[29]

Many critics regard Weil's attitude toward Christianity as bordering on heresy. For example, Paul West writes, "Her passionate attention to religions other than Christianity prevented her from becoming an Orthodox Christian. . . . She extracted too much of what she needed from too many places."[30] Others, enraged by her critical stance, independent spirit, and unconventional way of analyzing spiritual matters, label her work deviant. Weil's aversion to the Old Testament[31] and minimization of the Jewish contribution to the rise of Western civilization has also led to accusations that she cultivates anti-Semitic sentiment in her writings. In her works, she expresses a loathing for many Jewish characters in the Old Testament (except for Daniel, whom she considers a pure character). She also expresses a strong distaste for both Roman civilization and the Jewish people, again showing a preference for ancient Greece. Her dislike of Israel as the chosen people of God is evident when she accuses them of corrupting the Bible and killing Jesus. She is particularly judgmental toward Abraham, who she believes prostituted his wife when they fled to Egypt. Her criticism of "choses atroces"[32] ["crimes"] committed by the Jewish people in the name of God is blatant. On the publication of her posthumous works many French Jewish intellectuals, angered by her apparently anti-Semitic position, understandably reacted against her strongly.[33]

WEIL AND THE PROBLEM OF IDENTITY: NEITHER CHRISTIAN, NOR JEW, NOR FRENCH...

It has been argued that Weil's anti-Semitic sentiments likely stemmed from a sense of not belonging in a French society in which the state of Judaism remained uncertain, despite the declaration of its emancipation of Jews at the end of the eighteenth century. Weil had to confront complex identity issues relating to both Frenchness [*la francité*] and Jewisness [*la question juive*] in an anti-Semitic culture. According to Florence de Lussy, Weil must have suffered from a "mal être" or existential malaise as a French Jew.[34] Weil may well have internalized latent anti-Semitic views that were part of her religious upbringing in the Catholic school system, forcing her to distance herself from her ethnic origins, as is evident in her claim, "[J]e n'ai aucune attirance vers la religion juive, aucune attache avec la tradition juive"[35] ["I do not have either affection for the Jewish religion, nor connection with the Jewish tradition"]. Paul Giniewski argues that her anti-Semitism is profoundly Christian. This may well explain why, as Abosch advances, "Judaism represented something foreign to her," something "she sought to escape."[36] De Lussy suggests that like the Jewish intellectuals Adalbert de Chamisso and Hannah Arendt, Weil experienced "internal exile," struggling with her own sense of displacement and rootlessness. De Lussy also compares Weil's situation to that of Baruch de Spinoza who, belonging neither to the Jewish community nor to the Christian one, navigated with great difficulty between the two.[37]

Though ethnically and officially a Jew, Weil probably did not come to terms with her Jewish origins until 1940 when the Vichy government, promoting anti-Jewish laws, removed her from her teaching position as a professor of philosophy. Her assimilated parents had taught her nothing of her Jewish heritage. Following the occupation of France during World War II, however, Weil appeared to gain an awareness of her ambiguous Jewish situation. In a letter to the Minister of Education to protest her exclusion from the teaching profession, she insisted that she did not understand what it meant to be a Jew for she did not identify herself as such.[38] Nevertheless, in 1940, during the German occupation of France, she wrote to a former student about how painful it was for Jewish people (herself included) to endure racial prejudice.[39] The content of this letter stands in sharp contrast to the one in which she denied her Jewishness. Furthermore, despite Weil's denial of her Jewish identity when protesting her dismissal, she later wrote another letter to protest the Vichy government's mistreatment of the Jews. Therefore, Weil, who privately admitted her Jewish identity and criticized in her letters the French government's persecution of the Jews, published offensive remarks about her own people and their religious tradition.

Despite Weil's assault on Judaism, not all scholars consider her anti-Semitic. Some have proposed that she is, rather, anti-Judaic because of her knowledge and adoption of the Christian tradition. After all, Weil had no real contact with the Judaic tradition, for she admits in her correspondence that she had never set foot in a synagogue or witnessed any Jewish ceremonies or rituals. One could perhaps advance that Weil voluntarily turned toward Christianity for spiritual sustenance in the absence of any genuine knowledge of Jewish spirituality. In truth, Weil defies easy categorization in this area, since she displays the same kind of irreverence in her critical analysis of both Christianity and Judaism, always speaking from the periphery and reacting against what she believes to be any form of compromise. For Weil, personal spiritual experience, especially of a mystical nature, appears to be more authentic and reliable than any religious tradition.

WEIL AND THE MYSTICAL TRADITION

Weil's attraction to mysticism may be based not only in its privileging of individual spiritual experience and authority, but also because paradox and contradiction is inherent to the mystical tradition. Weil was particularly fascinated by the paradox of God as both an immanent and transcendent being, a subject that is central to much mystical writing. To Weil's mind, God is neither too far nor too close to humans, a conclusion reached, in part, because of her fusion of philosophical and religious conceptions of the Divine. Based on her study of Hinduism, Weil draws the conclusion that God is both personal and impersonal. As a Platonist, Weil conceives of God as personal to her in a mystical sense. As a Kantian reluctant to embrace any kind of dogmatism, she finds Him impersonal.

Much of Weil's writing reflects on God's presence in her life. She speaks in great detail about her mystical experience and proclaims her faith and salvation: "Dieu est l'unique chemin. Il est la voie"[40] ["God is the only way. He is the Way"]. In her *Autobiographie spirituelle*, a testament of faith, Weil recounts several occasions in which she distinctly felt God's presence. The first occurred in her early twenties when she was on a holiday in a small Portuguese village. While watching the villagers and listening to them sing during a religious precession, she reports having had a revelation: "Là, j'ai eu soudain la certitude que le christianisme est par excellence la religion des esclaves, que des esclaves ne peuvent pas ne pas y adhérer, et moi parmi les autres"[41] ["There, I suddenly realized that Christianity is ultimately the religion of slaves, that slaves cannot help belonging to it, I among them"]. Weil reports a second mystical incident during her trip to Assisi in 1937; when she journeyed to a small chapel where Saint Francis had prayed, she claims, "quelque chose de plus fort que moi m'a obligée . . . à me mettre à genoux"[42] ["something stronger than me pushed me . . . to kneel down"]. A year later, Weil recalls another spiritual experience she had during liturgical services for Easter at Solesmes: "Il va de soi qu'au cours de ces offices, la pensée de la Passion du Christ est entrée en moi une fois pour toutes"[43] ["It goes without saying that during the services, the thought of the Passion of Christ entered into my being once and for all"]. Weil's mystical experiences force her to confront her spiritual doubts, leading to her admission that she was deeply touched by her personal encounter with God, something she previously thought impossible. She then concludes, "quant à la direction spirituelle de mon âme, je pense que Dieu lui-même l'a prise en main dès le début"[44] ["as for the spiritual direction of my soul, I think God himself has taken it in hand from the beginning"]. However, as much as Weil claims to have felt the presence, or immanence, of God through mystical experience, she is also acutely aware of His distance, absence, and silence, which she sees manifested in human suffering.

The experience of affliction, or *malheur*, according to Weil, is what can bring us closer to God and/or distance us from Him. She explains that *malheur* is the supreme form of human suffering: "L'extrême malheur, qui est à la fois douleur physique, détresse de l'âme et dégradation sociale, constitue ce clou. La pointe est appliquée au centre même de l'âme. La tête du clou est toute la nécessité éparse à travers la totalité de l'espace et le temps"[45] ["Extreme affliction, which means physical pain, distress of the soul and social degradation, is the nail. Its tip is applied to the very center of the soul. The head of the nail is the whole scattered need throughout all space and time"]. With the image of the nail, Weil goes further to connect Christ's suffering on the cross with that of humanity and suggests that extreme suffering creates a distance between God and us, hence His absence in our lives and His seeming powerlessness. The Weil biographer Jacques Cabaud explains her idea of affliction in relation to the notion of God's absence: "*[M]alheur* . . . is not just a synonym for suffering; *malheur* takes possession of the soul and brands it to the depths with the mark of servitude. . . . It implies social degradation. . . . [A]s with a red-hot iron, with scorn, disgust, and self-loathing, *malheur* leaves . . . [one] writhing on the earth like a half-crushed worm. The principal effect of *malheur* is to render God absent for a time, more absent than one who has died."[46]

Weil ultimately connects redemptive suffering to God's distance and absence by focusing on His abandonment of Jesus on the cross. She equates the distance between God the father and God the son (Jesus) with that between God the father and His creation, suggesting that "Dieu ici-bas ne peut nous être parfaitement présent à cause de la chair. Mais il peut nous être, dans l'extrême malheur, presque parfaitement absent. C'est pour nous sur terre l'unique possibilité de perfection. C'est pourquoi la Croix est notre unique espoir"[47] ["God can never be perfectly present to us here below because of our flesh. But He can be almost perfectly absent from us in extreme affliction. This is for us on earth the only possibility of perfection. That is why the cross is our only hope"]. For Weil, the cross figuratively represents God's love through His presence and His absence, an abandonment experienced through suffering. In the process, Weil invests affliction/crucifixion with double meanings: presence/absence, love/abandonment: "Le vrai malheur... c'est la contemplation de la Croix du Christ.... Il n'y a rien d'autre.... Une mère, une épouse, une fiancée, qui savent celui qu'elles aiment dans la détresse et ne peuvent ni le secourir ni le rejoindre voudraient au moins subir des souffrances équivalentes aux siennes pour être moins séparées de lui.... Quiconque aime le Christ et se le représente sur la Croix doit éprouver un soulagement semblable"[48] ["True affliction is the contemplation of Christ's crucifixion.... There is nothing else.... A mother, a spouse, a fiancée, who know that their beloved one is in distress, but cannot rescue nor join him, would at least like to suffer like him in order to feel closer to him.... Anyone who loves Christ and imagines Him on the cross might experience a similar feeling of relief"].

Weil's paradoxical reflections on the crucifixion have been criticized for their apparent theological masochism or nihilism.[49] Susan Taubes, for instance, decries the alleged suicidal nuance in such passages of Weil's works and asks, "If affliction is the proof of God's supreme love, why should we not deliberately uproot, degrade, and destroy both ourselves and others? If we were created in order that we should de-create ourselves, why should we not choose suicide, or why should we try to avert or to assuage the suffering of others?"[50] Weil was, after all, known as a hard-core ascetic who practiced self-denial and self-sacrifice. She nurtured the idea of martyrdom and probably died of self-starvation, perhaps in an attempt to identify with the suffering of her people during the holocaust.[51] However, the idea that she crafted a theory of theological nihilism in regard to the crucifixion is rather overstated. It is fairer to say that Weil uses her subversive theological imagination to express in depth the intensity of her spiritual fervor. Like many mystics, Weil often relies on the discourse of extremes to characterize her spiritual pain and struggles, her writings seething with a series of intense emotions. In shaping her theology of the cross, and affliction more generally, Weil's ultimate desire is to be self-less and Christ-like. She can thus exclaim without hesitation, "[C]ar toutes les fois que je pense à la cruxificion du Christ, je commets le péché d'envie"[52] ["Every time I think of the crucifixion of Christ, I commit the sin of envy"]. Weil wishes to emulate Jesus's sacrificial act in order to feel closer to God, to sense His presence, which is not necessarily a masochistic impulse.

Weil's conception of affliction seems, in fact, far more life-giving than Taubes's commentary suggests, since it is directly implicated in what Weil calls "decreation": the idea of lowering ourselves and forgetting our ego in order to care for the sick, the poor, the oppressed, and the outcast.[53] During decreation or emptying of the self, the Divine is made present within us, enabling us to love others authentically. Weil writes, "Dans l'amour vrai, ce n'est pas nous qui aimons les malheureux en Dieu, c'est Dieu en nous qui aime les malheureux. Quand nous sommes dans le malheur c'est Dieu en nous qui aime ceux qui nous veulent du bien"[54] ["In true love, it is not we who love the afflicted in God, it is God in us who loves them. When we are afflicted, it is God in us who loves those who treat us well"]. In other words, Weil stresses the importance of showing compassion to the afflicted in the same way that God does for humans in their misery. She also implies that we are only capable of showing such love to those in need thanks to the divine grace given to us.

Weil's association of affliction and the absence / presence of God is seen in a deeply personal way in her encounter with the poem "Love" by George Herbert, a seventeenth-century English devotional poet well versed in both the languages of affliction and love. As she recited the poem, during a period in which she suffered from excruciating migraines, Weil writes, "le Christ lui-même est descendu et m'a prise"[55] ["Christ himself came and took hold of me"]. Anderson writes that the "God who reached out to Simone Weil" in such mystical moments was

> the God of the Cross, the God of the concentration camp, the God of slaves, the God of those in pain and despair, the God of the victims of poverty and contempt. For it is precisely when all the bogus protective structures have collapsed, when the soul is "pulverized" or nihilated, when it cries out, as the soul of Jesus did, in its helplessness and pain—it is precisely then that God is discovered in the darkness and love shapes itself in the void. That is what Simone Weil understood and that is how she understood.[56]

He adds, "[she] was perhaps more Christian than many who call themselves by that name. The center of her experience and her thought were occupied by the passion of Christ."[57]

Weil's emphasis on comtemplative waiting and attention without desire as a means to become closer to God—to feel His presence—is far less controversial than her association of *malheur* and divine immanence, though it is no less important. Such a practice is essential for the afflicted soul who can do nothing but "stand and wait."[58] Weil stresses the idea that the spiritual practice of this form of contemplation plays a crucial role in entering the presence of God and hearing His voice which is, paradoxically, figured as silence. Weil declares, "Celui qui est capable non pas seulement de crier, mais aussi d'écouter, entend la réponse. Cette réponse, c'est le silence.... La parole de Dieu est silence. La secrète parole d'amour de Dieu ne peut pas être autre chose que le silence"[59] ["Anyone who is capable not only of screaming, but also of listening, hears the answer. This response is silence. God's word is silence. . . . The secret word of God's love can be nothing but silence"]. This spiritual discipline can be seen as a measurement of spiritual progress and growth, when one accepts universal suffering as part of the human condition.

Despite her mystical experiences—her encounters with "the God of the Cross" in which she is privy to the language of divine silence—Weil, however, recognizes that she cannot explain why humans must endure affliction in this world, stating that "[l]e pourquoi du malheureux ne comporte aucune réponse, parce que nous vivons dans la nécessité et non dans la finalité. S'il y avait de la finalité dans ce monde, le lieu du bien ne serait pas dans l'autre monde"[60] ["there is no answer to the 'why' of the afflicted because the world is necessity and not purpose. If there were finality in the world, the place of the good would not be in the other world"]. She seems to echo George Herbert's dictum, "Affliction then is ours."[61]

CONCLUSION

Simone Weil believed that "[l]a fonction propre de l'intelligence exige une liberté totale, impliquant le droit de tout nier, et aucune domination"[62] ["the proper function of intelligence is to claim total freedom, including the right to resist and reject any domination"]. It is, therefore, hardly surprising that she was wary of religious institutions and traditions. While Weil embraces many elements of the Christian faith, she argues that faith and salvation can be achieved outside institutionalized religion:

> Il n'y a pas de salut sans "nouvelle naissance," sans illumination intérieure, sans présence du Christ et du Saint-Esprit dans l'âme. Si donc il y a possibilité de salut hors de l'Église, il y a possibilité de révélations individuelles ou collectives hors du christianisme. En ce cas, la vraie foi constitue une espèce d'adhésion très différente de celle qui consiste à croire telle ou telle opinion. Il faut penser à nouveau la notion de la foi.[63]

> There is no salvation without a "new birth," without inner illumination, without Christ's presence and the Holy Spirit in the soul. If then there is the possibility of salvation outside the church, there is the possibility of individual or collective revelations outside Christianity. In this case, true faith is different from the kind that consists in believing in this or that opinion. We need to think again about the notion of faith.

In light of this view, Weil constantly rebels against the Church to free herself from its dogmas, traditions, and teaching, just as she repeatedly questions the reliability of the Bible. Her ambivalent attitude, rooted in skepticism, toward Scripture and the God described within it was likely exacerbated by her pluralist exegetical practices. She strove to access God through Greek philosophy, a myriad of myths, and a range of religions, often ending up in a place of contradiction and inconsistency. Nevertheless, despite any contentious aspects of her work and the challenges of her thinking, Weil invites anyone searching for truth to ponder in new and unexpected ways difficult questions regarding God and the religious life. Unlike the secular thinkers of her day, Weil refuses to separate the intellectual from the spiritual and the social. For Weil, the scholar, who writes out of her own experience, the spiritual becomes personal and the personal becomes political. As a woman and a Jew facing double marginalization in France, she struggled to make her voice heard in a predominantly male intellectual circle. Despite the contradictions in her intellectual and spiritual life, Simone Weil is an example of a religious philosopher whose meditative work on God, love, extreme affliction or *malheur*, social justice, and oppression inspires the intellectual and spiritual development of her readers.

NOTES

1. Francine du Plessix Gray, "At Large and at Small: Loving and Hating Simone Weil," *American Scholar* 70, no. 3 (2001): 8.
2. Manichaeism is a sect of Christianity and Gnosticism is a form of religion that had a profound influence on some sects of Christianity. The dualist teachings of these sects (second to fourth centuries C.E.) distinguish the good spiritual world from the evil material world.
3. Heinz Abosch, *Simone Weil: An Introduction*, trans. Kimberly A. Kenny (New York: Pennbridge, 1994), 132.
4. D. Z. Phillips, preface to *Discussions of Simone Weil*, by Rush Rhees, ed. D. Z. Phillips (New York: State University of New York Press, 2000), vii.
5. See, for example, Leonard M. Marsak, ed., *French Philosophers from Descartes to Sartre* (Cleveland: The World Philosophy Company, 1961); Eric Matthews, ed., *Twentieth Century French Philosophy* (Oxford: Oxford University Press, 1996); and Gary Gutting, ed., *French Philosophy in the Twentieth Century* (Cambridge: Cambridge University Press, 2001).
6. Miklos Vetö, *The Religious Metaphysics of Simone Weil*, trans. Joan Dargan (New York: State University of New York Press, 1994), 153.
7. Rush Rhees, *Discussions of Simone Weil*, ed. D. Z. Phillips (New York: State University of New York Press, 2000), vii.
8. Albert Camus, quoted in John Hellman, *Simone Weil: An Introduction to Her Thought* (Waterloo, ON: Wilfrid Laurier University Press, 1982), 1.
9. Sarah K. Pinnock, "Mystical Selfhood and Women's Agency: Simone Weil and French Feminist Philosophy," in *The Relevance of the Radical: Simone Weil 100 Years Later*, ed. A. Rebecca Rozelle-Stone and E. Lucian Stone (New York: Continuum Books, 2010), 205.
10. Catharism is considered a heretic cult deriving from the Gnostic Manichean tradition of the East.
11. Simone Weil, *Lettre à un religieux* (Paris: Gallimard, 1951), 40.

12. J. M. Perrin and G. Thibon, *Simone Weil as We Knew Her* (London: Routledge and Kegan Paul, 1953), 146.

13. For example, in her judgment against the Church's orthodox teaching, she rejects the idea of an omnipresent and omnipotent God who reigns everywhere: "Les religions qui représentent la divinité commandant partout où elle en a le pouvoir sont fausses" (*Formes de l'amour implicite de Dieu*, in *Œuvres*, ed. Florence de Lussy [Paris: Gallimard, 1999], 724) ["Religions that represent God as ruling everywhere where he has the power are false"].

14. Simone Weil, "Autobiographie spirituelle," in *Attente de Dieu* (Paris: La Colombe, 1950), 45.

15. *Anathema sit*: "let him be anathema" (excommunicated).

16. Weil, *Lettre à un religieux*, 9–11.

17. See Emmet Kennedy, "Simone Weil: Secularism and Syncretism," *JHS* 5 (2005): 203–25.

18. Helen Cullen, "Simone Weil and Greece's Desire for the Ultimate Bridge to God: The Passion," *Faith and Philosophy* 16, no. 3 (July 1999): 353.

19. Simone Weil, *Commentaires de textes pythagoriciens,* in *Œuvres*, ed. de Lussy, 604.

20. Ibid., 595.

21. Ibid., 596.

22. Weil, *Lettre à un religieux*, 18.

23. For more information on Origen, see Edward Moore, "Origen of Alexandria (185–254 C.E.)," *Internet Encyclopedia of Philosophy*, www.iep.utm.edu/origen-of-alexandria/.

24. Jacques Cabaud, *Simone Weil: A Fellowship in Love* (New York: Channel Press, 1964), 207–8.

25. George A. Panichas, introduction to *The Simone Weil Reader* (New York: David McKay, 1981), xxii–xxiii.

26. Simone Weil, Letter to Jean Wahl (October 1942), in *Œuvres*, ed. de Lussy, 979.

27. Lesslie Newbigin, *The Gospel in a Pluralist Society* (Grand Rapids, MI: William B. Eerdmans; Geneva: WCC, 1989), 72.

28. Weil, Letter to Jean Wahl, 979.

29. Francis A. Schaeffer, *The Complete Works of Francis Schaeffer: A Christian Worldview, Volume 2: A Christian View of the Bible as Truth* (Wheaton, IL: Crossway, 1982), 4.

30. Paul West, *The Wine of Absurdity: Essays on Literature and Consolation* (University Park: Pennsylvania State University, 1966), 144.

31. Weil did admire some Old Testament books. In *Formes de l'amour implicite de Dieu*, she writes, "certain endroits de l'Ancien Testament, dans les Psaumes, dans le livre de Job, dans Isaïe, dans les livres sapientaux, enferment une expression incomparable de la beauté du monde" (732) ["certain passages in the Old Testament, in the Psalms, in the book of Job, in Isaiah, in the sapiential books, contain an unparalleled expression of the beauty of the world"].

32. Weil, *Lettre à un religieux*, 13.

33. See Emmanuel Levinas, "Simone Weil contre la Bible," in *Difficile liberté: Essais sur le judaïsme* (Paris: Albin Michel, 1976) and M. Kac, "Simone Weil ou la conspiration du silence autour d'un langage corrompu," *AMIF* 227, 228 (1974).

34. See de Lussy's introduction to the section "L'Antijudaïsme de Simone Weil" in *Œuvres*, ed. de Lussy, 961.

35. Letter to Xavier Vallat (October 18, 1941), in *Œuvres*, ed. de Lussy, 973.

36. Abosch, *Simone Weil: An Introduction*, 12.

37. De Lussy, introduction to "L'antijudaïsme de Simone Weil," 962.

38. Letter to Xavier Vallat, 973.

39. Letter to Huguette Baur (September 1940), in *Œuvres*, ed. de Lussy, 969.

40. Weil, *Commentaires de textes pythagoriciens*, 624.

41. Weil, "Autobiographie spirituelle," 37.

42. Ibid.

43. Ibid.

44. Ibid., 41.

45. Simone Weil, *L'Amour de Dieu et le malheur*, in *Pensées sans ordre concernant l'amour de Dieu* (Paris: Gallimard, 1962), 104.

46. Cabaud, *Simone Weil,* 209.
47. Weil, *L'Amour de Dieu et le malheur,* 96.
48. Ibid., 125.
49. Dorothée Soelle, *Suffering,* trans. Everett R. Kalin (Philadelphia: Fortress, 1975), 9–32.
50. Susan Anima Taubes, "The Absent God," in *Toward a New Christianity: Readings in the Death of God Theology,* ed. Thomas J. J. Altizer (New York: Harcourt, Brace, and World, 1967), 113.
51. There is also some evidence that suggests she may have died from a tuberculosis-related heart attack.
52. Weil, "Autobiographie spirituelle," 51.
53. There are different interpretations of Weil's idea of decreation. On this subject, see Anne Carson, "Decreation: How Women Like Sappho, Marguerite Porete and Simone Weil Tell God," *Common Knowledge* 8, no. 1 (Winter 2002): 188–201; and Timothy C. Baker, "Praying to an Absent God: The Poetic Revealing of Simone Weil," *Culture Theory and Critique* 47, no. 2 (2006): 133–47.
54. *Formes de l'amour implicite de Dieu,* 727.
55. Weil, "Autobiographie spirituelle," 38.
56. David Anderson, *Simone Weil* (London: S. C. M. Press, 1971), 61.
57. Ibid., 60.
58. This phrase is from John Milton's sonnet "On His Blindness."
59. Weil, *L'Amour de Dieu et le malheur,* 129.
60. Ibid., 128.
61. This line is taken from George Herbert's poem "Affliction [I]."
62. Weil, "Autobiographie spirituelle," 46.
63. Weil, *Lettre à un religieux,* 48–49.

Chapter Eight

Duras and the Desire for Spiritual Transformation

Kelsey L. Haskett

For many years, the writings of Marguerite Duras (1914–1996) appeared to embody the antithesis of a spiritual perspective, reflecting a vast cosmic void where any reference to God or spiritual values stood out by its absence. In *Marguerite Duras ou le temps de détruire*, published in 1972, Alain Vircondelet analyzes the negative themes of solitude, missing love, death, destruction, and despair that pervade Duras's works, all treated without hope, creating "a nihilism as much felt as reflected upon."[1] He and others perceive a familiar world being torn apart with nothing to replace it, certainly nothing spiritual: "It is a universe which continues to exist, but otherwise; no transcendence, no values, no virtue."[2] Nevertheless, two decades later, critics had begun discussing the spiritual side of Duras's writing, despite the seeming lack of spirituality in her works. In 1997, a year after her death, Vircondelet led an international colloquium titled "Duras, Dieu, et l'écrit" ["Duras, God, and Writing"] because, as his introduction to the proceedings explains, this combined notion seemed to be "for a long time already, at the heart of this work and its existential inquiry."[3] Thus, in the course of Duras's career as a writer, a radical shift had occurred in the literary criticism dealing with her works, such that by the end of her life the role of the spiritual in her writings, with its multitudinous facets, came to be fully recognized and acknowledged.

Although the approaches to the question of the spiritual in Duras's work have varied greatly, certain themes have emerged over the years that are undisputedly Durassien: the unending pursuit of an unattainable love or ultimate experience of passion, rendering ordinary life less than tolerable; the implicit fusion of this idealized love with a yearning for the absolute, the infinite, the eternal; the paradoxical expression of this search for an absolute of love through carnal means, apparently devoid of spirituality; the inexplicable pain and sorrow that overcomes the characters in the absence of any true experience of human or transcendent love which would fill and fulfill the individual. In *"Moderato cantabile" de Marguerite Duras*, an early study touching on the absolute nature of this quest for love, Henri Micciollo describes the essential longings that characterize not only the protagonist of this novel, Anne Desbaresdes, but most of Duras's female characters: "But, and this is true of all Duras's heroines, this woman who lives by relative values aspires to an absolute. And for her, there is only one absolute: that of love. Only love, lived in its totality, can bring about a fullness and complete realization of one's being."[4] Madeleine Alleins, also one of the first to highlight the spiritual quality of Duras's work, shows, in *Marguerite Duras: Médium du réel*, the author's "intuition of eternity"[5] which undergirds the particular manifestations of the search for love in her works. About a decade later, in 1993, the proceedings from a conference on Marguerite Duras given at the Centre Culturel International de Cerisy-la-Salle reveal a number of ways in which the desire for transcendence appears in Duras's writings. Danielle Bajomée concludes her paper from this conference by affirming that "for Duras, the here and now is not our true place. Texts and films do not cease to call for, to recall this quest for a place which is unapproachable, impossible to encompass (or define)."[6] The papers from the colloquium "Duras, Dieu et l'écrit" speak variously of her "mystical involvement," or "mystical vocation," while one author asks, "How can we reconcile the vocation of the sacred, the desire for an absolute, and the call to transcendence which motivate [Duras's] literary creation and the certainty of the absence of God which is so devastating to her?"[7] This fundamental question expresses not only the dilemma facing each of Duras's critics but also sums up effectively the basic notions underlying the spiritual nature of her work.

While much has now been written about the desire for transcendence manifested in often complex ways in Duras's works, the parallel desire for spiritual transformation which also inhabits many of her characters has remained virtually unexplored. It is important to remember that for Duras, aspirations tending outward toward the infinite are always the result of an inner void, revealing, rather, the opposite of an attempt to connect with a personal God or some kind of deity. In both *L'Amant* and *La Vie matérielle*, Duras presents a worldview which excludes any notion of a superior being in the universe: "On manque d'un dieu. Ce vide qu'on découvre un jour d'adolescence rien ne peut faire qu'il n'ait jamais eu lieu. L'alcool a été fait pour supporter le vide de l'univers, le balancement des planètes, leur rotation imperturbable dans l'espace, leur silencieuse indifférence à l'endroit de votre douleur"[8] ["We are lacking a god. This void that we discover one day in our teens, nothing can prevent it from occurring. Alcohol has been created so that we can cope with the emptiness in the universe, the motion of the planets, their imperturbable rotation in space, their silent indifference toward our pain"]. The individual's solitude is a solitude of cosmic proportions, that neither love nor alcohol can abate. Nothing can dull the pain of living in an impersonal, indifferent universe, although Duras's characters (mainly female, we should note) strive to overcome this reality through often desperate and futile means. The inner negation which defines their very beings is strikingly counterbalanced by the outer negation of the metaphysical world, both of which call for a presence to fill the unbearable absence. Not only do Duras's characters seek to encounter an absolute of love that would forever fill their empty lives, but they themselves long for an experience of personal renewal that could easily be described as spiritual. It is to the exploration of these intertwining aspirations, with a focus on the latter, that this chapter is devoted.

PHYSICAL AND METAPHYSICAL DESIRE

The notion of desire takes on many forms in Duras's works, but it refers mainly to sexual desire, which represents the only means of experiencing relationship that most of the characters possess. From Anne Desbaresdes to Lol V. Stein, from Anne-Marie Stretter to the young girl in *L'Amant*, the personal element of love is banished and replaced with an impersonal impulse that attaches itself to various objects of desire, not important in themselves. The impersonality of the universe is mirrored in the impersonality of these "love" relationships which drive the female characters on, but never satisfy them. Hence, an ongoing search for love appears in all of the novels, plays, and films, where the feelings of desire for one person transform into the desire for another, a replacement of the first, in a continuous cycle which perpetuates the longing while leaving it unfulfilled. As partners in relationships become nothing but substitutionary figures, however, the ideal of love sought for, in all its intensity and absoluteness, remains unchanged. It is in this incessant desire for a love beyond measure and beyond reach that the "aspiration for the eternal" can be found in Duras's works. Physical desire in fact discloses the deeper yearnings of the heart.[9]

Along with this deep-rooted longing for transcendence, the dream of inner transformation that also surfaces in the lives of some of Duras's female characters is manifested in at least three ways: a desire for radical renewal, expressed metaphorically as rebirth; a desire on the other hand for the finality and drama of death, whereby change is envisioned as possible only through some kind of suicidal means; and a generally unconscious desire for a complete reversal of identity, through the projection of one's self into that of another. These transformational desires touch the very core of being of Duras's characters, building on their profound sense of dissatisfaction with themselves and their need to escape the confines of self, to radically erase their inner person, and to step from unfulfilled existence into a new and different reality. As we now examine these basic expressions of transformational desire, we will also explore the soil in which they have sprung up, that is, the individual perceptions of self and life revealed by the characters.

SELF-REJECTION AND THE DESIRE FOR REBIRTH

Of all the female characters who experience profoundly negative feelings toward themselves, the most articulate in expressing them is Francine Veyrenattes, the narrator of *La Vie tranquille*, although others such as Lol V. Stein come close in their expression of inner negation. In relating her family's story, Francine reveals her painfully low self-esteem, based on the fact that she has been psychologically abandoned by her parents, and, in her perception of her youth, has let her brother's childhood replace her own, so that little remains of her own identity: "Je n'étais personne, je n'avais ni nom ni visage. En traversant l'août, j'étais: rien"[10] ["I was no one; I had no name or face. In living out the month of August I was: nothing"]. Her view of her relationship with Tiène, the man she loves and decides to marry, is equally crushing: "Je ne devais pas plus compter à ses yeux que Nicolas ou Luce. A y réfléchir, c'était comme s'il m'avait forcée à ne jamais l'aimer, à ne lui plaire qu'en restant pareille toujours, à n'être personne. Bientôt il me laisserait aux Bugues avec eux, avec rien" (*VT*, 70) ["I mustn't have counted more in his eyes than Nicolas or Luce. On thinking about it, it was as if he had forced me to never love him, to not please him except by always staying the same, by being no one. Soon he would leave me at the Bugues with them, with nothing"]. Her acute sense of worthlessness even prevents her from recognizing herself in the mirror at the seaside hotel where she mourns her brother's death. Her image is that of a stranger, contesting her identity and even further destabilizing her sense of self: "Qui étais-je, qui avais-je pris pour moi jusqu'à là?" (*VT*, 122) ["Who was I? Who had I taken to be me up until then?"]. Despite her narcissistic desire to love herself, embrace herself, even dance with herself, she feels irremediably detached from who she really is, incapable of connecting with her inner person, unable to identify with her own history or feel reassured by her name. While desiring an experience to claim as her own, one that would give her a sense of personhood and meaning, she finds herself trapped in an identity that is separate from her self, an identity that comes from without: "Je suis une certaine forme dans laquelle on a coulé une certaine histoire qui n'est pas à moi" (*VT*, 136) ["I am a certain form into which has been poured a certain history that doesn't belong to me"]. In the context of this identity crisis which is aggravated by her brother's death, Francine begins, nevertheless, to experience a sense of personal transformation through her contact with the sea, an instrument in her life of greater self-awareness and of a radical but temporary change in self-perception.

Francine's encounter with the sea evokes both her greatest fear and her greatest longing. The sea in all its vastness is frequently portrayed as a symbol of the eternal, of course, and for Francine, it connotes both the power of death and the power of life. In "Duras et le désir d'éternité," Bajomée equates the desire for eternity with the sea: "The desire for eternity corresponds to images that are explicitly related to the sea, that is, to the concept of the sea. In other words, that are related to this opening of space, this fullness which holds the secret of repetitive eternity, a wild and infinite space, the vastness of nothingness. 'To look at the sea is to look at the Whole,' says Duras (*Les Lieux de Marguerite Duras*)."[11] Duras confided to Ingrid Šafranek that the sea was "le néant" ["nothingness"], a term Šafranek understands to be both negative and positive.[12] For her, the sea in Duras's works is "the reverse of 'material life,' it is the negative of the earth, nothingness incarnate, the infinite present to our senses. Reflection of the heavens on earth [Reflet du ciel sur la terre], the sea here is the essential vehicle of spirituality."[13] Francine first experiences the negative side of the sea's infinity in its power to engulf, to envelop in death or nothingness. No longer does she see death merely as a little animal crouching inside her, of which she is daily aware, but rather as a roaring lion, spoiling for its prey:

> On est les yeux dans les yeux pour la première fois avec la mer. On sait avec les yeux d'un seul regard. Elle vous veut tout de suite, rugissante de désir. Elle est votre mort à vous, votre vieille gardienne. C'est donc elle qui depuis votre naissance vous suit, vous épie, dort sournoisement à vos côtés et qui maintenant se montre avec cette impudeur, avec ces hurlements? (*VT*, 145)

> [You are staring the sea in the eyes for the first time. You know with a single glance. She wants you right away, howling with desire. She is your own death, your old guardian. So it's she that since your birth has followed you, spied on you, slept slyly by your side and who shows herself now with this impudence, with this roaring.]

At the same time, however, she also recognizes the sea as a place of infinite beauty and oblivion, or permanent forgetfulness, where one's past and future are forever washed away: "Ce qui est passé et ce qui arrivera est enfoui dans la mer qui danse, danse en ce moment, au delà de tout passé, de tout avenir" (*VT*, 139) ["What has happened and what will happen is buried in the sea that dances, dances right now, beyond everything past and everything future"]. This spiritual need to erase the past and its hold on the future, to wipe the slate of one's life clean, finds an interesting parallel in the biblical picture of divine forgiveness, whereby the penitent sinner's faults are figuratively cast into the depths of the sea (Micah 7:19). It is only in confronting the sea in all its immensity that Francine becomes conscious of her inner self. The eternal mirror of the sea, and not the temporal mirror in her room which reflects back her narcissistic, superficial gaze, puts her in touch with her own reality and awakens in her a desire to be changed.

The absolute negation Francine's identity has suffered before her revitalizing contact with the sea cannot be stressed enough, if we are to truly grasp the significance of her new desire for transformation. As mentioned, Francine perceives herself as "nobody," as "nothing," as having no real existence; she imagines that with others she is "quelqu'un qui a à se faire pardonner d'oser être là, simplement" (*VT*, 98) ["someone who needs to be forgiven simply for daring to be there"]. While denying responsibility for her past and its consequences, she realizes she is irremediably tied to it and to her own, cumbersome body: "Cette histoire a commencé, elle me mène vers où elle veut, je ne sais pas où et je n'ai rien à y voir . . . Je suis à jamais prise au piège de cette histoire-ci, de ce visage-là, de ce corps-là, de cette tête-là" (*VT*, 126) ["This story has begun and is taking me where it wants to; I don't know where and I have nothing to do with it . . . I am forever trapped in this particular story, this particular face, body, and head"]. Her contact with the sea, however, heightens her desire for renewal and her need to detach herself from her current, stagnant state of being, a mental process she likens to the act of casting off a filthy dress, and to learning to dance with oneself:

> On regarde la mer . . . Je suis sûre qu'on pourrait en devenir folle. . . . Et pourtant à force de ne voir qu'elle, elle vous invite de plus en plus clairement dans son langage de sourde-muette à faire quelque chose de définitif. Peut-être à jeter toute votre pudeur, toute votre dignité en l'air comme une robe sale. Il faudrait oser se regarder soi-même jusqu'à danser une danse, pour soi seule, me guetter moi-même jusqu'à me danser, danser devant moi le triomphe de mon ignorance absolue de moi et de mon ignorance de tout. (*VT*, 160)
>
> [You look at the sea . . . I'm sure she could drive you crazy. . . . And yet, as you look only at her, she invites you more and more clearly in her language of a deaf mute to do something definitive. Perhaps throw all your modesty, all your dignity up in the air like a dirty dress. You have to dare to look at yourself to the point of being able to dance a dance, for yourself alone; to watch myself intently until I can dance with myself, dance in front of myself the triumph of my absolute ignorance of myself and of everything.]

In contemplating the sea, she recognizes her need to face her true inner being, to accept and even celebrate herself to the point of being able to dance both with herself and in front of her self, that is, in front of her own gaze. Sadly, even this expressive metaphor, profoundly narcissistic in its implications, does not allow her to come to terms with her identity, to imagine she can surmount her ignorance of self ("mon ignorance absolue de moi" ["my total ignorance of myself"]), or of existence ("mon ignorance de tout" ["my ignorance of everything"]), but only reinforces her sense of personal alienation.

When Francine finally enters the sea, she gives herself over to its overwhelming presence, allowing it to absorb her thoughts and her total being: "Peu à peu ça qui pense se mouille, s'imbibe d'opaque, d'une opaque toujours plus mouillé, plus calme et plus dansant. On est eau de la mer" (*VT*, 145) ["Little by little that which thinks becomes wet, becomes saturated with opaqueness, an opaqueness which is wetter and wetter, calmer, and more dancing. You become water of the sea"]. This fusion with the sea, an eternal womb, is a gratifying experience, which lets Francine lose herself in its all-encompassing ubiquity, happily spending hours wafting in a new freedom from her old self. Plunging into its depths, she emerges with a new sense of identity and the impression of having experienced a new birth:

> L'océan crache sa sève dans ces éclosions d'écume. J'ai fait des séjours dans des vestibules chauds et boueux de la terre qui m'a crachée de sa profondeur. Et me voilà arrivée. On vient à la surface. Il y a de la place assez pour que tout l'Océan vienne crever au soleil, que chaque partie d'eau épouse la forme de l'air et mûrisse à son contour. Il y a la mienne qui les regarde. Je suis fleur. Toutes les parties de mon corps ont éclaté sous la force du jour, mes doigts qui éclatent de la paume de ma main, mes jambes de mon ventre, et jusqu'au bout de mes cheveux, ma tête. J'éprouve la lassitude fière d'être née, d'être arrivée à bout de cette naissance. Avant moi, il n'y avait rien à ma place. Maintenant, il y a moi à la place de rien. (*VT*, 143)

> [The ocean spits out its life force in the birthing of the foam. I have sojourned in the hot and muddy vestibules of the earth, which spewed me out of its depths. And here I am. You come to the surface. There is enough room for the whole ocean to burst forth in the sunlight, for each particle of water to espouse the form of the air and to ripen at its contours. There's my form, which looks at them. I'm a flower. Every part of my body has exploded under the impulsion of the day; my fingers are bursting from the palms of my hands, my legs from my stomach, my head right up to the ends of my hair. I feel a proud weariness in being born, in having come to the end of this birth. Before me, there was nothing in my place. Now, there is me, in place of nothing.]

Proud to have gone through this birthing process, she is supremely conscious of the new person she believes she has become, of the new "moi" that has taken the place of "rien," the nothingness she once was. Her regenerative experience strikingly evokes the image of rebirth which the Gospels present as requisite to true spiritual life: "You must be born again" (John 3:7 NIV). As in baptism by immersion, a symbol of death and new life, Francine goes through a symbolic death in the ocean's deep, murky chambers, before arriving at its surface and being gently expulsed onto the land, like an infant in birth: "On glisse intelligemment avec la mer jusqu'à être versée sur la plage" (*VT*, 146) ["You glide intelligently with the sea until you are poured out onto the beach"]. Having passed through the purifying waters of the sea, she comes out renewed, reborn, at least in her own mind.

In the sea, Francine is transformed into a flower. She imagines her legs, the fingers on her hands, and the hair on her head spreading out like the petals of a flower, a totally new way of envisioning herself. She has finally achieved the goal of a transformative experience, a moment belonging uniquely to her, as long as she remains in the sea, her source of regeneration. Once she leaves its protective contours, however, it is not long before she begins to lose hold of her restorative experience and to fall back into her old ways of thinking, unable to hang on to this fleeting moment of *épanouissement* or blossoming. Like Narcissus, who returns unceasingly to the contemplation of his own image and is finally transformed into a flower, a symbol of death rather than life, Francine cannot maintain her sense of fulfillment for long, for her continuous introspection produces a morbid fixation with self and a regression into her past with all its destructive tendencies. Her attempts at renewal remain, in fact, limited to the physical plane, as will become clear, despite her desire for a spiritual experience which would produce deeper and more lasting results, but which is impossible, one could maintain, without an actual encounter with the Divine. The symbolism of the sea proves to be just that—a symbol with no real power for Francine.

Her desire for purification, however, is very real. While Francine appreciates the personal delight she finds in the sea, in the end she cannot overcome her displeasure with herself in the midst of the sea's perfection, which instead of reordering her life, causes her to feel by contrast like a worthless, smelly mess: "Près de la mer, en plein jour, c'est autre chose. On est dans la main de la mer. On est ce plaisir de respirer. Dans un ordre qui ne sent pas, on est ce rien de désordre qui sent" (*VT*, 168) ["By the sea, in plain daylight, it's something else. You are in the hand of the sea. You are that pleasure of breathing. In an order with no odor, you are a disorderly, smelly nothing"]. She realizes it is not outer but inner cleansing she desires, but perceives herself as totally impervious to this kind of change, metaphorically closed like a sealed bag: "Si je pouvais m'ouvrir et me nettoyer d'amer, de vent, de mer. Mais ma peau est scellée comme un sac" (*VT*, 179) ["If I could only open myself up and cleanse myself of bitterness, wind, and water. But my skin is sealed tight like a bag"]. While she waits for the renewal of her inward self, she longingly observes the beauty of the summer that outwardly surrounds her, knowing she is forever separated from its perfection in her deepest being, where the symbolic harshness of winter keeps her from experiencing its transformative, regenerating qualities: "Je voudrais que l'été soit en moi aussi parfait que dehors, réussir à oublier d'attendre toujours. Mais il n'y a pas d'été de l'âme. On regarde celui qui passe tandis qu'on reste dans son hiver" (*VT*, 179) ["I wish that summer were as perfect inside of me as it is on the outside, that I could forget about always waiting. But there is no summer of the soul. You observe the one that goes by while you remain in your own winter"]. Spiritual transformation remains out of reach for Francine, despite her ardent wish to be changed from the inside out. The contrast between her lifeless inner condition and the outer, natural world full of warmth, light, and the enduring wonder of the sea only heightens Francine's longing to pass from one state to another, without enabling her to achieve this goal. The metaphor of birth, fleetingly encountered, is ultimately denied its meaning for Francine.

In a later novel, *Le Vice-consul*, we once again meet a young woman who struggles to change her personal reality, until the circumstances of life and the passage of time render her attempts useless. The beggar-woman of Calcutta represents in many respects the physical portrait of the negative inner state of most of Duras's female characters, carried to the extreme. She is the image of walking death, both inwardly and outwardly. Her whole being disgusts and disturbs those who watch her beg for food, sleep with the lepers, swim like an animal in the Ganges River to catch fish, emerge covered with slimy mud, unable to communicate with her fellow human beings and devoid of language, except for a single word, that of her birthplace. Filthy, skeletal, virtually bald, dispossessed of her home, her family, her memory, and her identity, she is the polar opposite of the novel's other protagonist, Anne-Marie Stretter, the French ambassador's wife. Although the beggar-woman has now gone past the point of no return, in terms of reversing her mental and physical degeneration, she began her journey toward degradation with a strong desire for something better. As in Duras's autobiographical novels, the source of the daughter's problems is her troubled relationship with her mother, who in this novel casts her out of her home at an early age on account of an illegitimate pregnancy, forcing her to live for the rest of her life by begging and prostitution: "Demain au lever du soleil, va-t'en, vieille enfant enceinte qui vieillira sans mari, mon devoir est envers les survivants qui un jour, eux, nous quitteront"[14] ["Tomorrow at sunrise, get out of here, old, pregnant child who will grow old without a husband. My duty is toward the survivors, those who will leave us one day"].

In contrast to Francine's emotionally absent mother in *La Vie tranquille*, the beggar-woman's mother acts with absolute, tyrannical authority, holding in her hands the power of life and death for her daughter (like the sea in *La Vie tranquille*). She is merciless, unforgiving, unable to forget her daughter's wrongs, unwilling to identify with her shame, adamant in her refusal to let her daughter return home: "Si tu reviens, a dit la mère, je mettrai du poison dans ton riz pour te tuer" (*VC*, 10) ["If you come back, said the mother, I will put poison in your rice to kill you"]. And yet, in her broken state of rejection, the evicted daughter wants nothing more than to be reconciled to her mother, to see her family again, and to start life over before setting out for good, on her own terms. While seeking the road of separation from her past, in her conflicted inner state, she longs to return to her intransigent mother to tell her she has forgotten her, an obvious contradiction, revealing her inability to break the maternal tie. In this need to return to her childhood, to undo the past, to reroute her life, to obtain her mother's blessing rather than her curse, she displays a need for personal renewal akin to Francine's aspiration for inner change, but in a much more graphic way. In place of the sea, that immutable, eternal force, the all-powerful mother figure portrayed in this novel evokes the image of the Almighty, but in the role of judge rather than giver of new life. The huge womb from which Francine imagines herself emerging, reborn, now becomes the inversion of a protective, maternal space, a source of death and separation rather than life, an absolute authority to which the daughter must do subservience: "en aucun cas tu ne dois revenir . . . aucun . . . va-t-en très loin, si loin qu'il me soit impossible d'avoir de l'endroit où tu seras la moindre imagination . . . prosternez-vous devant votre mère et va-t-en" (*VC*, 10) ["Under no circumstances must you return . . . none . . . go far away, so far that it is impossible for me to have even the slightest idea of where you are . . . bow down before your mother and be gone"].

As both her hunger and her pregnancy advance, however, the young beggar-girl is driven back to her mother by necessity, at least mentally. In a hallucinatory state caused by near starvation, her desire becomes a kind of false reality, as she mistakenly perceives the members of her family in an open market place, before finally taking the road that separates her from them forever. Alternating between the rejection of her mother and an attraction to her because of her physical condition, she dreams of starting life over again, of experiencing birth along with her child. This child, though, is the one she blames for her hunger, as she senses her arms, her legs, her cheeks, and her whole body being eaten away through lack of nourishment, devoured by the being inside that is destroying her life, physically and metaphorically. Her longing to return to her mother is a desire to be delivered of this burden, separated from this gnawing parasite, discharged of her maternal responsibilities, by giving the child back to her mother, the one who bore her, the one whose female image she bears and even blames:

> Elle part, elle part pour chercher un endroit où le faire, un trou, quelqu'un qui le prenne à son arrivée et le sépare complètement, elle cherche sa mère fatiguée qui l'a chassée. Sous aucun prétexte tu ne dois revenir. Elle ne savait pas, cette femme, elle ne savait pas tout, mille kilomètres de montagnes, ce matin, ne m'empêcheraient pas de retourner, sale femme, cause de tout, je te rendrai

cet enfant et toi tu le prendras, je le jetterai vers toi et moi je me sauverai pour toujours. Avec cette lumière crépusculaire, des choses doivent s'achever et d'autres recommencer. C'est sa mère, sa mère qui opérera donc cette naissance. Et de celle-ci, elle, cette jeune fille, elle sortira aussi, une nouvelle fois, oiseau, pêcher en fleur? (*VC*, 25)

[She leaves, she leaves to find some place to do it, a hole, someone to take it at its birth and separate it completely, she seeks her tired mother who chased her away. You must not return under any pretext. She didn't know, this woman, she didn't know everything, a thousand kilometers of mountains, this morning, couldn't keep me from returning, filthy woman, the cause of everything, I will give you back this child and you will take it, I will throw it at you and I will escape forever. With this twilight glow, certain things must come to an end and others begin. So it's her mother, her mother who will take care of this birth. And out of it will also come this young girl, once again, a bird, a flowering peach tree?]

In her desire for freedom and a separation from the past, she identifies fully with the infant she is carrying (as indicated at the end of this quotation), imagining herself being born once again like her child, transformed into a new being as free and beautiful as a bird or a blossoming peach tree. She clearly wants to rediscover the innocence of lost childhood, to escape the weight of caring for a new life, and to reposition herself in her mother's affections so that she can become a child once again: "Cette lumière appelle, appelle la mère, le recommencement de l'irresponsabilité" (*VC*, 25) ["This light calls, calls for her mother, the return to irresponsibility"].

The desire of this young woman is essentially the same as that of Francine, in that both want to rid themselves of their past, of their negative feelings toward themselves, and begin life again as newborn babes, restored, transformed, and liberated from shame and rejection. Neither view themselves as being of any worth at all; Francine's debilitating mindset is mirrored in the beggar-woman's emaciated body and total dispossession of her inner self as her life continues. Failing to return to her point of origin, she finally gives birth to her daughter on her own, rejecting both her mother and eventually her own child, whom she leaves with a white woman along the way. Observing her child from outside the house where the white woman tries to bathe her and restore her to life, feeling as if she is observing her own life, she is hopeful this stranger will succeed, but finally comes to realize that it is too late, and once again identifies with her daughter in death as she had in birth: "elle rêve: elle est son enfant morte" (*VC*, 70) ["She dreams: she is her dead child"]. Plunged into the bath water, like Francine into the depths of the sea, the child fails to revive, like her young mother who from this point on begins to lose all consciousness of her existence, seeing herself as more dead than alive: "elle rêve qu'elle est morte à son tour, noyée" (*VC*, 70) ["She dreams she is dead in turn, drowned"]. Drowned rather than emerging from the water, submerged but not restored to life, the beggar-woman represents, in fact, the absolute failure of transformational desire, culminating in symbolic death: "la mort d'une vie en cours" (*VC*, 175) ["The death of a life still in progress"].

Water in Duras's works, including the waters of birth, thus appears as a significant metaphor relating to personal transformation, be it successful or not. In *Duras: Une Lecture des fantasmes*, Madeleine Borgomano reveals the use of this metaphor once again in her discussion of the main character's ambivalent relationship to the sea in *Les Petits chevaux de Tarquinia*. In this novel, Sara is vacationing with her husband and their friends at a seaside resort where she finds the scorching heat particularly oppressive, reacting nonetheless very passively to her circumstances, never taking any initiative to modify them. In the midst of her growing marital problems, however, she is drawn into a fleeting love affair with a man she meets on the beach, the owner of a magnificent motorboat and a symbol of the kind of freedom for which Sara longs. In the end, however, she turns her back on this passing relationship, returning to the confines of her stifling villa, where she falls asleep as usual at the foot of her young son's bed, dreaming of other holidays and desperately hoping for rain to alleviate the unbearable heat, a metaphor for her depressing condition. In an excursion in the man's boat with her friends, it becomes obvious that Sara is too timid to swim very far and too afraid to look at the bottom of the sea. Despite her continuous longing for rain, an apparent indication of her desire for a change in her life, Borgomano sees, rather, in Sara's fear of the ocean's depths the sign of her unwillingness to look deeply into herself and be transformed:

> It's only because of the pressing invitation of the man with the boat—her lover for a night—that Sara, who is "afraid of everything," agrees to look at the bottom of the sea. Quickly, she looks away, as she turns away from the man—the stranger, adventure—to come back to the calm and monotonous quiet of her life, worriedly refusing all change, and any self-analysis that is too deep: the depths of the sea are also fantasized as the fascinating but frightening place of metamorphoses where life and death meet.[15]

Thus, Sara's bourgeois existence, in contrast to the lives of Francine and the beggar-woman, appears to exemplify the very opposite of a life turned toward possible inner transformation, although fear more than lack of desire seems to motivate her actions. Instead of reveling in the sea as does Francine, she fails to embrace the ocean's depths as a possible source of liberation, choosing rather to maintain the status quo. Her passive longing for rain positions her, nevertheless, as one of many in a series of female characters who in one way or another hope to break out of their world, all the while awaiting an ill-defined change within themselves.

Before we examine the case of Anne Desbaresdes in *Moderato cantabile*, a woman of similar social standing to Sara, but who seeks death rather than change as a solution to an unhappy life, it is worth noting that even the oppressive mother figure in the novels *L'Amant* and *L'Amant de la Chine du Nord* displays momentary expressions of transformational desire and the will to eradicate the past when she suddenly decides to wash the house from top to bottom. Wanting to rid herself of depression and guilt, due largely to her older son's delinquency and aggressiveness toward the other children, a situation she allows to continue in her unhealthy, codependent relationship with him, she occasionally does an about face, setting aside her discouragement for the exhilaration of washing the entire house. Experiencing extreme mood swings which are little understood by her children, she goes from inertia and the neglect of her family to the exuberance of feverish activity, turning the house-washing ritual into a glorious party for all. As multiple buckets of water are brought in to pour over the floors and cleanse the house, her desire for purification becomes evident. For a brief moment she believes that both the home and the lives within it can be transformed by this process, "que l'on peut être heureux dans cette maison défigurée qui devient soudain un étang, un champ au bord d'une rivière, un gué, une plage"[16] ["that one can be happy in this disfigured house that suddenly becomes a pond, a field alongside a river, a ford, a beach"]. This illusion of seeking inner change through outer cleansing is similar to Francine's desire to purify herself by plunging into the waters of the sea. The narrator highlights the spiritual dimension of the ritual by using language which speaks of purity, innocence, and the joy the family experiences through this short-lived event: "La maison toute entière embaume . . . c'est une odeur qui rend fou de joie surtout quand elle est mélangée à l'autre odeur, celle du savon du Marseille, celle de la pureté, de l'honnêteté, celle du linge, celle de la blancheur, celle de notre mère, celle de la candeur de notre mère"[17] ["The whole house gives off a fragrance . . . it's an odor that fills you with joy, especially when it is mixed with that other scent, that of the soap of Marseille, of purity, of honesty, that of linens, of whiteness, that of our mother, of the candour of our mother"]. The rest of this woman's life, however, portrayed as a veritable desert, depicts a state deprived of "spiritual" water and of the life-giving elements needed for personal and familial wholeness, including a positive self-image, that vital missing piece haunting all the women discussed in this chapter.

DESPAIR AND THE DESIRE FOR TRANSFORMATION IN DEATH

The absence of life which characterizes the aging mother figure in these novels, who succumbs more often than not to depression and despair, is carried over into the lives of Duras's other female characters, such as Anne Desbaresdes, the young mother in *Moderato cantabile*. Anne's suffocating milieu, devoid of marital love and communication, is portrayed through the symbolic representation of her bourgeois home, where her isolated bedroom is separated from the rest of the house by a long hallway, while her only encounters with her husband occur in the semi-private areas of the home, the living and dining rooms. Her child's bedroom is the only room of any significance to Anne. Her bedroom windows are kept firmly closed, to shut out both the heady scent of the magnolias, a symbol of passion for Duras, and the powerful sounds of the sea. A large beech tree she has allowed to remain standing also prevents the sunlight from entering, while the only noise that occasionally penetrates this sterile environment is that of the privet hedge scratching against the windows during a storm. An ambiance of death reigns in this room which presents the perfect picture of Anne's claustrophobic existence, where her lonely, inner world is cut off from the outside, even as she strives to maintain the image of a faithful wife and mother, despite the growing emptiness of her heart. Chauvin, a man she begins to meet in a café and who reads her like a book, asserts that many women, past residents of this house, have heard the sounds of the privet hedge at night, "à la place de leur coeur"[18] ["in place of their heart"], and have died in their room. Anne's life is no different than her predecessors who have figuratively lost their lives in loveless marriages and empty, bourgeois existences, and her desperation no less.

Using her son's piano lessons across town as a pretext to escape from her oppressive home, she cringes as the overbearing piano teacher metes out her rigorous discipline to her son, constrained to submit, like him, to the dictates of the musical education she has chosen for him, all the while gazing out the window at the boats that pass by on the sea, a symbol once again of the freedom that eludes her. Nothing has prepared her for the sudden cry that resonates from the café below, piercing her heart with the revelation of a passion consummated in death, the peak of all experiences for Anne, who craves a kind of emotional high she never thought existed. When she descends to the café and catches a glimpse of the murderer clinging to the woman he loved, his mouth covered in blood, a whole new world opens up to Anne, one in which the "crime passionnel" she has witnessed comes to signify the ultimate experience, an absolute moment which nothing can ever change. Micciollo affirms that "murder is the guarantee of the absolute, its petrifaction."[19] Nothing can maintain a relationship at its height of passion if it is lived out in real life, Micciollo goes on to explain, for "all love, from the moment it is fleshed out in real life, gets stuck in daily life and is condemned to mediocrity."[20] Paradoxically, only death can prevent passion from dying, can freeze it in time, unlike everyday love, which dissipates with the years, as Anne has discovered. From the moment she receives this revelation onward, Anne begins to dream of copying the experience of the murdered lover, of dying at the hands of a man completely submitted to her outrageous desire, knowing that her life up to that point will never be the same, imagining that it can only be transformed through passion and death.

This suicidal longing is the second kind of transformational aspiration we see operating in Duras's works, a desire stemming from the life of the author herself, who admits in an interview with Xavière Gauthier that the fusion of the death-wish with the notion of love sprang from her own experience with a man,[21] adding a new dimension to her work: "J'ai traversé une crise qui était . . . suicidaire, c'est-à-dire . . . ce que je raconte dans *Moderato cantabile*, cette femme qui veut être tuée, je l'ai vécu . . . et à partir de là les livres ont changé"[22] ["I went through a crisis that was suicidal, that is . . . what I recount in *Moderato cantabile*, this woman who wants to be killed, I lived it . . . and from that point onward my books changed"]. While this obsession with death reveals a certain quest for the absolute, it reveals at the same time the latent masochism inherent in the Durassian search for love, which appears in novels in which the protagonist becomes increasingly self-abasing and self-destructive, particularly on a psychological level. Anne Desbaresdes herself becomes so impregnated with the idea of the other woman's death that she tries to mimic her, living her experience vicariously in the same café where the murder took place through the relationship she develops with Chauvin, her ideal partner in this dangerous game of love.

Motivated by the desire to radically change her life, to the point of even accepting death as the only means to achieve this end, Anne begins to imitate the other woman in her daily encounters with Chauvin, inventing with him this woman's (hypothetical) story, letting him reconstruct the events he claims led up to the murder, allowing him to insult her as he paints a picture of the crime and of the woman's absolute submission to her sadistic lover. Far from being scandalized by his interpretation of the woman's desires, Anne revels in the thought that she, too, may one day experience this same intensity of passion: "Morte, dit-elle, elle en souriait encore de joie" (*MC*, 60) ["Dead, she said, still smiling with joy"]. The spiritual desire for transformation has taken a strange turn, in that death, not life, has come to symbolize the epitome of that transformation. As is always the case with Duras, though, the outward manifestation of the inner spiritual need belies the true aspirations of her characters, proving to be the very opposite of what appears on the surface, where love is exchanged for passion and life for death. Anne and Chauvin limit their relationship to highly charged conversations in the café, playing out in words what the other couple accomplished in deed. When Chauvin declares in the end that he wishes Anne dead, she replies simply, "C'est fait" (*MC*, 114) ["It's done"], allowing this symbolic death to replace the suicide she hoped to experience at the hands of Chauvin. In many ways, the old Anne is dead, radically changed by her identification with the murdered woman and her rejection of her bourgeois way of life at home, although the consequences of her transformation are far from obvious as Anne leaves Chauvin and the café for the last time, heading for an unknown destiny. The reader is left to interpret the end of the novel either as a form of liberation for Anne, who appears to leave not only Chauvin but her former life behind, or a form of death that leaves her suspended in limbo, so to speak, with none of her passionate desires having been truly fulfilled, except symbolically.

DEFEAT AND THE DESIRE FOR THE IDENTITY OF ANOTHER

The need to identify so completely with another that one's own identity is abolished represents the final outworking of the aspiration for change that we have seen in this chapter. Following Anne Desbaresdes, other female characters try to live out their desires vicariously through the experiences of idealized women who have relationships with the men they love, or want to love. Maria, in *Dix heures et demie du soir en été*, is the perfect example of this type of woman, in that she has completely abandoned all hope of recovering her love relationship with her husband, and permits another woman to take her place, as long as she can observe the two of them together, imagining that she is somehow part of the relationship. On vacation in Spain with her husband, her young daughter, and Claire, a family friend, Maria melts into the shadows when she sees this woman embracing her husband, imagining that she is in her shoes, rather than ousting her from the role she lets her play on the trip. In order to experience love, Maria must efface herself and take on the identity of the other, incapable of understanding the ways of love herself, longing to be, in fact, the other, and willing to sacrifice her own identity in her desperate attempt to come close to love. The emptiness this mode of behavior necessarily creates in her leaves her farther than ever from the love she desires and more and more dispossessed of self, to the point of losing all hope for restoration. Madeleine Alleins comments that in this novel, Duras "thought she was telling the ordinary story of a woman being cheated on, when in reality, for the first time, she allowed the other's existence to triumph over the importance of self."[23] Self-replacement is another strategy used by Duras's heroines to transform their unsatisfactory lives into lives appearing to have some semblance of fulfillment, but in reality, nothing could be further from the truth.

The master of this line of conduct is certainly Lol V. Stein, whose practice of personal negation leads her more than any other of Duras's characters to the brink of psychological self-destruction in *Le Ravissement de Lol V. Stein*. While the means she uses to attain her desired ends could hardly be said to be spiritual in nature, her deepest longings are nonetheless no different than those of Duras's other female characters, who yearn to be inwardly changed in ways that would bring radical transformation to their lives and a greater acceptance of their inner self. While the ideal that Lol strives to integrate into her psyche is a woman so striking, so seductive, that her level of perfection is beyond the grasp of the ordinary woman, this "femme fatale" represents, once again, a kind of absolute, in that she is everything Lol imagines she needs to be to find love and knows she is not, or can never be. It is this woman who steals her fiancé one night at a ball, leaving a permanent hole in Lol's heart and mind which she strives to fill not with an authentic relationship for herself, but with the simulation of the love of this other couple, as if she could absorb them into her own mental and emotional space. Too unconscious of the workings of her psyche to ever articulate or even conceive of her needs, Lol employs strategies dictated by her subconscious to replace both herself and the male figure in the original love relationship with yet another couple she encounters, projecting herself mentally into the lives of these substitutional lovers while eliminating her actual self in her own mind, a necessary step of effacement for one who sees herself as totally unworthy of love. This mode of behavior is not too far removed, in fact, from those who seek love today through personal replacement in the virtual, animated world of cyberspace.

Lol's extreme self-rejection stems from the dramatic incident at the ball, where she is suddenly abandoned by her fiancé and replaced by the stunning older woman who has just entered the ballroom, the inimitable Anne-Marie Stretter. Both her fiancé and this woman are immediately idealized to the point of capturing Lol's entire imagination, leaving her emptied of self and completely invested in this new relationship which she must integrate into her own life, so she can experience their passion vicariously. Lol does not want merely to imitate the other woman; she wants to be her, to position herself mentally at the very center of the current of desire drawing this man to this woman, to transform them through her gaze into part of her own psyche. Tragically, she can never again overcome her fixation with the ball, in which the new couple's early morning departure together tears her from reality and cements her obsession with the lovers, although she can never fully complete her mental construct of their intimate moments, much to her frustration: "Elle n'est pas Dieu, elle n'est personne"[24] ["She is not God, she is nobody"]. Years later, as she attempts to reconstruct the relationship through her manipulation of two other lovers she observes and who become substitutes for the first, Lol becomes the man's mistress at the same time. She insists, however, that he maintain his ties with the first woman, a more "perfect" lover than Lol, who then envisions herself as this woman when she makes love to this man. Through a complex pattern of replacements, Lol is able to "become" the woman she has always held up as an idol, to see herself at last as the object of a man's desire, that ideal man who always chooses the most attractive woman and thus attains the perfect love relationship that alone can bring satisfaction, in Lol's perspective. The problem is, of course, that her needs can never be fulfilled in this way, any more than the absolute she desires can exist in real life, all of which throw Lol back onto her nothingness, her loss of identity, and her rejection of self, longing once again to be transformed into another, and to leave self behind. As she confusedly admits to her lover at one point, "Je ne comprends pas qui est à ma place"[25] ["I don't understand who is in my place"].

CONCLUSION

Lol's avowal pinpoints the tragedy that surfaces for the women in these novels who seek out substitutes for the inner self they deny—eventually they are deprived of any clear identity, having destroyed the very center of their own existence, through infinite replacements. The desire for transformation, as we saw in the beginning, can lead to life or death, but is always built upon a gaping void in the lives of Duras's characters, whether it be a critical lack of self-esteem, as is the case of Francine, or a desperate hungering for love, as is the case of most characters, including Anne Desbaresdes, Maria, and Lol V. Stein. While the dream of new birth is the most positive way forward for those who aspire to some kind of inner renewal, it remains out of reach for the women who entertain this possibility, because birth cannot come in a vacuum—a seed of love must be planted, life must spring from Life, and not from death, or even from self, but from the love of the Other. But this Love is precisely what is absent in Marguerite Duras's world, where desire constitutes a hollow replacement for the ineffable. Love, the object of all longing, never comes, however, like the rain in *Les Petits cheveaux de Tarquinia.* And while Sara waits passively for the rain to relieve her situation, others, like Anne Desbaresdes, eventually despair of waiting, driven to conceive of an absolute of love bound up in the absolute of death, a suicidal wish leading to a fatal transformation that denies all hope. This self-destructive tendency also emerges in the lives of those, like Lol, who latch on to an ideal persona to replace their shattered inner identity. In each case, no ordinary solution will provide the sought for transformation; extreme measures are required to lift the characters above depression, self-hatred, and the stagnation of everyday life, measures so extreme, in fact, that they can be understood as metaphysical longings, even if the means to the end are far removed from spiritual solutions. A link exists, however, between the discovery of self and of a greater spiritual reality, as Bajomée suggests, in speaking of the Durassian search for love: "This waiting for love is intimately linked to the search for self, or to a search for a state that allows one to pass, in uninterrupted motion, from the multiple, from the fleeting, to the eternal."[26]

This movement which Bajomée describes is akin to that of spiritual metamorphosis, of a transition from the earth-bound to the eternal, from unworthiness to perfection. In multiple ways, Duras does not hesitate to depict the search for the ideal, the unflawed, the pure, a word she claims is "un des mots sacrés de toutes les sociétés, de toutes les langues, de toutes les responsabilités"[27] ["one of the sacred words of all societies, of all languages, of all responsibilities"]. Whether it be through some form of purification associated with water or rebirth, or through the replacement of one's scarred identity by an imagined ideal, the profound desire for inner change in Duras's characters cannot be denied. Its spiritual connotations can be read into the various forms of transformation sought for, even in the suicidal wish that envisions transformation through passion culminating in death, although the means employed eliminate the possibility of regeneration, evoking the image of baptism with no resurrection. Duras herself sought transformation through her writing, which she often viewed as a form of salvation, a rampart against solitude and death, an incarnation of her inner self in the form of words which would outlast her mortal life: "J'écris pour me déplacer de moi au livre. . . . La solution de continuité, livre ou mort"[28] ["I write to displace myself from myself to the book. . . . The solution of continuation, a book or death"].

Like her characters, however, Duras operates out of herself alone; that is, her inner world is her point of departure and her point of return, with no significant, transformative encounter en route, despite her desire to transcend herself, to attain immortality. Christiane Blot-Labarrère sees that Duras explores the world using sensitivity rather than reason, and discovers unexpected, mysterious forms, "that of the divine with a human face . . . , of the sacred assessed from herself alone, of a form of religion that flows from her personal experience, to keep from completely abandoning life, a passive determination to orient oneself towards the absolute."[29] Hanging on to life, rather than abandoning it, is what spiritual transformation is all about for Duras; it is the desire to go beyond oneself, "se dépasser" through any means possible, to hope against all hope that there is *something more*, that one does not have to live life as it is, with all its disappointments, failures, and heartbreaks, but that some way out exists: a way to become another, to know love, and to find one's place in the world. In this quest, Blot-Labarrère concedes, there is a disconcerting distance between hope and reality, "a poignant contrast between the aspiration to drill into the spiritual and the disenchantment that follows."[30] For Micciollo, the pursuit of the absolute by Duras's characters is always "doomed to failure."[31] This disillusionment does not prevent them, though, from searching, as Duras did throughout her life, believing, possibly, as Pascal affirmed, that happiness once existed, that it has left its invisible mark on our lives, and that the infinite void can somehow be filled, and indeed, must be filled, if we are ever to be at home in the universe. It is to this end that all of Duras's heroines aspire.

NOTES

1. Alain Vircondelet, *Duras ou le temps de détruire* (Paris: Éditions Seghers, 1972), 43.
2. Ibid., 46.
3. Alain Vircondelet, introduction to *Duras, Dieu et l'écrit*, ed. Alain Vircondelet (Paris: Éditions du Rocher, 1998), 9.
4. Henri Micciollo, *"Moderato cantabile" de Marguerite Duras* (Paris: Hachette, 1979), 31.
5. Madeleine Alleins, *Marguerite Duras: medium du réel* (Lausanne: Editions de L'Age d'Homme, 1984), 13.
6. Danielle Bajomée, "Duras et le désir d'éternité," in *Marguerite Duras: Rencontres de Cerisy*, ed. Alain Vircondelet (Paris: Écriture, 1994), 271.
7. Alain Vircondelet, "Marguerite Duras, libre et captive," in *Duras, Dieu et l'Écrit*, ed. Vircondelet, 127; Ingrid Šafranek, "L'écriture absolue ou la dernière des romantiques," in *Duras, Dieu et l'écrit*, ed. Vircondelet, 245; Dominique Denes, "Marguerite Duras par-delà le bien et le mal," in *Duras, Dieu et l'écrit*, ed. Vircondelet, 203.
8. Marguerite Duras, *La Vie matérielle* (Paris: Gallimard, 1994), 22.
9. Alleins, *Marguerite Duras*, 81.
10. Marguerite Duras, *La Vie tranquille* (Paris: Gallimard, 1972), 71; subsequent references are to this edition and will appear parenthetically in the text by the acronym *VT* and page number.
11. Bajomée, "Duras et le désir d'éternité," 252.
12. Šafranek, "L'Écriture absolue," 252.
13. Ibid., 255.
14. Marguerite Duras, *Le Vice-consul* (Paris: Gallimard, 1966), 10; subsequent references are to this edition and will appear parenthetically in the text by the acronym *VC* and page number.
15. Madeleine Borgomano, *Duras: Une Lecture des fantasmes* (Petit Roeulx, Belgique: Cistre-Essais, 1985), 48.
16. Marguerite Duras, *L'Amant* (Paris: Editions de Minuit, 1984), 77.
17. Ibid.
18. Marguerite Duras, *Moderato cantabile* (Paris: Editions de Minuit, 1958), 58; subsequent references are to this edition and will appear parenthetically in the text by the acronym *MC* and page number.
19. Micciollo, *"Moderato cantabile" de Marguerite Duras*, 43.
20. Ibid.
21. The experience of Duras with Gérard Jarlot, who provided the masculine role model for this text, is described in detail in the biographies by Frédérique Lebellay and Laure Adler. In *Marguerite Duras* (Paris: Éditions Gallimard, 1998), Adler describes Jarlot as a very seductive

man, "light, charming, frivolous" (319), able to whittle away hours in a café like Chauvin. Like Anne and Chauvin, Duras and Jarlot met in a café and began a similar type of relationship: "They went from café to café, and in each from table to table . . . , coming home dead drunk and sleeping until noon" (319). Like the female model in the suicidal passion with which Anne Desbaresdes is obsessed, Duras experienced a violent relationship with Jarlot, which she saw as inescapable. In the end, Duras was transformed by the extreme nature of this relationship, admitting to Xavière Gauthier that from this point on her writing was not the same. Says Adler, "In *Moderato*, Marguerite's ambition is to tell the untellable" (321). This, I believe, is Duras's goal in relation to her own search for self. Anne's quest to understand the other woman's passion in the novel strikes me as Duras's quest to understand herself, in a dimension that is beyond what she can grasp.

22. Marguerite Duras and Xavière Gauthier, *Les Parleuses* (Paris: Editions de Minuit, 1974), 59.

23. Alleins, *Marguerite Duras*, 14.

24. Marguerite Duras, *Le Ravissement de Lol V. Stein* (Paris: Gallimard, 1964), 53.

25. Ibid., 160.

26. Danielle Bajomée, *Duras ou la douleur*, 2nd ed. (Paris-Bruxelles : Duculot, 1999), 28.

27. Marguerite Duras, *Écrire* (Paris: Gallimard, 1993), 132.

28. Duras expressed this notion in an interview with Jean Schuster which is included at the end of Vircondelet's study, *Duras ou le temps de détruire*, 179. In *Marguerite Duras et l'autobiographie* (Paris: Le Castor Astral, 1990), Arliette Armel reiterates this idea in discussing the desperately serious role that writing played in Duras's life: "For Marguerite Duras, writing comes first. It's that which saves the writer from death" (20).

29. Christiane Blot-Labarrère, "Dieu, un 'mot' chez Marguerite Duras?" in *Duras, Dieu et l'écrit*, ed. Vircondelet, 193.

30. Ibid.

31. Micciollo, *"Moderato cantabile" de Marguerite Duras*, 31.

Chapter Nine

Spiritual Desire and Domestic Life in Malika Mokeddem's *La Nuit de la lézarde*

Susan Udry

The fictional representation of domestic life by French women authors has often taken on two profiles in regard to the relationship between female spirituality and social structures: the representation of gender inequality or mistreatment under the law, which in turn demonstrates the spirituality of the victim,[1] or, alternatively, the representation of women's lives in a way that illustrates feminine attributes of spirituality as a counterpoint to more dominant patriarchal representations. The same rhetorical motives, however, are misleading if applied to portrayals of domestic life by Islamic Francophone writers, because of the relationship that traditionally exists between domestic life and the spiritual in Muslim society. In Islam, the gender roles of men and women are connected to their spirituality because their roles emanate from divine law and are contained in the Qur'an. Whereas biblical concepts of God-created gender have relatively little prescriptive influence on domestic duties in Western culture, Islamic representations of gender tend to be highly prescriptive and define social behavior for the believing Muslim. Through the study of a particular author and work in this chapter, I will argue that Muslim women writers of French expression are engaging fictional images of domestic life in a way that both supports the individual's pursuit of spirituality and represents the emergence of distinct modes of accommodating that pursuit in some Muslim societies. At the same time, however, the heroine's capacity to decide whether or not to accept a transcendent hope proves to be the prerequisite to personal and spiritual fulfillment.

For Muslim women writing in French, the extent to which radical Islamic religious thinking shapes women's participation in society makes the representation of domestic life a pressing political issue. Under conservative Islam, a woman's legal status is to be covered at all times by her husband, and her activity in the public sphere is to be restricted. The cultural and social position of women of Muslim origin writing in exile offers a dual perspective on the Islamic ordering of domestic life because these women are writing both from the margins of French society and its secular tradition, and from the margins of the koranic tradition. On the one hand, Western feminism has called for a complete rejection of the traditional ordering of the household and tied this rejection to achieving self-actualization and personal freedom, while Muslim feminism often calls for women to uphold tradition as a form of struggle against the colonial past.[2]

Whether used literally or symbolically, images of domestic space in literature play a role in enabling the reader to visualize the spiritual aspirations of the individual. The spiritual content of dreams has a long tradition in Islam, with the courtyard of the house often figuring prominently. In present-day Muslim culture, domestic imagery is still important in symbolizing individual transformation. For example, in a dream-like vision experienced by a North African converted to Christianity, the subject recounts finding himself seated in a house that is completely destroyed and looking across a space into a large house in which everything is clean and shining: "I longed to go from the demolished house into the new house, but I could not reach it. A shining white cloud appeared above the man and a voice said, 'Stretch out your hand to me.' I asked, 'How? I can't.' The voice replied, 'Try, if you truly love God.' I tried, but it was impossible. I could not reach Him though I tried and tried."[3] In the man's vision of two houses, one demolished and the other beautiful, images of domestic order and disorder are presented as a mental space in which the subject can express his desire to connect with an absent God; yet it does so in a way that avoids positioning the subject in relation to a dominant social structure. While it is unsurprising to find that images of domestic space are being used symbolically in the literature of protest emerging from Islamic Francophone writers, it is the way these authors use domestic imagery to avoid positioning the individual in opposition to social structures, be they religious or political in nature, that is both original and crucial to the ongoing discussion of the role of individual freedoms in the society. This is the case in the work of the contemporary French-Algerian writer Malika Mokeddem (b. 1949), who relies on domestic imagery to portray female desire for self-transformation and transcendence.

Mokeddem left Algeria for France in 1985 to escape civil violence and has since become well known in France and North America for novels about women who learn to reshape their lives in order to mediate between the dictates of traditional Islam and the demands of the modern professional world. She is part of a political and linguistic community of women who are dedicated to protesting the current Islamist influences in Algeria by writing in French about the lives of women under Islamist rule. In her portrayal of one woman's struggle to create an identity for herself after being expelled from her family, Mokeddem equates the woman's new domestic life with the intentional practice of creating a border space between the woman's past (and culture of origin) and her future. Quite specifically, domestic imagery in Mokeddem's work helps define a Muslim woman as an individual in relation to other individuals rather than as a member of a group.[4]

The Qur'an's statements on the nature of women as a distraction or temptation in relation to faith, and the commentary traditions (hadith) describing women as deficient in spiritual matters because of periods of impurity either during menstruation or following childbirth, have at times been interpreted in such a way as to serve as a basis for politically motivated violence toward women.[5] In Algerian society, where violence against women has been tacitly approved by some Islamist groups, the female body itself has been perceived both as the target of violence and as a spiritual refuge. In many of their works, Mokeddem and other Algerian writers juxtapose the extreme violence that strikes at the heart of the family, through the treatment of women, with images of feminine nurturing. In Mokeddem's *Le Siècle des sauterelles*, for example, the spirituality of the hero in the face of disaster is evoked by showing him engaged in a number of mundane domestic tasks after finding his wife has been murdered: preparing traditional nomadic cakes, feeding the daughter, caring for the tent site, and finally burying the corpse. What from an Islamic cultural perspective would be considered weakness, or even contaminating for a Muslim man to perform, is used here to indicate that a spiritual rebirth is taking place that allows the epic hero to emerge as a counter-cultural figure.

In the face of the intensity of civil violence in Algeria, including over twenty years of conflict and delayed human rights, Francophone women writers have had to overcome a major obstacle in deciding how to convey accurately the atrocity of the violence being suffered by women, without either exploiting the victims or alienating potential readers. Both social reform movements such as "vingt ans, Barakat" and the literary trends that characterize the writing of Algerian women authors have relied on the perspective of secular feminism in order to bear witness to the underlying connections between domestic law and political violence.[6] The direct way in which Algerian Francophone writers Mokeddem and Assia Djebar depict the plight of Algerian women has caused this style of writing to be categorized as "une littérature d'urgence" ["a literature of urgency"] by both French and Algerian critics. However, Mokeddem's fourth novel, *La Nuit de la lézarde* (*The Night of the Lizard*), has been criticized for shifting focus away from the political violence toward descriptions of everyday life, in a way that has been viewed by some as a betrayal of the pledge to bear witness, and as a gesture of appeasement.[7] In *La Nuit de la lézarde,* Mokeddem focuses on the relationship between domestic and political violence by presenting a heroine who has been divorced and renounced by her husband. The focus is not on the violence itself, but on its psychological and social effects. The novel narrates the inner struggle of a woman caught in the civil conflict, and evokes the image of transcendent love as a way of moving beyond the rhetoric of both fundamentalism and feminism that has dominated the debate up to this point. The author depicts the spirituality of Algerian women as emerging out of a tension between two opposite facets of love in the face of national trauma: the desire to affirm community and compassion through the traditional roles of wife and mother, and the desire to refuse all community in favor of seeking communion with a transcendent being.

FEMINIST IDENTIFICATION VS. SPIRITUAL WAITING IN *LA NUIT DE LA LÉZARDE*

In recent criticism, the concept of deterritorialization seeks to decenter social and cultural ideas about gender and race by finding within texts and language itself the means to decouple the subject from the stickiness of culture which makes it adhere to larger and more complex binary systems of meaning.[8] In deterritorialization, individuals can only achieve true identity through a definitive break with their past, usually brought about by engaging in conflict with an opposing political or social force.[9] In order to achieve true emancipation, the Muslim woman must set herself on a journey away from her origins, and create her new role in confrontation with stereotypes and traditional roles. In writing about Mokeddem's *L'Interdite,* Valerie Orlando notes that the author uses the contemporary political situation in Algeria to form the background of the protagonist's emerging identity: "It is only after confronting the forces around her that Sultana finally attains a certain purity of identity, resulting from a process of deterritorialization that enriches and liberates her."[10] Orlando argues that the relationship between identity and the social sphere in *L'Interdite* is less characterized by a definitive rupture with the past than by a subject who belongs to and partakes of two traditions at the same time. As such, the deterritorialized subject is neither traditional nor feminist, but inhabits the tension between competing ideologies: "Mokeddem tells not only the story of a woman fleeing her past, but rather the story of a woman caught between two traditions, two nations. Sultana exemplifies the woman who lives in two spheres in a world that is neither determined nor completed; it is a new space yet to be discovered."[11] The deterritorialized subject offers a new mode of political action that is neither feminist nor

Islamist based. Where feminist subject positions are defined by a process of identification with fixed discourses, either by opposition or alignment, the deterritorialized subject is fluid and intersects with dominant discourses at different points in time while remaining in a state of transformation. The literary image of the woman whose identity stems from the grafting in of two cultures but who is not defined by either one is reflected in society by the way women are heard in the debate over women's inequality in Algeria. In the debate over the Family Code, for example, women have been able to use the gap between their semi-status in the home and their voice in public politics to emerge at various historical moments as presenting a valid petition without ever being identified with any one discourse in particular.[12] As we will now see, the notion of deterritorialization clearly emerges in Mokeddem's *La Nuit de la lézarde*, where the author creates for her protagonist a new space from which to grapple with the essential questions of identity and fulfillment.

In *La Nuit de la lézarde*, the ksar (a fortified village in the desert made almost entirely of sand) serves as the transitional space between the nomadic origins of the main character and her emerging identity as a woman alone. After her husband rejects her because she has not borne him any children, Nour sets out on a journey across the desert and settles in the abandoned ksar, so that she will not have to answer any more questions about her situation. There, she creates a semi-fictitious life with a blind man, Sassi, telling him she has a lover who is temporarily away on a military mission in order to protect his family, but is expected back any day. Free from the burden of family life, she is able to reflect objectively on her past domestic role and on the possibilities offered by her present position: "Durant des années, Nour s'était appliquée à se forger à un destin d'épouse pour oublier des blessures, occulter des peurs. Sans y parvenir complètement. Pourquoi persisterait-elle dans ce rôle qui, pour le moins, l'ennuyait? Elle n'avait même plus de parents pour l'y contraindre. A quoi aspirait-elle réellement? Elle aurait été bien en peine de le dire"[13] ["For years, Nour had tried to create the calling of a wife for herself in order to forget her wounds, to hide her fears, without really succeeding. Why did she continue in this role that bored her at best? She did not even have any relatives to tie her down. But what did she really want? She would have been hard-pressed to say"]. Her discomfort with her previous role is equaled by her discomfort with her new identity as a "femme libre" ["free woman"], because her deepest aspirations seem to elude her. She returns the stares of the villagers with the gaze of a stranger, and begins to identify with her role as a dissident. Nour creates a domestic life based on her friendship with Sassi and love for certain children of the ksar that is parallel to family life, but completely estranged from it: "Libre, donc seule face aux autres, même lorsqu'elle était parmi eux. Au contact de ces familles, Nour avait mesuré l'ampleur de sa solitude, une solitude sans cesse aiguisée par l'exubérance des affections et les manifestations inhérentes à la vie des familles" (45) ["Free, and therefore alone in relation to others, even when she was among them. When she met these families, Nour felt the extent of her solitude, which was always made sharper by the exuberant affections and actions of family life"].

Nour's exile from her past propels her along two opposite courses: one that leads out toward the desert, "le reg," the other that is defined by her everyday life in the ksar. The impulse outward is frequently registered in the novel through Nour's gaze, which figures prominently in the way Nour is presented to the reader. Mokeddem reverses the gender dynamic of the male gaze on the female subject in the visual rhetoric that she uses to mark Nour's first appearance. Instead of being the object that is seen, she is the subject who sees, and gradually brings the landscape into focus. Nour's gaze is marked by episodes of daydreaming that constitute not a single, definitive break from her past, but a continuous irruption of her spiritual longing into the continuum of domestic activities she shares with Sassi. The first view of Nour is atop a ruined building looking out over a desolate landscape: "Perchée sur une terrasse comme une vigie guettant une apparition, Nour observe les environs. N'étaient deux taches vives, le safran de sa robe et l'indigo du turban emmêlé à ses nattes, sa silhouette se confondrait avec l'ocre des murs" (12) ["Perched on a roof like a sentry watching for a phantom, Nour takes in her surroundings. If it weren't for two bright patches, the saffron of her robe and the indigo of the turban mixed in with her plaits, her silhouette would blend in with the ochre of the walls"]. Her gaze doubles back on itself, so that she sees herself abstractly, as she would appear on the horizon through a camera lens, or on a canvas, as two dabs of color against the deep brown of the ruin's walls.

Nour's gaze in the novel defines the landscape as it sweeps across the wasteland between the ksar and the village looking for someone. But instead of looking toward the populated village, she turns her face toward the emptiness of the desert, having punctured a hole in the courtyard wall surrounding her house in an attempt to look out on its vastness (19). Her waiting causes immediate conflict with Sassi, not only because she claims to be waiting for another man, but because the one she is waiting for is more phantom than human. Perceiving Nour has once again directed her eyes to the horizon, Sassi exclaims, "Les fantômes ne peuvent hanter que le voisinage des vivants. Qu'attends-tu de ce monde de sable et de pierre? C'est du village qu'il arrivera, ton amoureux, quand il sera rentré. Tu vas finir par devenir dingue avec cette histoire" (87) ["Ghosts can only haunt the dwelling place of the living. What are you expecting from this sand and rock? When he comes home, your lover will come from the village. You are going to drive yourself crazy with this story"].

Day after day, Nour maintains the pretense that she is waiting for her lover to return from the war, and in doing so delays any decision she might otherwise have to make in regard to Sassi. The story that originally served the purpose of protecting her from male violence, however, becomes a surreal experience of waiting. She experiences night after night the same apocalyptic dream followed by a reassuring presence: "—Un rêve éveillé. J'avais encore dans les oreilles les échos de métal cassé et de sable en crue d'orage, quand mon aimé a poussé la porte et refermé ses bras sur moi. J'ai enfoui mon visage dans son cou et aussitôt me suis endormie" (84) ["A waking dream. The sound of broken metal and of sand in the fury of the storm was still echoing in my ears, when my beloved opened the door and put his arms around me. I buried my head in his neck and immediately fell asleep"]. The emotions of Nour's dream, in which she experiences first the horrors of war and then the reassuring presence of the beloved, are reflected in the compassion she feels for the orphan children of the ksar. It is as she is thinking about the children's experiences of war, and in turn her love for them, that her gaze is drawn back to the horizon: "Nour retourne les yeux vers l'horizon. Elle le scrute un moment et murmure: 'Je t'aime,' sur un ton de prière. Est-ce cette ardeur qui l'ébranle ainsi?" (79) ["Nour turns her eyes back to the horizon. She stares at it for a moment and murmurs, 'I love you,' in a prayerful way. Is it this passion that shakes her up like that?"]. The simple phrase, "je t'aime," encompasses here two different dimensions of Nour's desire; it expresses the maternal tenderness she feels for the unloved child, Alilou, and at the same time it is directed toward the horizon and the absent lover, whose identity begins to take on a metaphysical dimension. In speaking her love for Alilou, she expresses her love for the community stricken by violence, but that love is deflected to the horizon that receives her love as a petition. In response to Sassi's question as to whether she loves the one for whom she is waiting, Nour answers in terms of deliverance from fear, echoing the dream's description of deliverance from war: "Sans lui, je ne serais pas restée dans un ksar désert. Mais j'aurais continué à transporter le désert en moi. Sans lui, la nuit aurait fini par éteindre mes jours" (67) ["Without him, I would not have stayed in a deserted ksar. But I would have continued to carry the desert in me. Without him, night would have ended up extinguishing my days."]. As part of the pretense she uses to conceal the fact that she is a woman alone, Nour asks Sassi to join her in waiting for her lover, and not just to wait, but to join her in adopting a specific mental posture of hope: "Je veux dire attendre pour de bon comme quelqu'un qui te serait cher" (55) ["I mean really wait, as if it were someone who was dear to you"].

Nour's act of waiting serves as a means of deterritorializing her everyday domestic life and creating a new identity. Nour must deterritorialize domestic life in order to regain its spiritual value, or reterritorialize it as a source of spiritual strength. In a neutral space, domestic life such as that which takes place in the garden and in the doorways of Nour's home functions as an "espace de métissage," that is, an in-between space, or literally, a place where something is grafted onto something else, thereby creating a new area of growth. But the spirituality represented by Nour's engagement with Sassi in gardening, cooking, and even in her putative mothering role to the village children stands in contrast to the transcendent identity embodied in Nour's waiting, so that the two come into irresolvable conflict. Instead of simply opening up a space for female resistance to predetermined domestic roles, Nour's intentional act of waiting opens up a space for her to realize her identity through a relationship with a transcendent presence who loves her absolutely. The story she tells to herself and Sassi—that there is someone, rather than something, to wait for—invites the Absolute to come into both of their lives and offers Nour the possibility of truly decoupling herself from the world's logic and more tangible, material responses to need.

A POETICS OF DOMESTIC SPACE

For Muslim believers, the physical order and beauty of the spaces of domestic life are an outward expression of perfection in one's life with God. Religious perfection extends from God's house of which heaven is the roof, to the family life of the Prophet, his wives, and concubines, to the orderly arrangement of spaces for family, worship, and social interactions in the household of every believer. In communities peripheral to mainstream Islam, such as Bedouin communities, the house and its architecture represent the transition from a nomadic to a sedentary lifestyle. For Mokeddem, who herself was only one generation removed from Bedouin culture, the living areas of the ksar are domestic spaces that are representative of the nomadic lifestyle. Descriptions of the outer architecture of the abandoned ksar as well as its interior living spaces contribute to the creation of domestic backdrops against which Nour develops her identity. Living space and desert space flow into and out of the same image, erasing the boundary between desert and hearth.

Expelled from her home by her husband for her failure to have children, Nour moves from house to house, finally settling in a ksar that everyone else is leaving because of sectarian violence. The solitary life she establishes for herself separates her from her former life, although she opens her heart to Alilou and his friends, and to Dounia, a teenage girl in the ksar who tries to escape from her stifling life through her books. In her exile from family, Nour reassembles a household from the rubble of families destroyed by violence. She inhabits the house of a man who hanged himself, a place where her only companion is a lizard named Smicha. There she lives as a "femme libre," taking anonymous men into her bed, but at the same time adopting a routine of daily tasks that allow her to interact marginally with the life of the village.

Both the rocky landscape of the "reg" and the domestic landscape of the abandoned ksar are traced by trajectories of desire.[14] Carved out by the wind and the heat, the abandoned ksar itself is shaped by Nour's gaze as she watches the sun set over its walls. Similarly, the composition of Nour's household is determined not by law or social custom, but by her emotional life: her fantasies, her joy, and her grief. The everyday activities of life (gardening, marketing, house painting, drawing water) are also subject to Nour's desire, as well as to economic necessity. The gardening activity itself is an endless process of reclaiming space that is on the verge of ceasing to exist, or at least becoming something else, because of the ongoing problem of being covered with sand. Nour and Sassi's garden plot, situated at the edge of the ksar where it is most exposed to the desert, requires constant work to free it from sand. The unending sand removal or "désensablement" is mirrored in the give-and-take of Nour and Sassi's conversations; as they work the garden, each is also engaged in the continuous work of revealing the other's personality:

> Nour et Sassi ne cessent de se comparer, de se conter, de se contrer. A l'évidence, c'est leur façon d'apprivoiser leur singularité et leurs tourments. Et s'ils se reconnaissent différents à bien des égards, plusieurs traits de caractère les réunissent: la même application aux taches les plus banales du quotidien, la même aptitude, presque juvénile, à transposer le fastidieux en ludique, à tromper la tristesse. (85)
>
> [Nour and Sassi never stop comparing each other's lives, telling stories, contradicting each other. From all appearances it is their way of soothing their anxieties and becoming accustomed to each other's peculiarities. And if they prove different in many ways, a number of character traits unite them: the same dedication to the most tedious everyday tasks and the same childlike tendency to make fun of drudgery as a way of hiding sadness.]

The everyday work of sand removal, even though it seems Sisyphean, creates, in fact, a mental framework for transformation, in which Nour and Sassi learn to overcome hardship. Most of the work they do together consists of traditional forms of women's work in Islam, but here Mokeddem decenters them by having Sassi, Nour's blind companion, engaged in them as well. The spaces of their domestic life are revealed both in the surrounding physical structures of the ksar itself and in the wandering ellipses inscribed in the desert by Sassi's cane as he goes about his daily tasks. Whether or not this is a portrait of an idealized marriage or a romantic friendship, Mokeddem is careful to resist putting either Nour or Sassi into traditional "husband-wife-lover" roles, creating merely a transformative space for them to be together.

Three different domestic settings stage the interactions of Nour with Sassi, as well as providing her own places of being and becoming: the garden, which we have just examined; the "maison du pendu" ["house of the hanged man"]; and the marketplace. The "maison du pendu" offers her shelter from the wind and heat, as well as the spirit presence of its former owner, who interacts with her in some ways like a lover, and in some ways like a brother. In the "maison du pendu," Nour begins to shape her own reality in a domestic context, while dream and reality again begin to blend into one another. She has a dream which, although very different in style from the dream of rescue, also presents a mystical lover and a story of redemption, except that in this case, it is Nour who redeems the lover with her love: "Je le voyais pendu à la poutre centrale. Ses yeux révulsés se tournaient lentement et me fixaient. La langue pendante, il essayait de me dire quelque chose que je ne parvenais pas à comprendre. Je me levais. Je grimpais sur ma petite table et le détachais. Ensuite, je le portais, l'installais dans mon lit, le caressais pour le réanimer" (66) ["I saw him hanging from the main beam. His eyes that were rolled back in his head slowly turned to look at me. With his tongue hanging out, he tried to tell me something that I couldn't understand. I got up. I scrambled up on my little table and let him down. Then, I carried him to my bed and caressed him to revive him"]. In this passage, Nour confronts the horrors of war through a very personalized image. The hanged man's eyes fix their gaze on Nour, not in a dominant way, but in an attempt to communicate suffering. She carries the dead man to her bed and begins to make love to him, which revives him. The dream and the hanged man's house itself together form a space in which Nour invests her past domestic role with a new identity yet to be defined. Imitating the wife's role, she spends her days "beautifying his house" and distracting him with gossip from the town, even bringing in an old recording of Andalusian hymns so that the rapturous voices can "distract him from his sad fate" (66).

Mokeddem uses the idea of decadence (both moral and material) to draw a parallel between the wreckage of Nour's past family life, and the political violence that, although still remote from the ksar, encroaches on it with increasing vehemence. The decrepit condition of her environment reflects the state of Nour's life. Her spartan kitchen in particular becomes a place of protest, a place of contrast to the society outside:

> La cuisine est encore plus monastique. Quelques assiettes, des couverts, des pots à épices sont disposés sur une étagère suspendue au mur. Les surmonte un poste transistor rafistolé au sparadrap. Un jour, accablée par les morts égrenées sur les ondes, Nour l'avait laissé tomber pour aussitôt le reprendre, le recoller, s'assurer qu'il fonctionnait encore. (119)
>
> [The kitchen is even more monastic. Some plates, table settings, some spice containers are arranged on a shelf hanging from the wall. On top of this the transistor pole is affixed with tape. One day, overcome by the news of the dead that it kept churning out, Nour let the whole thing collapse, only to pick it up, retape it and make sure that it was working again.]

The portrait of her much-loved Dounia (her only possession besides the utilitarian mattresses in her great room), is described as enthroned upon a television that has not worked for a long time (118). Unlike the dream of the hanged man in which Nour's love and grief are unresolved, when she allows the radio transistor pole to collapse, it is a deliberate expression of grief at the civil unrest that surrounds her, although she quickly returns it to working order.

BECOMING MINOR AND MYSTICAL DISCOURSE: HOUSEHOLD STORIES AND THE POLITICS OF PURITY

According to Gilles Deleuze and Félix Guattari, fragmented language is the defining mark of the deterritorialized subject. The deterritorialized subject may be represented through the poetic use of an existing language, or by virtue of its position in relation to an oppressed people. When a language that once belonged to a nation or culture is deterritorialized, it can be said to "become minor." A national language that becomes minor is a language that bears the marks of national trauma such as colonization or war. Deterritorialized language should "become minor," and a deterritorialized subject should know how to make it "become minor," by using language in an intentionally fractured way so as to create dissonance in the dominant discourse. Muslim Francophone writers have abundantly made the case that French has become a minor language for Algerians,[15] making the point that the very fact that one writes in French marks a novelist as "anti-Islamic" and puts the writer at risk.[16] For Francophone writers living in exile, French is effectively a language of "becoming minor" in that it embodies the indeterminate discourse of the subject who embraces two countries and two traditions.

Mokeddem uses household tales of life in the ksar to reveal the connections between domestic life and religious / political rhetoric. While they do not directly address Islamist rhetoric, they expose attitudes of superstition and economic backwardness that are voiced by male characters in positions of power and influence in the ksar, and in particular by two local blowhards named l'Explication and Oualou. The language used to recount these tales could be called "minor" because, although it deals with the religious notion of purity, it stands apart from traditional modes of discourse, undermining society, and in particular male perceptions, through irony and rather dark humor.

Three tales about life in the ksar—the story of the well of El Ghazi, the story of the flies, and the story of the mail-order brides—identify negative social attitudes and influences that contribute to conflict in everyday life and to the disparagement of women. Each one of the tales focuses in on a different configuration of the idea of purity. Each story features a powerful figure who voices the purity theme followed by a secondary character or narrative that undermines it. In the tales, women's voices use laughter, mockery, and imagery to create dissonance in the dominant rhetoric of purity.

The story of El Ghazi exemplifies such attitudes in a tale that tells what happens when the ksar's wells go dry, thus offering one explanation for the ksar's abandonment. When the wells at El Ghazi become dry, the women begin to dispute and fight over the little water that is left (represented by the clatter and clash of water buckets in the dry well). A well driller is sent for, but he quickly becomes discouraged at the criticisms of the villagers, and gives up his task in frustration. The people then turn to the man named L'Explication for advice. L'Explication plays on village superstitions by suggesting that the man for whom the well is named (El Ghazi) must be offended because of an impurity. While the opposition between purity and pollution in Islam does not uniquely define women as the source of conflict, the association of women with impurity is a prominent feature of Islamic commentary traditions.[17] Through the character of L'Explication, Mokeddem subtly mocks cultural and theological debate in Islam about purity, and suggests that it is the debate itself that contributed to the destruction of the ksar. The preposterous nature of L'Explication's argument about impurity, however, does not keep his rhetoric from having the desired effect of reinforcing his audience's deeply held prejudice and superstition and pushing them to religious action: "Il n'empêche que le jour même, les habitants se sont hâtés de sacrifier un mouton et d'adonner des versets du Coran pour sanctifier El Ghazi et se purifier d'hypothétiques fautes ou du mauvais œil. On ne sait jamais" (81) ["This did not prevent the inhabitants from rushing to sacrifice a lamb that very day and saying extra prayers from the Qu'ran to sanctify El-Ghazi and to purify themselves from any hypothetical faults or the evil eye—after all, one never knows"].

The next two tales elaborate on the idea of purity and pollution directly as it relates to the treatment of women in the context of civil violence. They falsify the biased rhetoric offered by L'Explication by directly engaging the experiences of women and children with violence. The first tale, told by

Kamel, a friend of Alilou, recounts the fabulated story about how a group of female flies of many nationalities are attacked while meeting in Algiers. He mockingly describes how an Algerian fly resists her assailants and outlasts all her sisters even as she is being assaulted with a canister of insecticide: "Tu ne vois pas la bébête leur faire la danse du ventre au milieu du nuage? Ma parole! comme si elle respirait du kif. Elle soulève une aile, puis l'autre, puis la queue et continue son chiqué: 'Encore un peu ici, et là, sous mes aisselles, et entre mes cuisses, s'il vous plaît.' Les ninjas en perdent leur cagoule et s'arrêtent net" (97) ["Do you see that little one doing the belly dance in the middle of the cloud? My word! Like she was on kif (hash). She lifts one wing, then the other, then her tail and continues to chant: 'A little more here, and there, under my arms, and between my legs, if you please.' The ninjas lose their nerve and stop cold"]. Although the main import of this story is to show the toughness of Algerians, the tale is strongly tinged with suggestive wordplay and represents women as flies—albeit tough, upper-class flies who know how to use comical, subversive tactics to overcome attack. The woman parodied as a fly in the tale vitiates the soldiers' power by asserting her own words. She reverses the soldiers' expectations by acting out ridiculous words and gestures, thereby further fragmenting the opposition and the notions they hold to be true. Both her language, in its explicit sexuality, and the young narrator's language, in its juvenile attempt to impress, are made minor by the subjects' experience with civil violence (being a victim of assault and an orphan, respectively). Instead of purity versus pollution, the woman's voice in Kamel's story allows her to survive her assault by asserting pollution versus pollution, thus breaking down the binary categories and provoking laughter, at least among the story's child audience.

The third tale, the story of the mail-order bride, is the one that most directly engages cultural ideas about purity with secular feminist rhetoric. As Sassi and Nour are reflecting on the former residents of the ksar, he tells how Nour's protégée, Dounia, tricked a man named Omar into believing that a collection of pornographic tattoos in a tabloid was actually a catalogue offering "brides of the martyrs" in polygamous marriage: "Ce sont les femmes des martyrs de la guerre. Le gouvernement les expose ici pour que les hommes puissent en choisir et les commander. Il dit que dans ce cas, la polygamie est un devoir national!" (134) ["They are the widows of war martyrs. The government shows them here so that men can choose and order them. It says that in this case, polygamy is a national duty!"]. The tale uses humor to expose some of the most brutally misogynist statements about women at the heart of Islamist thinking, but also shows the female narrator (Dounia) using verbal cleverness to disarm brutality by turning it into a practical joke.

Nour's experience of transcendent waiting is also reflected in her use of language. As Nour pushes away from the world and deeper into a state of waiting, her language becomes more and more minor, using elements of colloquial Arab-French and elements of nonsense. She does not so much use language to communicate as to resist the violence that surrounds her. Nour's language is a kind of obscene inversion of holy language. She is found in the garden, cultivating beans and laughing: "Nour avait eu un rire plein de dérision et s'était exclamée: 'Jnane fou!' Ainsi prononce-t-elle 'je m'en fous.' Nour adore les fèves bien tendres, cuisinées avec leur peau. Dans son jardin, près du puits, elle les cultive avec un soin particulier. 'Jnane fou!' Il y va de la vie comme de la cuisine. Il y a ceux qui mangent par nécessité et ceux qui dégustent" (44) ["Nour had let out a derisive laugh and cried, 'Jnane fou!' her way of saying, 'je m'en fous.' Nour loves young and tender beans cooked in the pod. She grows them in her garden, next to the wells, with particular care. 'Jnane fou!' Life is like cooking. There are those who eat and those who really taste"]. Although standing in contrast to her prayer, "je t'aime," the vulgar interjection, "j'nane fou!" ("I don't care"), nevertheless has the same effect of "making minor" by disrupting the discursive function of language. While its immediate referent is the pain of her former marriage, it embodies her anger against the violence she has personally experienced and against the civil violence around her.

In her discussion of mysticism and women authors, Karma Lochrie has made the point that the language of mysticism may have political force when it embodies the subject's desire. Mystical discourse is more immediate and is a closer approximation of the embodiment of female voice than can be achieved by women through conventional religious texts or orthodox religion. Therefore in the context of women's political or religious oppression, mystical discourse can serve as a means of circumventing or cutting through the dominant religious or social discourse. In her conversations with Sassi, Nour uses the surreal image of snow in the desert to denote her experience with the transcendent, but it is also a means of blocking Sassi's attempts to counter or prevail over her experience. Nour's imagery of cat paws making tracks on a snowy layer of bean blossoms covering the garden is an evocation of transcendent beauty that has no other purpose than to transcend reality, in accordance with Nour's desire: "Jnane fou! La réalité du monde ne m'intéresse pas. Ce qui m'importe, c'est ce que j'en fais, comment je la vois" (146) ["I couldn't care less! The reality of the world does not interest me. What matters to me is what I do with it, how I see it."]

Later, as Nour is dying in the local hospital, her language becomes more fragmented, or disjoined from reality, embodying the breakdown of her body and the communion of her self with the transcendent, albeit a painfully absent transcendent being. When Nour is on her death bed, Sassi asks her to describe the lover she is waiting for, and she describes him in terms of the dissolution and fragmentation of her own parched body, thirsting for her lover, disintegrating in its desire for the unattainable presence of the Other:

—Tu sais ce que j'ai envie de raconter?
Dis!
—Les gerçures de mes mains par le manque de sa peau. La prison des immensités qu'il ne franchit pas.
—Dis, dis encore!
—Mes rires qui s'étranglent loin de sa voix. Le fiel de ma bouche sans ses lèvres. Mon corps entier morcelé en une multitude avide. Désert dans le désert. Dés
hérence éclatée en pierres, en sables, en poussières. Les mirages de l'attente qui me brulent les yeux au tréfonds. Et maintenant, le sceau de la mort à la source du sang. (204)

[—Do you know what I feel like saying?
Say!
—The cracking of my palms from the lack of his skin. The prison of infinite space he does not cross over.
—Say, say more!
—My stifled laughter far from his voice. The bitter taste in my mouth without his lips. My whole body broken into a hungry multitude. Desert inside of a desert. Disinheritance exploded into rocks, into sand, into dust. Mirages of waiting that burn my eyes to their very depths. And now, the seal of death at the spring of blood.]

The image of violent dismemberment in this passage is evocative of the violence experienced by women that forms the core of feminist writing from Algeria. The idea of a woman broken in pieces ("mon corps entier morcelé") certainly suggests that violence, but also bears witness to a love or passionate desire that transcends the violence, underscoring Nour's unquenchable spiritual longing. In the absence of inner fulfillment, she undergoes, in fact, a "spiritual dismemberment" that represents the complete deterritorialization of herself.

INFINITE WAITING

It is while she is in the hospital that Nour begins to question the idea of waiting for her lover to return, although she obviously comes back to this stance in the end, despite the lack of response to her waiting: "Maintenant, je pense que j'aurais dû partir vraiment, quitter la région . . . L'attente d'un absent peut être une joie, au pire une impatience. L'attente dans le vide n'est qu'une hallucination qui finit par te saccager le corps et l'esprit. Vois où ça m'a menée" (202) ["Now, I think that I should have really gone, left the region. . . . Waiting for a loved one can be a joy; at worst, a feeling of impatience. But waiting in emptiness is nothing but a hallucination that only finishes by ravaging the body and the spirit. Just look what it's done to me"].

The hospital becomes the setting for a pointed, if somewhat forced debate on the relative value of women's emancipation into full political participation at the price of family life, with the discourse centering on social action and prescribed religion. The character of Doctor Zeïneb represents the point of view of secular feminists disappointed with twenty years of waiting for equal representation in Algerian society. Although the text does not make any concrete references to the Algerian Family Code, the legalistic spirit of its Sharia underpinnings is implicitly attacked in Doctor Zeïneb's diatribe about women's solitude, as she recounts a dialogue that enraged her: "Ce qui devrait être péché, c'est qu'à quarante ans je dorme seule, sans homme, sans amour . . . et selon toi, je n'ai même pas le droit d'avoir des fleurs imprimées sur mes draps?" (186) ["What should be a sin is that at forty years old I sleep alone, without a man and without love . . . and according to you, I don't even have the right to have printed flowers on my sheets?"]. The problem, argues the doctor, is the turgidity of rhetorics:

> On parlait, tout à l'heure, de la boursouflure des mots. Elle ne fait que traduire celle des dogmes auxquels on a toujours sacrifié les doutes et l'intelligence. On nous a tellement cuit et recuit l'identité qu'on nous a disloqués. Solidarité dessoudée. Même la tradition y a laissé le burnous. On est passé sans transition de la vie tribale à des solitudes brisées. . . . Que des femmes, aussi différentes de tempérament, de conviction comme de classe sociale, se retrouvent à vivre seules! (186–87)

> [We were speaking, just now, about verbal pompousness; it does nothing but transpose the pompousness of dogmas to which we have always sacrificed our doubts and our intelligence. Our identity has been cooked and recooked until we are all dislocated, our solidarity broken apart. Even tradition has left its burnous (mantel) behind. We have passed without transition from tribal life to broken solitude. . . . How many women of different temperament, conviction, and social class find themselves living alone!]

The doctor's contention in this passage is that all feminist rhetoric has done is to increase women's isolation. She lays the blame for women's isolation on both secular and religious rhetoric for simply transposing the same old cultural oppressions into another form, leaving the underlying social problems untouched. Women have moved without education and without preparation from a traditional and even tribal way of life into the modern era.

In the end, Nour leaves the hospital without telling anyone, assisted by the three young boys of whom she is so fond. After making her way back to the ksar with them, she manages to offer them tea at Sassi's, while discussing the devaluation of language under fundamentalist rule. Before leaving the village for the ksar, however, she purchases a copy of Simone de Beauvoir's *Second Sex* for Dounia, when she notices it in a street bazaar, showing her desire to see the young woman arrive at her true identity by finding personal meaning and freedom. Nour herself has sought personal meaning within a community, while at the same time remaining independent from it, providing, perhaps, a kind of role model for her "spiritual" daughter. Earlier on in the narrative, Sassi has a significant dream of Nour, in which she appears to him transfigured, emerging from the water in a way suggestive either of baptism (as a sign of death and personal renewal) or entry into a kind of paradise:

> Soudain, il voit Nour, dans un lac aux berges ouatées de brun, d'or et de vert, un décor rappelant la fresque peinte sur ses murs. . . . Elle s'élance vers lui et s'écrie: "C'est ça que j'attendais, l'aube des beaux jours. Enfin nous avons traversé la nuit." Au son de sa voix, des colombes s'envolent et l'auréolent de leurs ailes d'argent. Elle fend le lac à grandes enjambées. L'eau perle sur sa peau et goutte de ses seins, de ses mains, de ses cheveux dénoués. (175)
>
> [All of a sudden he sees Nour, in a lake with fleecy shores of brown, gold, and green, a pattern reminiscent of the fresco painted on her walls. . . . She suddenly bursts toward him and cries out, "This is what I was waiting for, the dawn of beautiful days. Finally we made it through the night." At the sound of her voice, doves take flight and surround her with their silvery wings. She crosses the lake with great strides. The water makes pearls on her skin and drips from her breasts, her hands, her unbraided hair.]

In this passage, Nour appears to Sassi as the completely fulfilled beloved to the lover. Striding toward him through a lake, in contrast to the desert she has known, she is drenched in water that represents both her sensual fulfillment and her spiritual transformation. She speaks words that resonate as both Judeo-Christian and Islamic images of divine love, echoing the biblical Song of Songs. Her dreams are finally realized in the dream of Sassi, her blind companion, whose blindness may have allowed him to see her in her way that others could not. It is in his dream, in fact, that she finds fulfillment, passing from the dark of night into the light of dawn. It is Sassi, too, who closes her eyes in the end, moments after her passing in the garden of the ksar, and just after her gaze has scanned the horizon, reaching out to that elusive transcendent being she has sought for throughout the novel.

CONCLUSION

Mokeddem represents domestic life as a type of spiritual discipline that brings the subject through a purification of her identity. By stripping domestic life of the dominant discourses of both Islamism and feminism, it becomes a transformative space in which a new self is taking shape. The tension between Nour's "je t'aime" for the community stricken by violence and her openness to the transcendent opens up a mental space in which the national trauma can be confronted dispassionately, yet in a deeply personal manner. Nour's seeming rejection of solitude and waiting in a void point to the limitations of the deconstructed or deterritorialized subject. Without love, the deterritorialized subject, although disengaged from its origins, will nevertheless retain within itself a magnetic kernel of those origins, inevitably pulling it back into the cycle of trauma and symbolization, a cycle that only perpetuates the cultural system of binaries (i.e., feminism vs. Islamism; Islam vs. Islamism). Instead of waiting "in emptiness" for her country to achieve self-realization, Mokeddem recommends waiting with hope, "pour de bon," and calls on a different process of transformation, that is, realizing full personhood through a Transcendent Person. Nour's waiting, rather than separating her from her origins and inner self, brings her into direct contact with them, but in a transcendent form. At the same time, the very thought of the civil violence taking place elsewhere ultimately kills her, as her illness shows. In conclusion, Nour deterritorializes her domestic life by waiting, by refusing either to symbolize it or to reconcile herself to the trauma of her experience, insisting instead on loving the object of her undefined longing, by deliberately extending herself sacrificially into its consuming presence, even if this presence is portrayed as an absence, and an unknown lover still to be encountered.

NOTES

1. As seen, for example, in George Sand's *Indiana*, examined in the sixth chapter in this book.
2. Maryam Poya, *Women, Work, and Islamism: Ideology and Resistance in Iran* (London: Zed Books, 1999), 54–55.
3. An anonymous narrative recounted in a newsletter of a Non-Governmental Organization working in North Africa. The details of the publication are withheld for reasons of security at the NGO's request.
4. On the other hand, in *The Caged Virgin*, trans. Jane Brown (New York: The Free Press, 2006), Ayaan Hirsi Ali argues that Islam can be said to operate according to collective or tribal thinking that diminishes the individual in favor of the clan or tribe (56).
5. For the argument that Islam views women as deficient and is therefore able to rationalize violence toward them, see Patricia Geesey, "Violent Days: Algerian Women Writers and the Civil Crisis," *International Fiction Review* 27, nos. 1–2 (2000), journals.hil.unb.ca/index.php/IFR/article/view/7658/8715. The concept of purity in Islam covers a vast spectrum of thought, of which gender relations is only one part. For a discussion of purity and deficiency in relation to women's spirituality, see Anne Sofie Roald, *Women in Islam* (London: Routledge, 2001), 131ff.
6. Geesey, "Violent Days"; *Vingt Ans Barakat* (*Twenty Years Is Enough*) is the name given to one of the more prominent feminist movements dedicated to protesting revisions to the Algerian Family Code of 1984 that relied on a religious rather than a secular body to change the law.

7. Geesey, "Violent Days." In this regard, Franck Dalmas perceptively remarks: "Of all Mokeddem's books, this one is the least polemical, denunciatory, or violent; the one that instead uses poetry to defend life and love. Nevertheless, while appearing to appease, *La Nuit de la lèzarde* is also an engaged novel that denounces intolerance and the failings of society toward minorities, the oppressed, and the uprooted" ("Les Multiples visages de la guerre dans *La Nuit de la lézarde* de Malika Mokeddem." *Romance Notes* 45, no. 1 [Fall 2004]: 11).

8. The concept of deterritorialization is derived from the works of Gilles Deleuze and Félix Guattari, most notably *Mille plateaux: Capitalisme et schizophrénie* (Paris: Minuit, 1980). In their view, identity is represented as a series of flights or ruptures from the center, which then trace paths across national and gender boundaries, thus deterritorializing the subject by destroying old subjective categories and creating new subject positions.

9. Valerie Orlando, "Ecriture d'un autre lieu: La Déterritorialisation des nouveaux rôles féminins dans 'L'Interdite,'" in *Malika Mokeddem: Envers et contre tout*, ed. Yolande Aline Helm (Paris: L'Harmattan, 2000), 105.

10. Ibid., 108.

11. Ibid., 112.

12. Irina D. Mihalache, "Le Code de l'infamie: Algerian Women between Secularization and Islam," *Feminist Media Studies* 7, no. 4 (2007): 409.

13. Malika Mokeddem, *La Nuit de la lézarde* (Paris: Grasset, 1998), 41; subsequent references are to this edition and will appear parenthetically in the text by page number.

14. In *La Poétique de l'espace* (Paris: Presses Universitaires de la France, 1957), Gaston Bachelard maintains that physical space is not defined by objective boundaries or natural features but by human desire. He argues that the human subject is continually transforming its space into a symbolic representation as s/he moves through it.

15. See Gilles Deleuze and Félix Guattari, *Kafka: Toward a Minor Literature*, trans. Dana Polan (St. Paul: University of Minnesota Press, 1986), for the theory of minor discourse. In *Autobiographical Voices: Race, Gender, Self-Portraiture* (Ithaca: Cornell University Press, 1989) Françoise Lionnet puts forth the argument that to write in French is itself an act of defiance; see also Geesey's analysis of Djebar's *Oran, langue morte* in "Violent Days."

16. Geesey, "Violent Days."

17. Roald, *Women in Islam*, 126–30.

Bibliography

Abosch, Heinz. *Simone Weil: An Introduction*. Translated by Kimberly A. Kenny. New York: Pennbridge, 1994.
Adler, Laure. *Marguerite Duras*. Paris: Éditions Gallimard, 1998.
Albanese, Ralph Jr. "Aristocratic Ethos and Ideological Codes in *La Princesse de Clèves*." In *An Inimitable Example: The Case for the Princesse de Clèves*, edited by Patrick Henry, 87–103. Washington, DC: Catholic University of America Press, 1992.
Ali, Ayaan Hirsi. *The Caged Virgin*. Translated by Jane Brown. New York: The Free Press, 2006.
Alleins, Madeleine. *Marguerite Duras: Medium du réel*. Lausanne: Editions de L'Age d'Homme, 1984.
Allen, Prudence. *The Concept of Woman: Vol. II: The Early Humanist Reformation, 1250–1500, Part II*. Grand Rapids, MI: William B. Eerdmans, 2002.
Altmann, Barbara K. "Diversity and Coherence in Christine De Pizan's *Dit de Poissy*." *French Forum* 12, no. 3 (1987): 261–71.
Anderson, David. *Simone Weil*. London: S. C. M. Press, 1971.
Armel, Arliette. *Marguerite Duras et l'autobiographie*. Paris: Le Castor Astral, 1990.
Austin, J. L. *How to Do Things with Words*. Edited by J. O. Urmson and Marina Sbisà. Cambridge: Harvard University Press, 1975.
Bachelard, Gaston. *La Poétique de l'Éspace*. Paris: Presses Universitaires de la France, 1957.
Bajomée, Danielle. "Duras et le désir d'éternité." In *Marguerite Duras: Rencontres de Cerisy*, edited by Alain Vircondelet, 249–72. Paris: Écriture, 1994.
Baker, Timothy C. "Praying to an Absent God: The Poetic Revealing of Simone Weil." *Culture Theory and Critique* 47, no. 2 (2006): 133–47.
Bakhtin, M. M. *The Dialogic Imagination: Four Essays*. Edited by Michael Holquist. Translated by Caryl Emerson and Michael Holquist. Austin: University of Texas Press, 1981.
———. *Duras ou la douleur*. Brussels: De Boeck University, 1989.
Balthasar, Hans Urs von. *Love Alone Is Credible*. Translated by D. C. Schindler. 1963. Reprint, San Francisco: Ignatius Press, 2004.
Beasley, Faith E. *Revising Memory: Women's Fiction and Memoirs in Seventeenth-Century France*. New Brunswick: Rutgers University Press, 1990.
Bell, David. *The First Total War*. New York: Houghton Mifflin, 2007.
Benveniste, Emile. *Problèmes de linguistique générale*. Paris: Gallimard, 1966.
Birk, Bonnie. *Christine de Pizan and Biblical Wisdom: A Feminist Theological Point of View*. Milwaukee: Marquette University Press, 2005.
Blot-Labarrère, Christiane. "Dieu, un 'mot' chez Marguerite Duras?" In *Duras, Dieu et l'écrit*, edited by Alain Vircondelet, 177–99. Paris: Éditions du Rocher, 1998.

Boisdeffre, Pierre de. *George Sand à Nohant*. Paris: Christian Pirot, 2000.
Borgomano, Madeleine. *Duras: Une Lecture des fantasmes*. Petit Roeulx, Belgique: Cistre-Essais, 1985.
Boulton, Maureen. "'Nous deffens de feu, . . . de pestilence, de guerres': Christine de Pizan's Religious Works." In *Christine de Pizan: A Casebook*, edited by Barbara K. Altmann and Deborah L. McGrady, 215–58. London: Routledge, 2003.
Bourgeois, René. Introduction to *Le Compagnon du tour de France*, by George Sand, 5–27. Grenoble: Presses de l'Université de Grenoble, 1988.
Bowman, Frank Paul. "1799, 10 October: The Ideologists." In *A New History of French Literature*, edited by Denis Hollier, 596–602. Cambridge: Harvard University Press, 1989.
Bradley, Rita Mary. "Backgrounds of the Title *Speculum* in Medieval Literature." *Speculum* 29 (1954): 100–115.
Briçonnet, Guillaume, and Marguerite d'Angoulême. *Correspondance 1521–1524*. Edited by Christine Martineau, Michel Veissière, and Henry Heller. 2 vols. Geneva: Droz, 1975.
Brown-Grant, Rosalind. *Christine de Pizan and the Moral Defence of Women: Reading beyond Gender*. Cambridge: Cambridge University Press, 1999.
Brownlee, Kevin. "Structures of Authority in Christine de Pizan's *Ditié de Jehanne d'Arc*." In *Discourses of Authority in Medieval and Renaissance Literature*, edited by Kevin Brownlee and Walter Stephens, 131–50. Hanover: University Press of New England for Dartmouth College, 1989.
Bruneau, Marie-Florine. *Women Mystics Confront the Modern World*. Albany: State University of New York Press, 1998.
Cabaud, Jacques. *Simone Weil: A Fellowship in Love*. New York: Channel Press, 1964.
Campbell, John. *Questions of Interpretation in "La Princesse de Clèves."* Amsterdam: Rodopi, 1996.
Carson, Anne. "Decreation: How Women Like Sappho, Marguerite Porete and Simone Weil Tell God." *Common Knowledge* 8, no. 1 (Winter 2002): 188–201.
Chadwick, Harold, ed. *The Best of Fénelon*. Gainesville, FL: Bridge-Logos, 2002.
Charnes, Jean-Antoine, abbé de. *Conversations sur la critique de "La Princesse de Clèves."* 1679. Edited by François Weil et al. Tours: Université de Tours, 1973.
Charrière, Isabelle de. *Caliste: Lettres écrites de Lausanne*. Paris: Editions des Femmes, 1979.
———. *Lettres de Mistress Henley publiées par son amie*. New York: MLA, 1993.
Chastellain, Georges. *Œuvres*. Edited by Kervyn de Lettenhove. 8 vols. Brussels, 1863–1866.
Christophe, Paul. *George Sand et Jésus: une inlassable recherche spirituelle*. Paris: Les Éditions du Cerf, 2003.
Cottin, Madame de. *Claire d'Albe*. Paris: Régine Desforges, 1976.
Craveri, Benedetta. *The Age of Conversation*. Translated by Teresa Waugh. New York: New York Review Books, 2005.
Cullen, Helen. "Simone Weil and Greece's Desire for the Ultimate Bridge to God: The Passion." *Faith and Philosophy* 16, no. 3 (July 1999): 352–67.
Dalmas, Franck. "Les Multiples visages de la guerre dans *La Nuit de la lézarde* de Malika Mokeddem." *Romance Notes* 45, no. 1 (Fall 2004): 11–22.
Danahy, Michael. *The Feminization of the Novel*. Gainesville: University of Florida Press, 1991.
Darnton, Robert. *The Forbidden Best-Sellers of Pre-revolutionary France*. New York: Norton, 1995.
Davis, James Herbert. *Fénelon*. Boston: Twayne, 1979.
Decottignies, Jean. "Les Romans de Madame de Tencin: Fable et fiction." In *La Littérature des lumières en France et en Pologne: Esthétique, terminologie, échanges*. Actes du colloque franco-polonais organisé par l'Université de Wrocław et l'Université de Varsovie en collaboration avec l'Institut de Recherches Littéraires de l'Académie Polonaise des Sciences, 249–64. Wroclaw: Panstwowe Wydawnictwo Naukowe, 1976.
Delacomptée, J.-M. *"La Princesse de Clèves": La Mère et le courtisan*. Paris: Presses Universitaires de France, 1990.
Deleuze, Gilles, and Félix Guattari. *Kafka: Toward a Minor Literature*. Translated by Dana Polan. St. Paul: University of Minnesota Press, 1986.

———. *Mille plateaux: Capitalisme et schizophrénie*. Paris: Minuit, 1980.
Delforge, Frédéric. *La Bible en France et dans la francophonie: Histoire, traduction, diffusion*. Paris, Société biblique française, 1991.
Denes, Dominique. "Marguerite Duras par-delà le bien et le mal." In *Duras, Dieu et l'écrit*, edited by Alain Vircondelet, 201–17. Paris: Éditions du Rocher, 1998.
Doubrovsky, Serge. "*La Princesse de Clèves:* Une Interprétation existentielle." *La Table ronde* 138 (1959): 36–51.
Duras, Marguerite. *L'Amant*. Paris: Editions de Minuit, 1984.
———. *L'Amant de la Chine du Nord*. Paris: Gallimard, 1991.
———. *Dix heures et demie du soir en été*. Paris: Gallimard, 1960.
———. *Écrire*. Paris: Gallimard, 1993.
———. *Moderato cantabile*. Paris: Editions de Minuit, 1958.
———. *Les Petits chevaux de Tarquinia*. Paris: Gallimard, 1953.
———. *Le Ravissement de Lol V. Stein*. Paris: Gallimard, 1964.
———. *Le Vice-consul*. Paris: Gallimard, 1966.
———. *La Vie matérielle*. Paris: Gallimard, 1994.
———. *La Vie tranquille*. Paris: Gallimard, 1944.
Duras, Marguerite, and Michelle Porte. *Les Lieux de Marguerite Duras*. Paris: Editions de Minuit, 1977.
Duras, Marguerite, and Xavière Gauthier. *Les Parleuses*. Paris: Editions de Minuit, 1974.
Erasmus. *The Erasmus Reader*. Edited by Erika Rummel. Toronto: University of Toronto Press, 1990.
Ferguson, Gary. *Mirroring Belief: Marguerite de Navarre's Devotional Poetry*. Edinburgh: Edinburgh University Press, 1992.
Frelick, Nancy M. "Fetishism and Storytelling in *Nouvelle 57* of Marguerite de Navarre's *Heptaméron*." In *Distant Voices Still Heard: Contemporary Readings of French Renaissance Literature*, edited by John O'Brien and Malcolm Quainton, 138–54. Liverpool: Liverpool University Press, 2000.
Gauthier, Ursula. "La Nouvelle quête de Dieu." *Le Nouvel Observateur* 2032 (2003): 12–26.
Geesey, Patricia. "Violent Days: Algerian Women Writers and the Civil Crisis." *International Fiction Review* 27, nos. 1–2 (2000): 48–59. journals.hil.unb.ca/index.php/IFR/article/view/7658/8715.
Genlis, Madame de. *La Duchesse de la Vallière*. Paris: Librairie Fontaine, 1983.
———. *Mathilde*. Paris: Imprimerie de P. Gueffier, 1820.
Giniewski, Paul. *Simone Weil ou la haine de soi*. Paris: Berg International, 1978.
Godechot, Jacques. *Les Revolutions*. Paris: PUF, Nouvelle Clio, 1986.
Godwin-Jones, Robert. *Romantic Vision: The Novels of George Sand*. Birmingham, AL: Summa, 1995.
Gossman, Lionel. "1761, December: What Was Enlightenment?" In *A New History of French Literature*, edited by Denis Hollier, 487–95. Cambridge: Harvard University Press, 1989.
Graham, Ruth. "Women versus Clergy, Women pro Clergy." In *French Women and the Age of Enlightenment*, edited by Samia I. Spencer, 128–40. Bloomington: Indiana University Press, 1984.
Gray, Francine du Plessix. "At Large and at Small: Loving and Hating Simone Weil." *American Scholar* 70, no. 3 (2001): 5–11.
Grossir, Claudine. "Une chapelle en restauration." In *"Le Compagnon du tour de France" de George Sand*," edited by Martine Watrelo and Michèle Hecquet, 143–52. Lille: Presses de l'Université Charles-de-Gaulle—Lille 3, 2009.
Gutting, Gary. *French Philosophy in the Twentieth Century*. Cambridge: Cambridge University Press, 2001.
Guyon, Jeanne Marie Bouvier de la Motte. *Le Moyen court et très facile de faire l'oraison*. Edited by Marie-Louise Gondal. Grenoble: Jerôme Millon, 1995.
———. *A Short and Easy Method of Prayer*. London: Allenson, n.d. [1907].
Haase-Dubosc, Danielle. "La Filiation maternelle et la femme-sujet au 17e siècle: lecture plurielle de *La Princesse de Clèves*." *Romanic Review* 78 (1987): 432–60.
Hamon, Bernard. *George Sand et la politique*. Paris: L'Harmattan, 2001.

———. *George Sand face aux Églises*. Paris: L'Harmattan, 2005.
Hastings, James, and John A. Selbie, eds. *Encyclopedia of Religion and Ethics*. New York: Charles Scribner and Sons, 1932.
Heller, Henry. "Marguerite de Navarre and the Reformers of Meaux." *Bibliothèque d'Humanisme et Renaissance* 33 (1971): 271–310.
Hellman, John. *Simone Weil: An Introduction to Her Thought*. Waterloo, ON: Wilfrid Laurier University Press, 1982.
Henry, Patrick. Introduction to *An Inimitable Example: The Case for the Princesse de Clèves*, edited by Patrick Henry, 1–11. Washington, DC: Catholic University of America Press, 1992.
Hiddleston, Janet. *George Sand: Indiana, Mauprat*. Glasgow: University of Glasgow French and German Publications, 2000.
Holy Bible. Authorized King James Version. Nashville: Thomas Nelson, 1970.
Holy Bible. New International Version. Grand Rapids, MI: Zondervan, 1984.
Jackson, Susan K. "The Novels of Isabelle de Charrière, or, a Woman's Work Is Never Done." *Studies in Eighteenth-Century Culture* 14 (1995): 299–306.
Johnson, Jan. *Madame Guyon*. Minneapolis: Bethany House, 1998.
Jones, Rufus M. "Quietism." *Harvard Theological Review* 10, no. 1 (1917): 1–51.
Kac, M. "Simone Weil ou la conspiration du silence autour d'un langage corrompu." *AMIF* 227, 228 (1974).
Kamuf, Peggy. *Fictions of Feminine Desire: Disclosures of Heloise*. Lincoln: University of Nebraska Press, 1982.
Kay, Sarah. "Courts, Clerks, and Courtly Love." In *The Cambridge Companion to Medieval Romance*, edited by Roberta L. Krueger, 81–96. Cambridge: Cambridge University Press, 2000.
Kearney, Richard. *On Paul Ricœur: The Owl of Minerva*. Aldershot: Ashgate, 2004.
Kempis, Thomas à. *The Imitation of Christ*. Translated by William Benham. London, 1874.
Kennedy, Emmet. "Simone Weil: Secularism and Syncretism." *JHS* 5 (2005): 203–25.
Kenny, Anthony. *An Illustrated Brief History of Western Philosophy*. 2nd ed. Malden, MA: Blackwell, 2006.
Knowles, David. *The Evolution of Medieval Thought*. 2nd ed. London: Longman, 1988.
Kuizenga, Donna. "*The Princess of Clèves*: An Inimitable Model." In *An Inimitable Example: The Case for the Princesse de Clèves*, edited by Patrick Henry, 71–83. Washington, DC: Catholic University of America Press, 1992.
Lacoste, Jean-Yves, ed. *Encyclopedia of Christian Theology*. Vol. 2. New York: Routledge, 2005.
Laden, Marie-Paule. "Virtue and Civility in *La Princesse de Clèves*." In *Approaches to Teaching Lafayette's "La Princesse de Clèves."* Edited by Faith E. Beasley and Katharine Ann Jensen, 54–59. New York: Modern Language Association, 1998.
Lafayette, Mme de. *La Princesse de Clèves*. In *Romans et Nouvelles*, 241–395. Paris: Editions Garnier, 1961.
Landy, Francis. "Lamentations." In *The Literary Guide to the Bible*, edited by Robert Alter and Frank Kermode, 329–34. Cambridge: The Belknap Press of Harvard University Press, 1987.
Lanser, Susan S. "Courting Death: Roman, Romantisme, and Mistress Henley's Narrative Practices." *Eighteenth-Century Life* 13, no. 1 (1989): 49–59.
Laugaa, Maurice. *Lectures de Mme de Lafayette*. Paris: Armand Colin, 1971.
Lebellay, Frédérique. *Marguerite Duras ou le poids d'une plume*. Paris: Grasset, 1994.
LeBrun, Jacques. *La Jouissance et le trouble: Recherches sur la littérature chrétienne de l'âge classique*. Genève: Droz, 2004.
Levi, Anthony. "*La Princesse de Clèves* and the Querelle des Anciens et des Modernes." *Journal of European Studies* 10 (1980): 62–70.
Levinas, Emmanuel. "Simone Weil contre la Bible." In *Difficile liberté: Essais sur le judaïsme*, by Emmanuel Levinas, 177–88. Paris: Albin Michel, 1976.
Lewis, C. S. *The Allegory of Love: A Study in Medieval Tradition*. 1936. Reprint, Oxford: Oxford University Press, 1977.

Lionnet, Françoise. *Autobiographical Voices: Race, Gender, Self-Portraiture*. Ithaca: Cornell University Press, 1989.
Lochrie, Karma. *Margery Kempe and Translations of the Flesh*. Philadelphia: University of Pennsylvania Press, 1991.
Lord, F. Townley. *Great Women in Christian History*. London: Cassell and Company, 1940.
Lussy, Florence de, ed. *Simone Weil: Œuvres*. Paris: Quarto Gallimard, 1999.
Marks, Herbert. "The Twelve Prophets." In *The Literary Guide to the Bible*, edited by Robert Alter and Frank Kermode, 207–32. Cambridge: The Belknap Press of Harvard University Press, 1987.
Marot, Jehan. *Les Deux recueils*. Edited by Gérard Defaux and Thierry Mantovani. Genève: Droz, 1999.
Marsak, Leonard M., ed. *French Philosophers from Descartes to Sartre*. Cleveland: The World Philosophy Company, 1961.
Matthews, Eric. *Twentieth Century French Philosophy*. Oxford: Oxford University Press, 1996.
McGuire, Brian Patrick. Introduction to *Jean Gerson: Early Works*. Translated and introduced by Brian Patrick McGuire, 1–74. New York: Paulist Press, 1998.
Micciollo, Henri. "*Moderato cantabile*" *de Marguerite Duras*. Paris: Hachette, 1979.
Middlebrook, Leah "'Tout mon office': Body Politics and Family Dynamics in the verse épîtres of Marguerite de Navarre." *Renaissance Quarterly* 54, no. 4 (2001): 1108–41.
Mihalache, Irina D. "Le Code de l'infamie: Algerian Women between Secularization and Islam." *Feminist Media Studies* 7, no. 4 (2007): 397–411.
Miller, Nancy K. "1735: The Gender of the Memoir-Novel." In *A New History of French Literature*, edited by Denis Hollier, 436–42. Cambridge: Harvard University Press, 1989.
Mistacco, Vicki. *Les Femmes et la tradition littéraire: Anthologie du Moyen Age à nos jours. Première partie: XII–XVIIIe siècles*. New Haven: Yale University Press, 2006.
Mokeddem, Malika. *L'Interdite*. Paris: Grasset, 1993.
———. *La Nuit de la lézarde*. Paris: Grasset, 1998.
———. *Le Siècle des sauterelles*. Paris: Ramsay, 1992.
Molinos, Michael de. *The Spiritual Guide that Disentangles the Soul and Brings It by the Inward Way to the Getting of Perfect Contemplation and the Rich Treasure of Internal Peace*. Translated from the Italian copy, printed at Venice, 1685. London, 1688. www.adamford.com/molinos/src/s-guide.pdf.
Moore, Edward. "Origen of Alexandria (185–254 C.E.)." In *Internet Encyclopedia of Philosophy*, www.iep.utm.edu/origen-of-alexandria/.
Naginski, Isabelle Hoog. *George Sand mythographe*. Clermont-Ferrand: Presses Universitaires de Blaise Pascal, 2007.
Navarre, Marguerite de. *Le Miroir de lame pecheresse. Ouquel elle recognoist ses faultes et pechez. Aussi les graces et benefices a elle faictz par Jesuchrist son espoux*. Edited by Simon Du Bois. Alençon, 1531.
———. *Le Miroir de l'âme pécheresse*. Edited by Joseph L. Allaire. Munich: Fink, 1972.
———. *Le Miroir de l'âme pécheresse*. Edited by Renja Salminen. Helsinki: Academia Scientiarum Fennica, 1979.
The New Oxford Annotated Bible with the Apocrypha. Revised Standard. Edited Herbert G. May and Bruce M. Metzger. New York: Oxford University Press, 1977.
Newbigin, Lesslie. *The Gospel in a Pluralist Society*. Grand Rapids, MI: William B. Eerdmans; Geneva: WCC, 1989.
Newman, Barbara. *God and the Goddesses: Vision, Poetry, and Belief in the Middle Ages*. Philadelphia: University of Pennsylvania Press, 2003.
Oergel, Maike. *The Return of King Arthur and the Nibelungen: National Myth in Nineteenth-Century English and German Literature*. Berlin: Walter de Gruyter, 1998.
Orlando, Valerie. "Ecriture d'un autre lieu: La Déterritorialisation des nouveaux rôles féminins dans *L'Interdite*." In *Malika Mokeddem: Envers et contre tout*, edited by Yolande Aline Helm, 105–15. Paris: L'Harmattan, 2000.
Oxford English Dictionary Online. Oxford University Press, 1989. www.oed.com.
Panichas, George A. Introduction to *The Simone Weil Reader*, edited by George A. Panichas, xvii–xxxiii. New York: David McKay, 1981.

Perrin, J. M., and G. Thibon. *Simone Weil as We Knew Her*. London: Routledge and Kegan Paul, 1953.
Peylet, Gérard. *Le Musée imaginaire de George Sand: l'ouverture et la médiation*. Saint Genouph: Librairie Nizet, 2005.
Phillips, D. Z. Preface to *Discussions of Simone Weil*, by Rush Rhees. Edited by D. Z. Phillips. New York: State University of New York Press, 2000.
Picard, Raymond. *De Racine au Parthénon: Essais sur la littérature et l'art à l'âge classique*. Paris: Gallimard, 1977.
Pinnock, Sarah K. "Mystical Selfhood and Women's Agency: Simone Weil and French Feminist Philosophy." In *The Relevance of the Radical: Simone Weil 100 Years Later*, edited by A. Rebecca Rozelle-Stone and E. Lucian Stone, 205–20. New York: Continuum Books, 2010.
Pizan, Christine de. *The Book of Deeds of Arms and of Chivalry*. Edited by Charity Cannon Willard. Translated by Sumner Willard. University Park: Pennsylvania State University Press, 1999.
———. *The Book of the Body Politic*. Translated and edited by Kate Langdon Forhan. Cambridge: Cambridge University Press, 1994.
———. *The Book of the City of Ladies*. Translated by Earl Jeffrey Richards. New York: Persea, 1982.
———. *Letter of Othea to Hector*. Translated by Jane Chance. 1990. Reprint, Cambridge: D. S. Brewer, 1997.
———. *The Selected Writings of Christine de Pizan*. Edited by Renate Blumenfeld-Kosinski. Translated by Renate Blumenfeld-Kosinski and Kevin Brownlee. New York: Norton, 1997.
———. *The Treasure of the City of Ladies; or The Book of the Three Virtues*. Translated by Sarah Lawson. London: Penguin, 1985.
———. *The Vision of Christine de Pizan*. Translated by Glenda McLeod and Charity Cannon Willard. Woodbridge: D. S. Brewer, 2005.
———. *The Writings of Christine de Pizan*. Edited by Charity Cannon Willard. New York: Persea, 1994.
Pope Innocent XI. "Coelestis Pastor." Apostolic Constitution issued November 20, 1687. Papal Encyclicals Online. www.papalencyclicals.net/Innoc11/i11coel.htm.
Powell, David A. *George Sand*. Boston: Twayne, 1990.
Poya, Maryam. *Women, Work, and Islamism: Ideology and Resistance in Iran*. London: Zed Books, 1999.
Prud'homme, J.-G. *Vingt chefs d'œuvres jugés par les contemporains (du Cid à Madame Bovary)*. Paris: Librairie Stock, 1930.
Pseudo-Dionysius (the Areopagite). *The Divine Names and Mystical Theology*. Translated and edited by John D. Jones. Milwaukee: Marquette University Press, 1980.
Reid, Jonathan A. *King's Sister—Queen of Dissent: Marguerite of Navarre (1492–1549) and Her Evangelical Network*. 2 vols. (Leiden: Brill, 2009).
Rhees, Rush. *Discussions of Simone Weil*. Edited by D. Z. Phillips. New York: State University of New York Press, 2000.
Riccoboni, Marie-Jeanne. *Lettres de Milday Juliette Catesby à Milady Henriette Campley, son amie*. Paris: Desjonquères, 1983.
———. *Lettres de Mistress Fanni Butlerd*. Geneva: Librairie Droz, 1979.
Richards, Earl Jeffrey. Introduction to *The Book of the City of Ladies*, translated by Earl Jeffrey Richards, xix–li. New York: Persea, 1982.
———. "Somewhere between Destructive Glosses and Chaos: Christine de Pizan and Medieval Theology." In *Christine de Pizan: A Casebook*, edited by Barbara K. Altmann and Deborah L. McGrady, 43–55. London: Routledge, 2003.
Ricœur, Paul. *Figuring the Sacred: Religion, Narrative, and Imagination*. Edited by Mark I. Wallace. Translated by David Pellauer. Minneapolis: Augsburg Fortress, 1995.
Roald, Anne Sofie. *Women in Islam*. London: Routledge, 2001.
Rogers, Katharine M. "Fantasy and Reality in Fictional Convents of the Eighteenth Century." *Comparative Literature Studies* 22, no. 3 (1985): 297–316.
Sabbah, Hélène et al. *Itinéraires littéraires: XIXe siècle*. Paris: Hatier, 1988.

Šafranek, Ingrid. "L'Écriture absolue ou la dernière des romantiques." In *Duras, Dieu et l'écrit*, edited by Alain Vircondelet, 243–76. Paris: Éditions du Rocher, 1998.
Sand, George. *Le Compagnon du tour de France*. Grenoble: Presses de l'Université de Grenoble, 1988.
———. *Indiana*. Paris: Gallimard, 1984.
Sanders, E. K. *Fénelon: His Friends and His Enemies*. London: Longmans, 1901.
Sandrier, Jean-Claude. *George Sand: Le Parti du people*. Sury en Vaux: A à Z Patrimoine, 2004.
Sartori, Eva Martin. "Claudine-Alexandrine Guérin de Tencin (1682–1749)." In *French Women Writers*, edited by Eva Martin Sartori and Dorothy Wynne Zimmerman, 473–83. Westport, CT: Greenwood, 1991.
Schaeffer, Francis A. *The Complete Works of Francis Schaeffer: A Christian Worldview, Volume 2: A Christian View of the Bible as Truth*. Wheaton, IL: Crossway, 1982.
Sears, Theresa Ann. *Clio, Eros, Thanatos: The "Novela Sentimental" in Context*. New York: Peter Lang, 2001.
Semple, Benjamin. "Critique of Knowledge as Power: The Limits of Philosophy and Theology in Christine de Pizan." In *Christine de Pizan and the Categories of Difference*, edited by Marilynn Desmond, 108–27. Minneapolis: University of Minnesota Press, 1998.
Sévigné, Mme de. *Madame de Sévigné: Correspondance*. Edited by Roger Duchêne. 3 vols. Paris: Gallimard, 1974.
Sharon-Zisser, Shirley. *Critical Essays on Shakespeare's "A Lover's Complaint": Suffering Ecstasy*. Aldershot: Ashgate, 2006.
Sluhovsky, Moshe. *Believe Not Every Spirit: Possession, Mysticism, and Discernment in Early Modern Catholicism*. Chicago: University of Chicago Press, 2007.
Soelle, Dorothee. *Suffering*. Translated by Everett R. Kalin. Philadelphia: Fortress, 1975.
Sommers, Paula. *Celestial Ladders: Readings in Marguerite de Navarre's Poetry of Spiritual Ascent*. Genève: Droz, 1989.
Spencer, Samia I. "Sophie Cottin (1770–1807)." In *French Women Writers*, edited by Eva Martin Sartori and Dorothy Wynne Zimmerman, 90–97. Westport, CT: Greenwood, 1991.
Starobinski, Jean. "*Les Lettres écrites de Lausanne* de Madame de Charrière: Inhibition psychique et interdit social." In *Roman et lumières au XVIIIe siècle*, 130–51. Paris: Editions Sociales, 1970.
Stewart, Joan H. "Isabelle de Charrière Publishes *Caliste*: Designing Women." In *A New History of French Literature*, edited by Denis Hollier, 553–58. Cambridge: Harvard University Press, 1989.
———. "The Novelists and Their Fictions." In *French Women and the Age of Enlightenment*, edited by Samia I. Spencer, 197–211. Bloomington: Indiana University Press, 1984.
Stone, Brian. Introduction to *Medieval English Verse*, translated by Brian Stone, 12–22. 1964. Reprint with revisions, Harmondsworth: Penguin, 1971.
Summers, Claude J. "Herrick, Vaughan, and the Poetry of Anglican Survivalism." In *New Perspectives on the Seventeenth-Century English Religious Lyric*, edited by John R. Roberts, 46–74. Columbia: University of Missouri Press, 1994.
Taubes, Susan Anima. "The Absent God." In *Toward a New Christianity: Readings in the Death of God Theology*, edited by Thomas J. J. Altizer, 107–19. New York: Harcourt, Brace, and World, 1967.
Tencin, Claudine-Alexandrine Guérin de. *Les Malheurs de l'amour*. Paris: Editions Desjonquères, 2001.
———. *Mémoires du Comte de Comminges*. Paris: Editions Desjonquères, 1996.
Thomas, Ruth P. "The Death of an Ideal: Female Suicides in the Eighteenth Century French Novel." In *French Women and the Age of Enlightenment*, edited by Samia I. Spencer, 321–31. Bloomington: Indiana University Press, 1984.
Valincour, Jean-Baptiste Trousset de. *Lettres à Mme la Marquise de **** au sujet de la "Princesse de Clèves."* Edited by Jacques Chupeau. Tours: Université de Tours, 1972.
Vermeylen, Pierre. *Les Idées politiques et sociales de George Sand*. Bruxelles: Université de Bruxelles, 1984.

Vetö, Miklos. *The Religious Metaphysics of Simone Weil*. Translated by Joan Dargan. New York: State University of New York Press, 1994.
Viard, Bruno. "Sand et Leroux devant la question de la perfectibilité." In *"Le Compagnon du tour de France" de George Sand*, edited by Martine Watrelo and Michèle Hecquet, 53–60. Lille: Presses de l'Université Charles de Gaulle—Lille 3, 2009.
Villon, François. *Œuvres*. Edited by Jean Dufournet and André Mary. Paris: Garnier, 1970.
Vincent-Munnia, Nathalie. "Poésie du peuple, poétique sandienne dans *Le Compagnon du tour de France*." In *"Le Compagnon du tour de France" de George Sand*, edited by Martine Watrelo and Michèle Hecquet, 115–28. Lille: Presses de l'Université Charles-de-Gaulle—Lille 3, 2009.
Vircondelet, Alain. *Duras ou le temps de détruire*. Paris: Éditions Seghers, 1972.
———. Introduction to *Duras, Dieu et l'écrit*, edited by Alain Vircondelet, 9–12. Paris: Éditions du Rocher, 1998.
———. "Marguerite Duras, libre et captive." *Duras, Dieu et l'écrit*. Edited by Alain Vircondelet, 127–46. Paris: Éditions du Rocher, 1998.
Wallace, Mark I. "The European Enlightenment." In *World Spirituality: An Encyclopedic History of the Religious Quest*, edited by Peter Van Ness, 75–101. Vol. 22. New York: Crossroad, 1996.
Ward, Patricia. "Madame Guyon and Experiential Theology." *Church History* 67, no. 3 (1998): 484–98.
Watrelot, Martine, and Michèle Hecquet, eds. *"Le Compagnon du tour de France" de George Sand*. Lille: Presses de l'Université Charles-de-Gaulle—Lille 3, 2009.
Weil, Simone. *Attente de Dieu*. Paris: La Colombe, 1950.
———. *Lettre à un religieux*. Paris: Gallimard, 1951.
———. *Œuvres*. Edited by Florence de Lussy. Paris: Gallimard, 1999.
———. *Pensées sans ordre concernant l'amour de Dieu*. Paris: Gallimard, 1962.
Wells, Byron R. "The King, the Court, the Country: Theme and Structure in *La Princesse de Clèves*." *PFSCL* 12 (1985): 543–58.
West, Paul. *The Wine of Absurdity: Essays on Literature and Consolation*. University Park: Pennsylvania State University, 1966.
Whatley, Janet. "Isabelle de Charriere (1740–1805)." In *French Women Writers*, edited by Eva Martin Sartori and Dorothy Wynne Zimmerman. Westport, CT: Greenwood, 1991.
Willard, Charity Cannon. "The Dominican Abbey of Poissy in 1400." In *Christine de Pizan 2000: Studies on Christine de Pizan in Honour of Angus J. Kennedy*, ed. John Campbell and Nadia Margolis, 209–18. Amsterdam: Rodopi, 2000.
———. Introductions and Notes to *The Writings of Christine de Pizan*, edited by Charity Cannon Willard, *passim*. New York: Persea, 1994.
Williams, James G. "Proverbs and Ecclesiastes." In *The Literary Guide to the Bible*, edited by Robert Alter and Frank Kermode, 263–65. Cambridge: The Belknap Press of Harvard University Press, 1987.
Wingård Vareille, Kristina. *Socialité, sexualité et les impasses de l'histoire: L'Évolution de la thématique sandienne d'Indiana (1832) à Mauprat (1837)*. Uppsala: Université d' Uppsala, 1987.
Wiseman, Josette A. "The Resurrection according to Christine de Pizan." *Religion and the Arts: A Journal from Boston College* 4, no. 3 (2000): 337–58.

Index

Abosch, Heinz, 132, 139
absence: contrasted with presence, 9–10, 141–143, 151, 188, 188n1; from court, 79; of a lover, 79, 176, 188; of faith, 11, 96, 149; of forgiveness, 97; of God, 9–10, 44, 97, 141–143, 149–150; of life and fulfillment, 162, 185; of love, 73, 96, 108, 149–151, 162, 166, 176; of spiritual values, 10–11, 96, 149–151
absolute(s), search for, 1, 8, 10–11, 109, 114, 116, 126, 128n18, 132, 149–151, 162–163, 165–168
abuse of women, 112, 162–163, 171
Adler, Laure, 168n21
afterlife, 7, 12, 100–101, 113–114. *See also* heaven
Alain, Emile, 132, 137
Alexis, Guillaume, 39
Ali, Ayaan Hirsi, 188n4
Allaire, Joseph L., 37
allegory, 18, 31n76
Alleins, Madeleine, 150, 164
Allen, Prudence, 17, 20, 30n45
Altmann, Barbara K., 17
ambivalence, moral or theological, 9, 90, 131, 160
Anderson, David, 143
Angoulême. *See* Navarre, Marguerite de
anti-Islamic, 181
anti-Judaic, 137–140
anti-Semitic, 9–10, 138–139

apocalypse, 22, 24, 31n69, 177
appearances, false, 6, 73–74, 84n16
Aquinas. *See* Thomas Aquinas, Saint
Arendt, Hannah, 139
aristocracy, 6, 8, 20, 24, 28, 35, 51, 81, 102n16, 107, 117, 119–120, 123–124, 130n37
Aristotle, 19; *Nicomachean Ethics*, 19
Armel, Arliette, 169n28
Articles of Issy. *See* Issy Conferences
Augustine, Saint, 19
Austin, J. L., 45

Bachelard, Gaston, 189n14
Bajomée, Danielle, 150, 153, 167
Bakhtin, M. M., 15
Balthasar, Hans Urs von, 19
Balzac, Honoré de, 120, 127n4
baptism, 45, 46, 113–114, 134, 155, 167, 187. *See also* sea; water
Beasley, Faith, 84n13
Beauvais, Vincent de, 39
Beauvoir, Simone de, 186
Benveniste, Emile, 45
Bethune-Charost, Duchesse de, 51–52
Bible, 4–5, 17–18, 20–23, 37–38, 41, 46, 51, 56–57, 60, 117, 122, 136–138, 145; *1 Corinthians*, 38; *Ezekiel*, 25; *Genesis*, 45, 138; *Isaiah*, 111, 146n31; *Jeremiah*, 23; *Job*, 24, 146n31; *John, Gospel of*, 155; *Lamentations*, 23–24; *Matthew,*

Gospel of, 23, 56; *Micah*, 154; *Proverbs*, 18, 22; *Psalms*, 22, 146n31; *Revelation*, 57; *Song of Songs*, 187; *Wisdom of Solomon*, 22
Birk, Bonnie A., 15, 22, 25, 30n24, 31n78–32n79
Blanc, Louis, 106
Blot-Labarrère, Christiane, 167–168
Blumenfeld-Kosinski, Renate, 20
Boethius, 20, 30n40; *On the Consolation of Philosophy*, 20, 30n40
Boisdeffre, Pierre de, 130n40
Borgomano, Madeleine, 160
Bossuet, Jacques-Bénigne, 5, 49, 52
Boulton, Maureen, 15, 26
Bourges, Michel de, 116, 127n5
Bowman, Frank Paul, 103n19, 104n30
Briçonnet, Guillaume, Bishop of Meaux, 33–35, 36, 47
Brown-Grant, Rosalind, 15, 18, 21, 25
Brownlee, Kevin, 26
Bruneau, Marie-Florine, 51
Bubel, Katharine, 3, 15, 207
Bussy, comte de. *See* Rabutin, Roger de comte de Bussy

Cabaud, Jacques, 137, 141
Calvin, John, 34
Campbell, John, 73, 81, 83
Camus, Albert, 134
carte de Tendre, 74, 81–82
Castiglione, Baldassare, 84n16
Catholic: Church, 2–3, 5, 16, 33–34, 47, 89, 126n1, 127n12, 134, 136–137; doctrines and practices, 26, 37, 47, 52–53, 89, 113, 127n12, 134, 137; education, 51, 106, 139
Chamisso, Adalbert de, 139
Chantal, Madame de, 51
Charles V (King), 20
Charrière, Isabelle de, 7, 91, 95–99, 101, 102n14, 103n19; *Caliste, ou suite des lettres écrites de Lausanne*, 96–99, 103n19; *Lettres de Mistress Henley, publiées par son amie*, 95–96
Chastellain, Georges, 39–40; *Le miroir de mort*, 39–40
Chateaubriand, François-René de, 109

chivalry, 18, 30n20. *See also* courtly love tradition
Christ, 34–36, 56, 116–118, 135–136, 138, 141–144
Christ figure, 8, 112, 116–118
Christianity, 2–3, 9, 28, 122, 127n12, 131–132, 134–140, 144, 145n2, 172
Christophe, Paul, 106, 126n1, 126n3, 127n11–127n13, 128n17
civilization, 109, 112–114, 138
class, in George Sand's novels, 8, 105, 130n40
community: Bedouin, 178; and female experience, 12, 173–174, 177, 187; political and linguistic, 173; religious, 22, 139; separation from, 12
compassion, 2, 46, 77, 93, 102n8, 110, 118, 127n12, 143, 174, 177
confession, 46, 63, 69–71, 77, 86n39, 86n46, 92, 97, 103n17
confessional background, 21
convent: as an educational institution, 51, 90, 102n9, 106; criticism of, 89–90, 103n17; domestic imitation of life in a, 90–91, 93–95, 99–100; forced entry into, 90; as a means of escape or retreat, 7, 90, 102n8, 102n10, 104n36; as a place for spiritual growth, 27, 89–91
Cottin, Sophie de, 7, 91, 93–95, 103n19, 104n31, 104n37; *Claire d'Albe* , 7, 93–96, 99–100; *Malvina* , 104n30
Counter-Reformation, 53
countryside, retreat to, 69–71, 74, 77
court, the, 5–6, 33, 49, 63, 87n55; as antagonist, 64–66, 72–74; and Christian spirituality, 17–18, 29n15
courtly love tradition, the, 3, 18, 64–66, 75, 79
Craveri, Benedetta, 104n36

Dalmas, Franck, 189n7
Danahy, Michael, 85n31
Dante Alighieri, 20, 25, 27
Decottignies, Jean, 102n8, 102n10
decreation, 143, 147n53
Deleuze, Gilles, 181, 189n8, 189n15
democracy, 9, 107, 117, 119, 123, 125
Descartes, René, 98

Index

desert (literal and symbolic), 11–12, 93–94, 161, 175–179, 184–185, 187
desire: for death, 11–12, 112, 151, 162–164; for earthly happiness, 114, 123; for freedom, 115, 159, 186; for the identity of another, 151–152, 164–166; religious or ethical, 4, 12, 58, 61, 66, 83, 94, 106, 113–114, 142–143, 172; for romantic love, 8, 17, 114; for transformation or transcendence, 2, 8, 11–12, 113, 123, 150–154, 157, 159–160, 165–166, 171, 188n1; unfulfilled, 7, 114, 151–152, 157, 164, 166
d'Étaples, Jacques Lefèvre, 4, 37
deterritorialization, 174–175, 189n8
devotio moderna, 44
devotional literature, 26–28, 35, 44, 143
Dieu. *See* God
Diderot, Denis, 89–91, 100–101; *La Religieuse*, 89
Djebar, Assia, 173
domestic life, 91, 93, 95, 108, 171–173, 175–179, 181, 187–188, 208
dream vision, 20
Du Bois, Simon, 34–37, 40
Duras, Marguerite, ix, 2, 10–12, 149, 169n31, 207; *L'Amant*, 150–151, 161; *L'Amant de la Chine du Nord*, 161; *Dix heures et demie du soir en été*, 11, 164; *Moderato cantabile*, 11–12, 150, 161–164; *Les Petits chevaux de Tarquinia*, 160, 166; *Le Ravissement de Lol V. Stein*, 151–152, 165–166; *Le Vice-consul*, 157–160; *La Vie matérielle*, 150; *La Vie tranquille*, 152–157

Ecclesiasticus, 22
editorial strategies, 33, 48n23
education: for all, 8; in convents, 51, 102n9, 106; equality through, 118–119, 129n26–129n28; for females, 33, 90, 97–98, 102n9, 106, 186
educational treatise, 41
Enlightenment, the, 8, 89, 98, 101, 104n37, 104n40, 105–106, 119, 122
equality: sexual, 8, 114–115, 129n35; social or economic, 2, 8, 105, 109, 111, 114–115, 117, 122–126, 127n12, 129n35; through education, 118–119, 129n27–129n28
Erasmus, Desiderius, 34, 40
eternity, 7, 31n69, 81, 94, 99, 114, 150, 153. *See also* afterlife; heaven
ethics, 1, 3, 15, 19–22, 23, 25, 27–28, 31n77, 90
evangelism, 46, 125
existentialism, 9–10

Family Code, the, 175
feminism, ix, 8, 63, 98, 104n37, 105–106, 115, 128n14, 134, 172–178, 183, 185–187, 188n1, 188n6
Fénélon, François de Salignac de la Mothe, 5, 49, 52–53
Fontenelle, Bernard le Bovier de, 63
fragmentation, of language, 181, 184
France: eighteenth-century, 7, 102n16; late medieval, 3, 15, 23–26; nineteenth century, 8, 107, 112, 116, 126; religious culture in, 2, 12; religious and ethnic persecution in, 37, 51–52, 54, 145; seventeenth-century, 5, 51–52; sixteenth-century, 4, 33–34; spiritual reformation of, 4; twentieth-century, 9, 132, 139, 172
Francis I (King), 4, 33, 41, 43, 47
François, Anne, 9, 131, 147n63, 207
fraternity, 8, 12, 122, 126
freedom, 2, 8, 108, 109, 111, 115, 119, 128n23, 129n27, 129n35, 130n40, 139, 144, 155, 159–160, 162, 172, 174, 186
Frelick, Nancy M., 17
French Renaissance, the, 4, 33
French Revolution, the, 116, 118

Gauthier, Xavière, 163, 169n22
Geesey, Patricia, 188n5
Genlis, Madame de, 90, 100; *La Duchesse de la Vallière*, 90; *Mathilde*, 90, 100
Gerson, Jean, 21, 27
Gilson, M. Etienne, 21
Giniewski, Paul, 139
Gnosticism, 137–138, 145n2
God: absence of. *See* absence: attributes of, 8, 17, 19, 24–26, 28, 35, 45, 111, 115, 123; and ethics, philosophy, or

theology, 19–20, 28, 127n12, 131, 135–138; faith in, 21, 105, 110, 122–123, 127n13, 134, 136; in relation to a human void, 94, 100, 149–150; laws or principles of, 28, 30n20, 85n34; peace with or rest in, 8, 94–95; perspectives on, 9–10, 89–90, 98, 101, 133–134, 140, 145, 146n13; relationship with, 4–6, 10, 12, 27, 41, 45–46, 81, 83, 101, 109–110, 113–114, 140–144, 172, 178, 188; and religion, 110–111, 113; search for, 9, 35, 89, 128n17, 131; service or devotion to, 3–4, 7, 16–17, 20, 32n79, 34, 83; thoughts of, 7, 96, 98, 100; union with, 5, 35, 49–51, 53–56, 58–61, 91
Godet-Desmarais, Paul de, 52
Godwin-Jones, Robert, 108, 127n5, 128n19, 128n24, 129n26, 130n37
Gossman, Lionel, 104n40
Graffigny, Françoise de, 89
Graham, Ruth, 102n16
Gray, Francine du Plessix, 132
Greek philosophy, 9, 19, 131, 135–136, 138, 145
Grossir, Claudine, 128n21, 129n25
Guattari, Félix, 181, 189n8, 189n15
Guyon, Jeanne Marie Bouvier de la Motte, 49, 62n25; *Explanations and Reflections on the Bible*, 51; *A Short and Easy Method of Prayer*, 49, 62n25; *Spiritual Torrents*, 51

Hales, John, 53
Hamon, Bernard, 126n1, 129n28
Haskett, Kelsey L., ix, 1–12, 105, 130n40, 149, 169n31, 207
heaven: on earth, 41, 114, 123–125, 153; paradise, 16, 22, 31n76, 94–95, 100–101, 178
hell, 39, 43, 44, 89
Hellenism, 135–137. *See also* Greek philosophy
Herbert, George, 143–144, 147n61
Hiddleston, Janet, 129n34
Hugh of Saint Victor, 38–39
Hugo, Victor, 127n4, 129n25
Huguenots, 117
humanism, 2, 37, 40

humility, 28, 39, 44, 46–47, 116–117, 137
Hundred Years War, the, 3

ideals: courtly, 16–18; Enlightenment and Romantic, 105–106; feminist, 7, 105; humanitarian, 105, 134; revolutionary (non-violent), 8, 105, 130n40; romantic, 149–151, 165–167, 180; scriptural, 16–18; socioeconomic, 8, 105, 130n40; spiritual, 7, 9, 126
identity, female, 10–11, 16, 26, 44–46, 113, 139, 142, 152, 154–157, 164, 166–167, 172–175, 178, 186–187, 189n8
ideology, 2, 174; communist, 106; enlightenment, 104n37, 106; feminist, 103n19, 106, 174; socialist, 105–106, 116, 128n20; utopian, 106, 125, 129n35
illumination/*illuminatio*, 35, 41, 144
imagination, 11, 53, 94–95, 125, 142, 165
imago dei, 58
inequality, sexual, 105, 171, 175
Innocent XI (Pope), 54
Inquisition, the, 54
interiority, 5, 33, 36, 38–40, 46, 51, 59, 178
Islam, 2, 12, 171, 189n17
Issy Conferences, the, 52

Jansenism, 81, 102n16
Jaspers, Karl, 24
Jones, Rufus M., 53
journey, spiritual, 38, 50–51, 57, 59, 61, 157
justice, 1–2, 8, 18, 25, 106, 115–116, 118–122, 132–134, 145n1

Kant, Immanuel, 132, 140
Kay, Sarah, 17
Kempis, Thomas à, 40, 53; *Imitatio Christi*, 40
King, Martin Luther, Jr., 28
Knowles, David, 19, 21

La Combe, François, 51–52
Laden, Marie-Paul, 84n16
Lafayette, Marie Madeleine Pioche de la Vergne, comtesse de, 3, 5–7, 12, 63, 87n55; *La Princesse de Clèves*, 5–7, 12,

63, 87n55
Lammenais, Hugues Felicité Robert de, 106, 126n3
Landy, Francis, 23
La Rochefoucauld, François de, 81
Lebellay, Fréderique, 168n21
Lefèvre d'Étaples, Jacques, 4, 37
Leroux, Pierre, 106, 116, 126n1, 126n3–127n5, 129n35, 130n37
Levi, Anthony, 80
Lewis, C. S., 29n15
l'Hermite, Tristan, 70
l'Incarnation, Marie de, 57
Lionnet, Françoise, 189n15
Lochrie, Karma, 184
Louis XIV (King), 5, 49, 52
Logos, 19, 22
love: absent. *See* absence: absolute, 8, 126, 11–12, 114, 116, 126, 149–151, 166, 178; courtly, 3, 16–17, 65, 81, 84n18; divine, 10, 12, 41, 53, 56–57, 59, 83, 94, 100, 142–143; for God, 5, 17, 21, 35, 50–51, 53–54; fraternal or familial, 41, 112, 117–118, 123–125, 175–177; human, flawed, destructive, 109, 112, 163; ideal, pure, sincere, 7–9, 12, 65, 82, 100, 105–109, 112–115, 123–124; marital, 11, 71, 87n54, 107, 128n14, 164; narcissistic, 152, 166; passionate, 6–7, 63, 67–74, 76–79, 86n39, 91–93, 162–163; platonic, 122; searching or waiting for, 108, 128n17, 150–151, 167–168, 174, 177, 184–185, 188; unfulfilled, 63, 100, 151, 166; vicarious, 164–166
Lussy, Florence de, 139
Luther, Martin, 139

Maintenon, Madame de, 5, 52
malheur, 10, 141, 143, 145. *See also* suffering
Manichaeism, 145n2. *See also* Gnosticism
Marks, Herbert, 25
Marot, Jehan, 41
marriage, 6–8, 23, 51, 57, 70–72, 75, 77, 90, 92, 95–98, 102n10, 103n17, 105–109, 112, 114–115, 124–125, 127n11, 128n14, 162, 180, 183–184
Mary (Virgin), 17

Mary of Berry, 21, 28
McKeown, Joanne M., 7–8, 89, 104n40, 207
metaphysics, 9, 44, 131–133, 138, 151, 167
Micciollo, Henri, 150, 162–163, 168
Michelet, Jules, 127n4
Miller, Nancy K., 90, 98, 103n17–103n19, 104n27
mirror literature. *See* speculum literature
misogyny, 23, 32n79, 183. *See also* patriarchy
Mistacco, Vicki, 91, 102n14, 103n22, 103n26
Mokeddem, Malika, 2, 12, 171, 189n17; *La Nuit de la lézarde*, 11, 173–188; *Le Siècle des sauterelles*, 173; *L'Interdite*, 174
Molinet, Jean, 39
Molinos, Michael de, 53–56
moral aesthetic, 18, 28, 121
moral agency and authority, 3, 20–22, 25–27, 32n79, 40
moral dilemmas, debates, or danger, 4, 52, 54, 66, 69, 70–71, 81, 111, 127n12
moral philosophy or theology, 19–20, 25
moral wisdom or action, 3, 6, 12, 19, 21, 23, 26–27, 31n78, 32n79, 39, 64–66, 104n31, 104n36, 120
Muslim: culture, 171–173; faith, 11, 171, 178; women, 171–174. *See also* Islam
mysticism, 10, 35, 53, 57, 61, 100, 105–106, 131–135, 140, 144

Naginski, Isabelle Hoog, 127n4
Napoleon, 107, 116
Navarre, Marguerite de, 3–5, 12, 33, 48n23; *Le Miroir de l'âme pécheresse*, 4, 34, 48n23
Nelson, Holly Faith, 1–12, 15, 32n102, 208
Newbigin, Lesslie, 137
Newman, Barbara, 31n57
Noailles (Bishop), 52
novel (genre): Christian, 80–83; New, 10; pastoral, 105; psychological, 6; sentimental, 71

Origen of Alexandria, 136
Orlando, Valerie, 174

other: take on the identity of the, 164; transformation of, 46–47
otherness, religious, 9, 131

Panichas, George A., 137
paradise. *See* heaven
Pascal, Blaise, 81, 168n1
passion, 6, 9, 11–12, 55, 65–82
Passion, the, 9, 27, 142, 144
passive: images, 58; longing or determination, 160, 167; prayer, 56; in tension with active, 50
patriarchy, 89, 92, 103n26, 171
Paul, Saint, 21
peace: the art of, 26, 117; inner (emotional), 6–8, 73, 75; political, 26, 41, 132; in and through prayer, 7, 58, 61, 90; spiritual, 1–2, 8, 90, 92, 94, 99, 118, 123; threats to, 65, 81, 98
perfection/*perfecto*: in and through love, 11, 112–116; spiritual or absolute, 4, 35, 38, 83, 141–142, 156, 165, 167, 178
Perrin, Joseph-Marie, 134
Peylet, Gérard, 129n35
Phillips, D. Z., 132
Philomela, 103n26
philophes, 7, 98–99
Pinnock, Sarah K., 134
Pizan, Christine de, 2–6, 12, 15, 32n102; *The Book of Deeds of Arms and of Chivalry*, 30n20; *The Book of Peace*, 20; *The Book of the Body Politic*, 17, 19, 22, 28, 32n97; *The Book of the City of Ladies*, 25, 31n76–32n79; *The Book of the Mutation of Fortune*, 24, 30n40; *Dit de Poissy*, 17; *The God of Love's Letter*, 17; *The Hours of Contemplation on the Passion of Our Lord*, 27; *The Lamentation on the Evils That Have Befallen France*, 23; *Letter of Othea to Hector*, 18–20, 22, 30n24; *The Letter on the Prison of Human Life*, 21, 28; *The Path of Long Study*, 20–21, 24, 25; *The Poem of Joan of Arc*, 24, 26–27; *Prayers to Our Lady*, 27; *The Tale of the Shepherdess*, 17, 29n18; *The Treasure of the City of Ladies; or The Book of the Three Virtues*, 16; *The Vision of Christine de Pizan*, 16, 20, 27, 31n78
Platonic thought, 38, 53, 119, 135, 140
postmodernism, 131
Powell, David, 128n20
prayer: contemplative or inner, 5, 51, 53–55, 57, 61, 177, 184; intercessory, 24, 92–93; meditative, 53, 55; *oraison*, 55–61; passive, 50–51, 53, 56; as a spiritual exercise, 2–3, 7, 22, 26–27, 35, 40, 49–50, 99–101
Procne, 103n26
proletariat, 8, 117, 120, 125
prophecy, 22–28, 111, 128n23, 130n40
Protestantism, 37, 117, 126n1, 134
proto-feminism, 15, 31n57
Pseudo-Dionysius, 35
purgation/purgation, 35, 44

quest: for an absolute, 10, 12, 163, 168; for love, 150; spiritual, 1–12, 27, 131, 135; for transcendence or inner transformation, 1
quietism, 5, 49–54
quietist prayer guide, by Mme Guyon, 49, 51–61

Rabutin, Roger de comte de Bussy, 63
Racine, Jean, 119
rationalism, 2, 9, 49
reason: absence of or distancing from, 69, 167; autonomous, 98–99, 101; as an instrument of deceit, 78; participatory, 98–99; and spiritual belief, 100; and spirituality and the novel, 98–100; as a virtue and source of truth, 18, 77–78, 89, 129n28
rebirth, 11, 155, 167, 173
Reformation, the, 33, 37
réforme évangélique, 33
religion, 2–12, 17, 80, 83, 91, 115, 126n1, 128n17, 131, 134, 138, 140; institutionalized, 89, 101, 103n17, 105–106, 110–111, 115, 121, 126, 134, 139, 144–145, 146n13, 184, 186; language of, 15–17, 28; of love, 16–17, 29n15; natural, 113; personal, 167; true, 109–111
repos. *See* peace
resurrection, 114. *See also* rebirth

Index

revelation: of passion, 11, 162–163; spiritual, 19, 26, 123, 140, 144. *See also* visions
Rhees, Rush, 133
rhetorical strategies, 15, 23–24, 33, 48n23, 50, 57, 176, 181–183, 186
Riccoboni, Marie-Jeanne, 89–90, 100; *Lettres de Milady Juliette Catesby à Milady Henriette Campley, son amie*, 100; *Lettres de Mistress Fanni Butlerd*, 90
Richards, Earl Jeffrey, 15, 27–28, 31n76–31n77, 32n96
Ricœur, Paul, 16, 19, 24
Roald, Anne Sofie, 188n5
romanticism, 8, 12, 106–108, 111–113
Rotrou, Jean, 70
Rousseau, Jean-Jacques, 104n30, 122, 137
Roy, Maurice, 27

Šafranek, Ingrid, 153
Saint Cyr school, 5, 52
Saint-Pierre, Bernardin de, 109
Sales, François de, 51; *Introduction to the Devout Life*, 51
Salminen, Renja, 37
Sand, George, ix, 6, 8–9, 12, 103n19, 105, 130n40, 188n1; *Le Compagnon du tour de France*, 8, 105, 116, 128n21, 126; *Consuelo*, 105–106; *Indiana*, ix, 3, 6, 105–116, 125; *Simon*, 128n20; *Valentine*, 128n20
sapiential tradition, 22, 23
Sartori, Eva Martin, 102n8, 103n17, 104n30
Savoie, Louise de, 41, 43
Schaeffer, Francis A., 138
Scripture. *See* Bible
sea (literal and symbolic), 11, 153–157, 159–162. *See also* baptism; water
secular, the, 2, 5, 9, 15–18, 27, 90–91, 100, 128n21, 145, 172–173, 186, 188n6
self: abasement and rejection, 10–11, 141, 152, 163; analysis, 6, 160; awareness and actualization, 41, 43, 68–69, 154, 165, 167, 169n22, 172, 184, 187–188; deception, 82; denial and renunciation, 53, 59, 114, 142–143; destruction and rejection, 165–167; dispossession, 156,

159, 164–165; examination, 40; interest, 73–74, 85n38, 86n41, 87n51, 107; replacement, 11, 151, 164–166
Semple, Benjamin, 27
sharia, 186
sibyl, 25–26
sin, 21, 81, 142
slavery, 111, 114, 128n14, 140, 143
social idealism. *See* ideals
social justice. *See* justice
socialism, 105–106, 116, 128n20
solitude, 11, 70, 73–74, 90–91, 149–151, 167, 176, 186, 188
Sommers, Paula, 35
Sophia (wisdom), 19, 22–23
Sorbonne, the, 4, 33, 37, 47
Spanish Civil War, the, 132
speculum literary tradition, 4, 38–45
Spencer, Samia I., 104n31, 104n37
spirituality, 1–2, 5–6, 8, 10, 16, 89, 91, 98–101, 105–106, 115, 126, 126n1, 135–136, 140, 149–150, 153, 171–174, 178, 188n5
Spinoza, Baruch de, 139
Stewart, Joan H., 98, 101, 103n19, 104n27
St. John of the Cross, 53
Stone, Brian, 29n15
suffering: emotional, 7–8, 12, 85n29, 91–95, 113–115, 150–151; for a cause, 122; human, 16, 144; in marriage, 125, 162, 184; mental, 94; through persecution, 5, 139; physical, 94, 138, 184–185; purpose of, 100, 143; spiritual, 141–144
Sullivan-Trainor, Deborah, 5, 49, 62n25, 208
Summers, Claude J., 31n69
surreal, the, 177, 184
surrealism, 9
syncretism, religious, 131

Taubes, Susan Anima, 142
Tencin, Claudine-Alexandrine Guérin de, 7, 90–93, 98, 102n8, 103n17–103n18; *Les Malheurs de l'amour*, 90; *Mémoires du Comte de Comminges*, 7, 90–93, 98
Teresa of Avila, Saint, 53
Thomas Aquinas, Saint, 19, 32n96, 135

Thomassy, Raimond, 27
Tournes, Jean de, 36
transcendence, 1, 10, 12, 149–151, 172
transformation, 1, 4, 9–12, 45, 46, 105, 115, 150–154, 157, 160–161, 163–167, 172, 175, 179, 187–188
translation, 62n23, 138; biblical, 37
trauma, personal and national, 21, 31n69, 90, 174, 181, 188. *See also* suffering
Trinity, 41
Tristan, Flora, 128n16
Tronso, Superior of Saint Sulpice, 52

Udry, Susan, 11, 171, 189n17, 208

Valincour, Jean-Baptiste Trousset de, 64
Vanderpool, Sinda, 4, 33, 48n23, 208
Vaughan, Henry, 31n69
Vermeylen, Pierre, 126, 126n1, 127n4, 128n14, 128n18, 129n27
Vetö, Miklos, 133
Viard, Bruno, 127n4, 130n37
Villon, François, 44
Vincent-Munnia, Nathalie, 128n23, 130n38
vingt ans, Barakat, 173, 188n6
violence: condemnation of, 130n37, 132; emotional, 73, 79, 87n48; military, 21; women and, 12, 132
Vircondelet, Alain, 149
vision(s): social, 105, 108, 110, 114–115, 123, 125; spiritual or ethical, 9, 22, 25, 31n69, 80, 115, 119, 123, 133, 172
Voltaire, 134, 137

waiting, 11–12, 54, 92, 125, 108, 143, 156, 166–167, 176–178, 183–187
Wallace, Mark I., 98
water (literal and symbolic), 155–156, 160–161, 167, 179, 182, 187. *See also* baptism; sea
Weil, André, 131
Weil, Simone, 9–10, 12, 131, 147n63; *L'Amour de Dieu et le malheur*, 141, 142, 144; *Attente de Dieu*, 131; *Autobiographie spirituelle*, 131, 135–136, 140, 142–144; *Commentaires de textes Pythagoriciens*, 135–136, 140–141; *L'Enracinement*, 131, 136; *Formes de l'amour implicite de Dieu*, 131, 143, 146n13, 146n31; *L'Iliade ou le poème de force*, 135; "Letter to Huguette Baur" (in *Œuvres*), 139; "Letter to Jean Wahl" (in *Œuvres*), 137–138; "Letter to Xavier Vallat" (in *Œuvres*), 139; *Lettres à un religieux*, 131, 134–136, 138, 144
West, Paul, 138
Whatley, Janet, 101
Willard, Charity Cannon, 15, 25, 27
Williams, James G., 22
Wingård Vareille, Kristina, 115, 127n5, 127n8
wisdom, 18–24, 28, 31n78, 40, 66, 71, 76, 119. *See also* virtue
Wiseman, Josette A., 15
Wood, Hadley, 6–7, 63, 87n55, 208

About the Contributors

Katharine Bubel, MA (Trinity Western University), is a PhD candidate in the English Department of the University of Victoria in Canada. Her current research focuses on the intersection of aesthetics, spirituality, and ecology. She has published a number of articles on religion and literature in journals such as *Renascence: Essays on Values in Literature, Illumine,* and *North Wind: A Journal of George MacDonald Studies.*

Anne M. François, PhD (New York University), is professor of French and Francophone literature at Eastern University. Her research focuses on French-Caribbean and postcolonial literature. Her work has appeared in *African Caribbeans: A Reference Guide*, and *Calabash: A Journal of Caribbean Arts and Letters.* Her monograph *Rewriting the Return to Africa: Voices of Francophone Caribbean Women Writers* was published in 2011.

Kelsey L. Haskett, PhD (Laval University), is associate professor of French and chair of the Modern Language Department at Trinity Western University, where she developed the French program. Her areas of research include French women's literature and twentieth-century French literature, on which she has published several articles. She has also published a book chapter on an approach to Modern Languages. Her monograph on the novels of Marguerite Duras, *Dans le miroir des mots: identité féminine et relations familiales dans l'œuvre romanesque de Marguerite Duras,* was published in 2011.

Joanne M. McKeown, PhD (University of Virginia), professor of French language and literature, is currently in her twenty-fourth year at Moravian College in Bethlehem, Pennsylvania, where she teaches French language, foreign language teaching methodologies, and the literature of the seventeenth and eighteenth centuries. She is the primary translator and editor of *Despine and the Evolution of Psychology: Historical and Medical Perspectives on Dissociative Disorders*, and has published related articles about translating Antoine Despine and about the understanding and literary representation of visions.

Holly Faith Nelson, PhD (Simon Fraser University), professor and chair of English and codirector of the Gender Studies Institute at Trinity Western University, has published widely on European literature, from the medieval through the romantic periods. Her most recent publications include the edited collection *Through a Glass Darkly: Suffering, the Sacred, and the Sublime in Literature and Theory* and book chapters on the proto-scientific works of early-modern women writers.

Deborah Sullivan-Trainor, PhD (University of California, Irvine), is currently serving as associate dean of General Education and Faculty Development at Bethel University in St. Paul, Minnesota. She assumed this role after having served as chair of Bethel's Modern World Languages Department for five years. Her primary research areas are Flora Tristan, Jeanne Guyon, and foreign language pedagogy.

Susan Udry, PhD (Indiana University), whose doctoral dissertation addressed female domesticity in late medieval French texts composed by male authors, has published articles on medieval French writers in *Essays in Medieval Studies*, *European Medieval Drama*, and *The ORB: On-line Reference Book for Medieval Studies*.

Sinda Vanderpool, PhD (Princeton University), serves as the assistant vice provost for Enrollment Management at Baylor University. She also teaches courses in the French division of the Modern Foreign Languages Department and the Honors College. Her work primarily focuses on women authors of the Renaissance. She has written on female expressions of religious belief, feminist approaches to knowledge, and contemporary foreign language learning.

Hadley Wood, PhD (Harvard University), is professor of French at Point Loma Nazarene University. Her articles have appeared in the *Journal of Christianity and Foreign Languages*, *Romanic Review*, and *French Studies*. She has written a number of French textbooks and workbooks for Houghton Mifflin.